Praise for *Salsa, Soul, and Spirit*

"This wonderful book made me want to dance with joy. In Western society, we suffer from a loss of community and spirit because we're so disconnected. American Indian, Latino, and African American cultures have never forgotten that we need to be together, and that diversity is not a problem, but a blessing. May this book lead you to discover what we've been missing— each other."

—Margaret J. Wheatley,
author of *Leadership and the New Science*

"Juana Bordas has broken new ground. She has documented and analyzed the effective and unique practices of Latino, Black, and American Indian leaders. Salsa, Soul, and Spirit is a fascinating read that shows us the road to leadership for a multicultural America."

—John Echohawk, Pawnee,
Executive Director,
The Native American Rights Fund

"A penetrating, highly personal study of American Indian, Black, and Latino leadership, presented in a manner that should attract a wide readership. A multicultural study at its best."

—James MacGregor Burns,
Pulitzer Prize-winning Presidential biographer
and author of *Leadership*

"Juana Bordas clearly understands that building an inclusive America requires leadership forms that respect and resonate with our growing diversity. Salsa, Soul, and Spirit provides an excellent roadmap that can transform and energize leadership into an authentic multicultural form that is truly representative of our great nation and its unifying ideals."

—Honorable Anna Escobedo Cabral,
Treasurer of the United States

"The politics of inclusion is not just some politically correct idea. It's essential to the adaptability of any organization or society that must rely on new ideas and synthesis in a changing world. Juana Bordas has given us a first-hand inspirational primer, full of wisdom and insight, for anyone practicing leadership that challenges people to thrive anew."

—Dr. Ron Heifetz, Cofounder,
Center for Public Leadership at Harvard's
John F. Kennedy School of Government

"Salsa, Soul, and Spirit is a refreshing and inspiring vision of a new form of leadership for the 21st Century. Bordas captures the unique but successful models of leadership developed by racial and ethnic minorities. Our nation would greatly benefit from leaders who embody these traits."

— Honorable Federico Peña,
former Mayor of Denver,
US Secretary of Transportation,
and US Secretary of Energy

"Salsa, Soul, and Spirit fills a necessary void in the study of leadership with its integration of the common elements of spiritual and programmatic leadership that are typical of minority approaches to social problems and which also build the basis for coalition politics."

—Dr. Ronald W. Walters,
author of *African American Leadership*

"To be relevant—let alone thrive—in the 21st Century, business leaders need a new awareness of our interdependency and a new leadership paradigm like that described in Salsa, Soul, and Spirit."

—Jack Lowe, Board Chair,
TDIndustries

"Reflecting the traditions of Black, Latino, and Native American cultures, Salsa Soul, and Spirit fashions a leadership model based on community, generosity, and a commitment to work for the common good. These proven leadership practices that sustained communities of color for generations are a source of strength, hope, and wisdom which will guide us through the turbulence of the 21st century."

—LaDonna Harris, Comanche,
President and Founder,
Americans for Indian Opportunity

"It is empowerment time in America—a time to live up to the basic values of equality and justice. Empowerment means closing the racial divide and opening the doors to leadership at all levels, so it represents our great and dynamic diversity. Salsa, Soul, and Spirit is a roadmap to guide us on this journey and invites us to work together to create an America that benefits from the beauty and potential of all its people."

—Marc H. Morial, President and CEO,
National Urban League
and former Mayor of New Orleans

"Frequently, people say it is too hard to have both excellence and diversity. Salsa, Soul, and Spirit shows not only why it doesn't have to be that hard, but also why it is critically important at this moment in history to develop organizational leadership that is both excellent and diverse. People need to read this book."

—John Hickenlooper, Mayor of Denver

"Salsa, Soul, and Spirit is a compelling, vibrant, and engaging exploration of the deep roots of multicultural leadership. It will challenge your view on leadership. Bordas' personal journey to integrate her Hispanic culture into her own leadership witnesses the great benefits of blending cultures rather than assimilating them."

—John Izzo, author
of Awakening Corporate Soul and Value Shift

"The new America is a web of myriad cultures and traditions. In this new era, we must enlarge our vision of what it means to be an American as well as embrace our identity as world citizens. This inspirational book can guide us to this multicultural future and sets forth a visionary leadership model that is founded on both our democratic traditions and our great diversity."

— Dr. James Joseph, former Ambassador to
South Africa and author of Remaking America:
How Benevolent Traditions of Many Cultures Are
Transforming Our National Life

"Juana Bordas is one of our nation's most effective facilitators of Leadership Development. Salsa, Soul, and Spirit brings together her years of experience and insights. Her book is unique because it offers principles for leading in an increasingly diverse America. A must-read for those interested in becoming leaders of our multicultural society."

—Raul Yzaguirre, President Emeritus,
National Council of La Raza

Salsa, Soul, and Spirit

Salsa, Soul, and Spirit

Leadership
for a
Multicultural Age

Juana Bordas

BERRETT-KOEHLER PUBLISHERS, INC.
San Francisco

Berrett-Koehler Publishers, Inc.
235 Montgomery Street, Suite 650
San Francisco, CA 94104-2916
Tel: (415) 288-0260 Fax: (415) 362-2512   www.bkconnection.com

Ordering Information

Quantity sales. Special discounts are available on quantity purchases by corporations, associations, and others. For details, contact the "Special Sales Department" at the Berrett-Koehler address above.

Individual sales. Berrett-Koehler publications are available through most bookstores. They can also be ordered directly from Berrett-Koehler: Tel: (800) 929-2929; Fax: (802) 864-7626; www.bkconnection.com

Orders for college textbook/course adoption use. Please contact Berrett-Koehler: Tel: (800) 929-2929; Fax: (802) 864-7626.

Orders by U.S. trade bookstores and wholesalers. Please contact Ingram Publisher Services, Tel: (800) 509-4887; Fax: (800) 838-1149; E-mail: customer.service@ingrampublisherservices.com; or visit www.ingrampublisherservices.com/Ordering for details about electronic ordering.

Berrett-Koehler and the BK logo are registered trademarks of Berrett-Koehler Publishers, Inc.

Printed in the United States of America

Berrett-Koehler books are printed on long-lasting acid-free paper. When it is available, we choose paper that has been manufactured by environmentally responsible processes. These may include using trees grown in sustainable forests, incorporating recycled paper, minimizing chlorine in bleaching, or recycling the energy produced at the paper mill.

Library of Congress Cataloging-in-Publication Data

Bordas, Juana.
  Salsa, soul, and spirit : leadership for a multicultural age / Juana Bordas.
— 1st ed.
      p. cm.
  Includes bibliographical references and index.
  ISBN-13: 978-1-57675-432-0 (pbk.)
  1 . Community leadership—United States. 2. African Americans.
3. Hispanic Americans. 4. Indians of North America. I. Title.
HM781.B67 2007
305.800973—dc22   2007001487

First Edition
12 11 10 09   10 9 8 7 6 5 4

Book producer: Dianne Platner. Cover designer: Barbara Jellow. Interior designers and compositors: Seventeenth Street Studios. Proofreader: Laurie Dunne. Copyeditor: Kristi Hein. Indexer: Medea Minnich.

Para mi Madre, mis Hermanas, mis Hijas, y mis Comadres

You have been the cradle and the substance of my life.

Contents

Preface

THE RAPIDLY INCREASING cultural and racial diversity of the U.S. workforce, consumer base, and citizenry is propelling leadership to better reflect the values, worldviews, and principles inherent in our multicultural age. As the world becomes flatter and globalization creates a world village, leaders must have the cultural flexibility and adaptability to inspire and guide people who represent the whole rainbow of humanity. For many years I have searched for materials that draw on multicultural approaches. Such materials continue to be extremely scarce. Today's leadership models, although they may differ from person to person and method to method, generally have a common bias toward Western- or European-influenced ways of thinking and approaches. Contemporary leadership theories center on the dominant or mainstream culture and exclude the enormous contributions, potential learning, and valuable insights that come from leaders in diverse communities. However, the task of integrating leadership from these communities into the American mainstream does not fall to Anglo leaders or authors. To be authentic and effective, this information must emerge from leaders and scholars in communities of color.

I have been asked why I, as a Latina, am writing a book on multicultural leadership, rather than leadership that springs from my community. Although it is insightful to look at Latino, or Black, or American Indian leadership separately, this continues to imply that leadership in each of these communities is pertinent only to that one group and is not relevant and generic enough for widespread application. Latino leadership is seen to be of interest only to people who are involved or work with this population. Black leadership is not regarded as applicable to mainstream organizations, although there is significant literature on its widespread effectiveness. Likewise, American Indian spirituality is not understood as the very essence of their leadership that can enrich all cultures.

Multicultural leadership has broad relevance and application to the diverse world that we live in. A culturally integrated model has *greater impact, influence, and scope.* Delving into leadership models from specific communities will certainly enhance a person's ability to relate more effectively with that population but will not necessarily be applicable to the growing diversity that exists. A multicultural leadership approach, on the other hand, offers practices and tools that will be effective with many populations.

Furthermore, even though Blacks, Latinos, and American Indians have distinct ways of leading, there are key *points of convergence.* As will be noted, a number of core cultural dynamics are shared by communities of color. Their history as colonized people is a common denominator that engenders leadership forms that are people-centered, community-focused, and advocacy-oriented. All three cultures center on collective or group welfare and value generosity and reciprocity. By identifying such points of convergence, multicultural leadership that integrates Black, Latino, and American Indian strengths can be brought forth.

These unifying factors lay the foundation for eight principles formulated in this book. Articulating these commonalities will cultivate a greater sense of unity among communities of color. By working together to find common ground and develop a collective force, these communities can proactively influence a more culturally inclusive leadership form. As the Hopi elders have prophesied, "The time of the lone wolf is over."[1] The future of communities of color lies in their unity and collective force.

Focusing on the cultural crossroads that shape multicultural leadership in no way denies the power or importance of leadership within the Black, Latino, or American Indian communities. Recognizing common abilities and celebrating differences are two of the touchstones of diversity. I hope this book will inspire people to deepen their understanding about the unique gifts that many cultures bring to leadership.

I feel uniquely qualified to discuss leadership in Black, Latino, and American Indian communities. I was the first president and CEO of the National Hispana Leadership Institute and have directed Latino organizations for over twenty years. Through the Chevron Management Institute, I designed a leadership program that trained ninety Urban League presidents. Spellman College's Center for Leadership and Civic Engagement honored me with their Legacy Award. I was initiated into the Colorado Women's Hall of Fame and presented the Wise Woman Award by the Center for Women's Policy Studies. I also taught at the Center for Creative Leadership in the Leadership Development Program, the most highly utilized corporate training program in the world. The U.S. Peace Corps acknowledged me with the Franklin Miller Award for my lifelong commitment to advancing communities of color. Most important, I have listened to the voices of diverse leaders, many of whom I have worked with closely. This book reflects the composite of our experiences and ways of leading.

My own background is also multicultural: Central American Indian, Spanish, and French. My grandmother was indigenous—her long braids hung down her back, as she never cut her hair. Coming from the Caribbean coast of Nicaragua, I have Black and Latino relatives. Through marriage, my daughters are of Hispanic, Irish, and Norwegian ancestry. My adopted daughter is African American and Anglo. I have had the enriching experience of living in an integrated neighborhood for twenty-five years. The multicultural zenith of our family is my Black, Latino, Irish, Blackfoot Indian, French, and English grandson, who represents our global future.

In this book, my use of the term *communities of color* refers to African Americans, Latinos, and American Indians. These communities also have preferences on how they describe themselves, although these have changed over time. I use the term *Hispanic* as well as *Latino*. For African Americans, I also use the term *Black* as a descriptor in usages such as Black History Month or the Black community. I refer to American Indians in general and indicate tribal membership whenever appropriate; I also use the term *Indian*, as this is a short form accepted within that community. These terms are intended to distinguish people, honor their identity, and highlight their cultural characteristics.

Other groups, such as Asian Americans, may wonder why they are not included in this book. Asian Americans, for instance, come from many different countries with numerous languages, customs, and histories. The complexity and scope of these groups merit their own volumes on their leadership experiences and styles. In addition, my limited experience with these groups would not do justice to their rich history and contributions. My hope is that this book will start a dialogue on multicultural leadership with the Asian American community, as well as others, who will expand the conversation. Creating authentic multicultural leadership is an ongoing and organic process that will enrich and expand American leadership in more representative and inclusive directions. This book offers a framework within which multicultural leadership can continue evolving as other groups in our global community bring their contributions to the forefront.

In communities of color, age is venerated and respected. The leaders interviewed for this book are largely elders and stand as beacons who have guided their communities for many decades. Most grew out of the civil rights era and thus incorporate a social responsibility that reaches beyond their communities into the realm of building the good and just society. They represent a noble American legacy. I hope that many younger leaders, particularly in communities of color, will be inspired to continue on the path forged by these great men and women.

Each principle section starts with a story from my life, which allows me to include my voice with those of the other leaders who have graciously shared their knowledge and wisdom. The first part of my life, for instance, mirrors many of the experiences that shaped leaders since the civil rights movement, when young people of color stood up in unprecedented numbers and answered the call to leadership. Each principle section ends with suggestions and exercises for using the principle in practical ways and can assist you in developing multicultural ways of leading.

Acknowledgments

IN THE LEADERSHIP FIELD, there are practitioners and scholars. Practitioners design, implement, and teach in leadership programs, as I have done for the past twenty years. Scholars research and formulate leadership theories and models, then write books on their findings. As a first-time author, I am a crossover, bringing many years of practical experience to this book. However, I had not thought about writing until Dr. Larraine Matusak, who was the director of the Kellogg National Fellows Program, invited me to be part of the Leadership Scholars she was bringing together. Exchanging ideas and dialoguing with authors such as Bernie Bass, James MacGregor Burns, Ron Heifetz, Barbara Kellerman, and Gill Hickman gave me a new perspective on how influential leadership books could be. These authors encouraged me to write about my experiences and perspectives in communities of color, as a needed addition to the leadership field. Without their encouragement, I would not been brave enough to venture on the long and tremulous journey of becoming a leadership author.

When I summoned up the courage to tell people I was writing a book, my friend Bob Grabowski immediately plunked down fifty dollars. "I want the first two copies!" This is an example of the unswerving faith my friends have had in my work. If I ever doubted I could do it—they didn't! They were fountains of hope I could draw on, and of course, once I said I was going to do it, I couldn't let them down. The public announcement, in front of your community and friends, that you are going to accomplish something is a surefire way to ensure that you *will* do what you said you would do!

It is impossible to thank all the people who have helped me with this venture. However, a few folks warrant special appreciation. Let me start with my *familia*, who have supported me in being a Latina maverick who strayed from traditional roles, and my many, many *comadres* across the country with whom I have shared my life's path.

The early conceptual work for the book was done in the breathtaking Rocky Mountains; my gratitude to Raydean Acevedo, Anne Padilla, and Dr. Margaret Hecht for their hospitality in lending me their mountain homes. Then there are those who graciously read my manuscript. A special *gracias* to David Perkins, Arnie Langberg, Lynette Murphy, and Rich Chavez for their guidance on the manuscript. To Lillian Jimenez, executive director from the Latino Educational Media Center, thank you for assisting me in capturing the wisdom of Dr. Antonia Pantoja.

A heartfelt appreciation to my professional colleagues, mentors, and authors who encouraged me and wrote endorsement letters: Jim Maloney, Larry Spears, Frances Hesselbein, Dr. Roger Sublett, Dr. David Altman, Dr. Larraine Matusak, Rima Matsumoto, Dr. John Burkhardt, Dr. Nancy Huber, Anita Luera, and Dr. Ron Heifetz. To Larry Spears, thank you for encouraging me to write my first published article.

To Steve Piersanti, the best editor in the world, and to the staff at Berrett-Koehler, thank you for your brilliance in shaping this work.

All of you have been my muses. I am blessed with an extended family like this and am forever grateful. You are indeed my relatives.

Juana Bordas
Denver, Colorado
January 2007

Special Contributions: Profiles of Leaders

$\int$ INCE THE CIVIL RIGHTS MOVEMENT, there has been a virtual renaissance in the leadership of communities of color. Leaders have stepped forward in unprecedented numbers and answered the call to serve, and they are guiding their communities with a deep sense of purpose. Yet these leaders are relatively unknown outside of their communities, particularly in mainstream America. Their incredible leadership journeys and the many lessons they offer remain largely invisible. I believe these leaders hold up a lantern of hope that can guide us over the troubled waters of the twenty-first century. Their integrity and deep compassion for humanity can help to shape a more caring and responsible world.

It has been my privilege to interview a number of these outstanding and visionary leaders, profiled below, and to draw from their wisdom and experience in writing this book. It is my hope that the book brings their inspiring stories to a wider audience and integrates their contributions into a new direction for leadership. (Unless otherwise noted, all the quotations from these special contributors that appear in this book come from personal interviews conducted with them, transcribed verbatim, and then coded for common themes and patterns.)

African American Leaders

Dr. Jim Joseph has served four U.S. presidents. Most recently, President Clinton appointed him to be chairman of the Corporation for National Service and U.S. ambassador to South Africa. He was formerly president and CEO of the Council on

Foundations and is currently director of the United States–Southern Africa Center for Leadership and Public Values at Duke University. Dr. Joseph has authored two books: *Charitable Impulse* and *Remaking America.*

Dr. Lea Williams is executive director of the National African-American Women's Leadership Institute, a nonprofit that helps women discover their leadership talents and use these in community service. She is currently the interim associate vice chancellor of academic affairs at North Carolina's A&T University. Dr. Williams began her career in higher education at the United Negro College Fund. She authored *Servants of the People: The 1960s Legacy of African American Leadership.*

Andrew Young was a top aide to Martin Luther King Jr. and a frontrunner in the civil rights movement. As vice president of the Southern Christian Leadership Conference, he was instrumental in crafting the Voting Rights Act. Young was elected to the U.S. House of Representatives and later served as the U.S. ambassador to the UN under President Carter. Upon returning to Atlanta, he served as mayor for two terms and led an economic rebirth. An ordained minister, he served as the head of the National Council of Churches. Young has authored two books, *A Way Out of No Way* and *An Easy Burden.* He has been awarded the Presidential Medal of Freedom.

American Indian Leaders

Ada Deer was the first woman to head the U.S. Bureau of Indian Affairs. Under her leadership, tribal sovereignty was advanced to 180 additional tribes. As the first woman elected chair of the Menominee Nation, she led the movement for federal recognition of her tribe. Deer currently directs the American Indian Studies Program in the School of Social Work at the University of Wisconsin, Madison, and was the first Native American woman to run for the U.S. Congress in Wisconsin.

John Echohawk is a cofounder and executive director of the Native American Rights Fund (NARF). A member of the Pawnee Nation of Oklahoma, he has worked to correct centuries-old injustices for Indian tribes for over thirty years. Since 1988 Echohawk has been recognized as one of the 100 most influential lawyers in America by the *National Law Journal*. He has received numerous service awards for his leadership in the field of Indian law.

LaDonna Harris, Comanche, is one of the most influential, inspired, and determined American Indians in politics. She has served as president of Americans for Indian Opportunity since 1970. Her publications include *To Govern or Be Governed: Indian Tribes at a Crossroads, Partnerships for the Protection of Tribal Environments, Indian Business Opportunities and the Defense Sector, Alternatives for Agriculture: Successful Tribal Farms,* and *Tribal Governments in the U.S. Federal System.*

Benny Shendo Jr., a native of the Jemez Pueblo, was appointed by Governor Bill Richardson as Cabinet Secretary of the New Mexico Indian Affairs Department. Secretary Shendo was the senior manager of Native American Programs for the University of New Mexico and director of the American Indian and Alaskan Native program at Stanford University. He serves on the National Institute for Native Leadership in Higher Education and cofounded the Riverside School in Jemez Pueblo—the first charter school on an Indian reservation.

Latino Leaders

Anna Escobedo Cabral currently holds the office of Treasurer of the United States. Previously, she directed the Smithsonian Institution's Center for Latino Initiatives. Cabral also served as president and CEO of the Hispanic Association on Corporate Responsibility, a coalition of the fourteen largest Hispanic nonprofits that advance Hispanic representation in corporate America. From 1993 to 1999, she was deputy staff director for the U.S. Senate Judiciary Committee under Chairman Orrin G. Hatch and executive staff director of the Senate Republican Task Force on Hispanic Affairs.

Dr. Antonia Pantoja, the first lady of the Puerto Rican civil rights movement, described herself as an "institution builder." Though she passed away in 2002, her profound legacy continues shaping Puerto Rican youth through ASPIRA (to aspire), which instills cultural pride, leadership, and motivation. Dr. Pantoja was the first Puerto Rican woman to receive the Presidential Medal of Freedom and the John W. Gardner Leadership Award. It was my honor to work with her on the curriculum for the National Hispana Leadership Institute and to review interviews for a film on her life—*Antonia Pantoja: Abriendo Caminos* (Opening Pathways, 2006). Her autobiography, *Memoir of a Visionary*, was published by Arte Publico Press in 2002.

Federico Peña, elected mayor of Denver in 1983 and 1987, was the first Latino mayor of a city with a minority Hispanic population. He revitalized Denver's economic health by initiating such projects as Denver International Airport, a new convention center, and Coors Baseball Stadium. A civil rights lawyer, Peña served in the Colorado House of Representatives and as U.S. Secretary of Transportation and U.S. Secretary of Energy during the Clinton administration. Peña is currently the managing director for Vestar Capital Partners.

Raul Yzaguirre served as president of the National Council of La Raza for more than thirty years, building it into the largest national Hispanic civil rights and advocacy organization in America. He is a founder of the Hispanic Association for Corporate Responsibility, the New American Alliance, and the National Hispanic Leadership Agenda. Recognized as one of one of the most influential Hispanic leaders of the twentieth century, Yzaguirre was the first Hispanic to receive a Rockefeller Award for Outstanding Public Service from the trustees of Princeton University and the John W. Gardner Leadership Award.

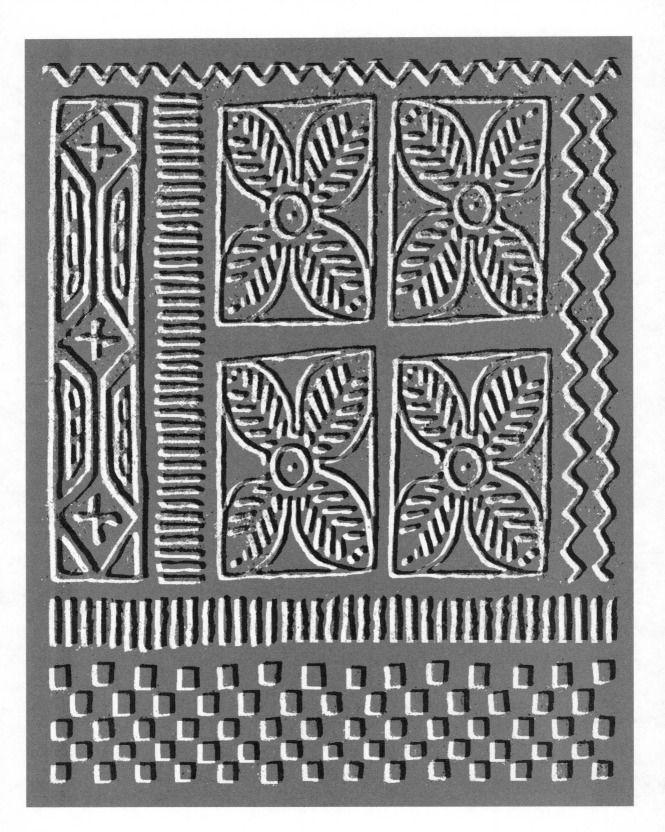

Diversity is Transforming Leadership

MY MOTHER, FOUR BROTHERS, MY SISTER, AND I stood on the edge of the ship's rail watching the image of our beloved Nicaragua become smaller and smaller and then finally disappear into the Caribbean Sea. In the hull of a banana boat, we rocked and swayed, across *El Golfo de Mexico*. The voyage was as endless as the torrential rains of the hurricanes that had erased the coastline of *Cabo Gracias a Dios* where my family had lived for generations. We docked in Tampa, Florida, and fell into the welcoming arms of *mi Papa*. He had arrived earlier, earning money to bring his *familia* to America so his children could have a better life.

This immigrant dream has been the promise of America and the wellspring of its greatness. "You should always be thankful you are here," my father would remind me.

My parents were relentless about unlocking the doors of opportunity for their children. The key, they knew, was education. Like the majority of Hispanics, we were devout

1

Catholics. My mother knew just where to look for help. With her soulful eyes and broken English, she approached the parish priest: "I can cook, clean, and take care of children. Can you give me a job to help my family?" How could he refuse a pure and selfless soul like that? Cooking and cleaning in the school cafeteria, she got her children tuition scholarships so they could get *una buena educación*.

When I became a teenager, there was no Catholic school on the outskirts of Tampa where we lived, but this did not deter my parents. My mother boarded a bus with me in tow and journeyed across town. Humbly, she entreated the nuns at the Academy of Holy Names to give her daughter a scholarship. Every Sunday we would go together to babysit children during services at Christ the King Church so I could earn the remaining part of my tuition. It took me a while to realize that many of my school classmates were going to college. I would never have thought of that, but, hey, my parents told me we came here so I could get a good education. College sounded like a great idea to me.

I could hardly speak, I was so excited. "*Mama y Papá*, I got accepted to college!" Their response shook my world. "Where did this idea come from?" My mother, with her fifth-grade education, thought a high school diploma was *una buena educación*. The University of Florida was only 120 miles away, but to my parents, this was as far as their distant homeland. And a girl, alone? In the old country, she would have been chaperoned or lived with family. "Besides, shouldn't it be your brothers who go to college?" my father lamented. But seeing my determination, my parents in their loving and humble way gave me their blessing.

I worked my way through college. And the land of opportunity made good on its promise. The vision, faith, perseverance, and selfless service of my parents were an endless source of inspiration and strength. They were the greatest leaders any young person could hope to emulate and the source of all the goodness that has been my life.

During my forty years of working in communities of color, I have listened to thousands of such life stories, and I know mine is not unique. Our stories are a collective journey that reflects the times in which we live. Like small streams forming a powerful river, these journeys are coalescing into a dynamic force that is restructuring our country into a multicultural society and transforming American leadership.

The Movements of Our Time

I T WAS A HOT AND HUMID DAY in May 1963. I was sitting outside of my dormitory when I saw my political science professor, Dr. Kantor, in a long line of people walking toward the administration building. I ran up to him and asked, "What are you doing?" He responded solemnly, "We are marching to integrate the University of Florida." I jumped into the line and joined a whole generation of people who believed that America should live up to its founding values.

Just as I was the first in my family to go to college, young people from communities of color across the country did likewise. Universities were being desegregated, and attaining a college degree was finally a possibility for us. For the first time in history, a whole generation could become educated at universities and learn how to operate effectively in dominant cultural systems. A great illustration is the life of John Echohawk, the long-time director of the Native American Rights Fund. He was part of the first cadre of Indian lawyers who interpreted the old treaties and won sovereign rights for their people.

The civil rights movement was a training ground for leaders, empowering communities of color to establish their identity and to seek their birthright as full and equal citizens. Black, Latino, and American Indian organizations flourished and developed culturally effective leadership models based on the values embedded in these communities. These unique models represent a bountiful harvest that can nourish multicultural leadership today.

As a Latina, I am also part of the demographic revolution that is altering our nation's complexion. Population growth is happening so fast in communities of color that by 2010 they will compose almost 35 percent of the U.S. population.[1] My own immigration story is part of that growth. America is a nation of immigrants. The first wave was Anglo European; today, immigrants look more like my family and represent the diverse spectrum of the world's people. In the spirit of ensuring that history is accurately depicted, we must remember that American Indians were indigenous to this land, and that most of the ancestors of African Americans arrived shackled on slave ships.

The movements of our time—immigration, civil rights, demographic shifts, and educational opportunity—imprinted the early phases of my life and the lives of a whole generation in communities of color. These movements spawned a diverse leadership core that reflected the history, challenges, and cultural values of their communities. This book's purpose is to provide practical insights that incorporate these dynamics into an inclusive view of leadership—a view that offers effective ways of leading our diverse society.

Diversity Is Destiny

A number of additional dynamics are beckoning America toward embracing culturally inclusive leadership. Businesses today understand the phenomenal growth in communities of color and desire to access these lucrative and growing markets. Tapping the potential of the changing workforce, consumer base, and citizenry requires leadership approaches that resonate with and are representative of a much broader population base. Mainstream leaders must be able to use practices and approaches that are effective with the many cultures that make up the U.S. population.

Globalization is also fueling diversity. The world is fast becoming a virtual community, where a technological network connects us like next-door neighbors. People are crisscrossing the world and traversing national boundaries. In today's global environment, in which people from widely varying backgrounds live and work side by side, cultural flexibility and adaptability are needed leadership traits. Frances Hesselbein, former president and CEO of the National Girl Scouts, speaks to this urgency: "Perhaps the biggest question in today's world is 'How do we help people deal with their deepest differences?' Governance amid diversity is the world's greatest challenge."[2] A survey conducted by Dr. Joanne Ciulla, professor at the University of Maryland's Jepson School of Leadership, indicates that world leaders are rising to this challenge. She found that 45 percent of heads of state had been educated in another country—and this experience, she notes, allowed them to build bridges and to expand their ability to work with people from many cultures.[3]

 The realization of full democracy contains within it the vision of a pluralistic society. Our democracy is fashioned on the principle of inclusive governance originally utilized by the Iroquois Indians.

Furthermore, the realization of full democracy includes the vision of a pluralistic society. Our democracy is fashioned on the principle of inclusive governance originally used by the Iroquois Indians. Yet when the Constitution was written, only free men were allowed to vote. Black men, as slaves, were counted as only *three-fifths of a person*, and women were not allowed to vote until the passage of the nineteenth amendment in 1920.[4] The discrepancy between the vision of democracy and the reality of racial and cultural segregation has caused a continuing tension in U.S. society. These inconsistencies are most apparent in leadership that is not reflective of our multicultural nation.

Dr. Martin Luther King Jr. believed that America had a date with destiny. America's destiny, he elucidated, was to fulfill the democratic principles inherent in our country's founding and unfold a society that established equality and domestic tranquility for all people and for generations to come. Leadership in communities of color reflects democratic values such as justice and promoting the common welfare, and it uses practical approaches that engage and empower people. This participatory form of leadership can replenish American democracy right at a time when involvement is faltering. Much as King envisioned, the dynamics urging America to embrace her great diversity and to fulfill her destiny as a democratic nation are now shaping leadership into a multicultural form.

These dynamics can be summarized as follows: (1) demographic changes leading to a diversified workforce and consumer base, (2) the civil rights movement, (3) immigration, (4) globalization, (5) America's democratic tradition, (6) the education of leaders from diverse communities, and (7) the development of diverse leadership models in communities of color. Together these factors have transformed our nation from a White homogeneous society to one in which the TV anchors on our nightly news, the football players, the students on college campuses, film stars and performers, and an increasing number of political leaders reflect our burgeoning diversity. Because of these changes, today there is a mandate for political correctness, which means that inclusion and the fostering of diversity are commonly seen as a social responsibility and a function of leadership. Even the president of the United States would not appoint only White cabinet members and staff.

Our eighth dynamic has evolved over fifty years of social change in America—diversity today is seen as politically correct, the right thing to do, and culturally desirable. Particularly for young people, multicultural and mixed cultural groups and activities are hip—the *in thing*—and sought after. Young people are in tune with the creativity, excitement, and learning that cultural interchange offers. Diversity is birthing a new interracial culture. This is evidenced by the 6.8 million Americans who identified themselves as multiracial in the 2000 Census.[5] Promoting social and economic equity is in tune with our values, religious traditions, and political foundation. As a result, leadership is challenged to be culturally relevant and incorporate the inclusive values and principles inherent in our diverse nation. This book offers a multicultural model for evolving leadership to be in step with the dynamic changes that are transforming our country.

The Global Connection

Although this book's emphasis is on Black, Latino, and American Indian communities in the United States, it is important to recognize that the multicultural principles I describe are applicable to many countries and contexts in which leaders are addressing the challenges of a diverse society. Even in countries such as the former Soviet Union, whose populations are distinct from those in the United States, the process used for identifying multicultural principles can be a model for fashioning their own diverse forms of leadership. Furthermore, Black, Latino, and American Indians have historical antecedents and current-day connections across the globe.

Latinos, for instance, are linked to twenty-three countries where Spanish is the primary language and are related to the Portuguese and the Italians, who share their Mediterranean ancestry. These cultures center on the extended family, have traditionally espoused the Catholic faith, and value the emotional or feeling aspects of human nature. In addition, the Moors, who occupied Spain for over 800 years, left their cultural imprint on music, architecture, and philosophy, and this cultural cross-pollination with Northern Africa is still evident; for example, fully one-quarter of all Spanish words are of Arab origin.[6]

It is estimated that during the African Diaspora twelve million people were taken to the western hemisphere.[7] African culture was embedded in many countries, including Barbados, Haiti, Jamaica, Trinidad, Cuba, Puerto Rico, and, of course, Brazil. The racial heterogeneity in Brazil birthed a diverse, rhythmic, and unique culture whose population is 39 percent mulatto and 6 percent Black. Brazil, which is the fifth largest country in the world and has the fifth largest population, is one of the best examples of a multicultural nation combining Black, Latino, and European influences. The principles overviewed in this book offer a rich resource for countries like Brazil that are addressing their own multicultural challenges, as well as others across Latin America, for which population statistics indicate 17 percent have mixed African ancestry and 5 percent identify as Black.

Through the dark night of slavery, African slaves fashioned a unique culture that sang of their tribal ancestry and the collective values of their homeland. Not only did their spirit of community survive, but new forms and meanings evolved from their African heritage. The leadership forms cultivated by Blacks in America are rooted in the African soil and offer contemporary models on leading from an Afro perspective. Certainly the South African movement that ended apartheid grew out of King's and Mahatma Gandhi's work and is indicative of how leadership in one country can be the fountain from which another freedom movement flows. We must remember that when the Berlin Wall fell, the Germans were singing "We Shall Overcome."

American Indians are kin to indigenous people in the western hemisphere and on every continent. They often share similar worldviews, a nature-based spirituality, and communal values whereby the good of the tribe supercedes the individual. These traditions have been passed from generation to generation. The pre-Columbian western hemisphere, as will be explored in this book, was resplendent with thousands of unique indigenous cultures. Mexico today is still 30 percent indigenous, and 60 percent identify as mestizo or mixtures of European, predominately Spanish, and Indian.[8] Across Latin America today, the native or indigenous population is estimated at 12 percent, with 23 percent mestizos.[9]

The western hemisphere, then, is a rich jambalaya of African, Spanish, and indigenous cultures. The principles presented in this book have direct applicability to the many countries where multicultural populations reside and where leading diversity is a critical issue. Even countries such as England, which historically was predominately Anglo-Saxon, now has significant Black and East Indian populations and could benefit from using inclusive leadership principles.

The migration, expansion, and settlement of societies is a phenomenon as old as human history; it has led to the intertwining of many cultures that share common roots. Going way back, all cultures have indigenous antecedents. The principles gleaned from Black, Latino, and American Indian cultures come from these ancient traditions that emphasized humanity's common bonds and counsel us to look out for one another. Multicultural leadership principles flow from this tradition and offer the potential to cultivate a strong sense of world community.

The western hemisphere is a rich jambalaya of African, Spanish, and indigenous cultures. The principles presented in this book have direct applicability to the many countries where multicultural populations reside and where leading diversity is a critical issue.

Crafting a Multicultural Leadership Model

ETHNOCENTRICITY IS SEEING THE WORLD from one cultural orientation and believing it to be the universal standard—or even superior. American leadership, which has been culled largely from White male perspectives, centers on White or mainstream cultural values and thus reflects an ethnocentric orientation. A multicultural leadership orientation, on the other hand, incorporates many cultural perspectives, appreciates differences, values the unique contributions of diverse groups, and promotes learning from many orientations. People are encouraged to maintain their cultural identity while at the same time participating in and contributing to the larger society.

Multicultural leadership is uniquely suited to our mosaic world because it incorporates the influences, practices, and values of a variety of cultures in a respectful and productive manner. Multicultural leadership encourages an inclusive and adaptable style that cultivates the ability to bring out the best in our diverse workforce and to fashion a sense of community with people from many parts of the globe. This inclusive form of leadership is in sync with many cultures, enabling a wide spectrum of people to actively engage, contribute, and tap their potential. Multicultural leadership brings a commitment to advance people who reflect the vitality, values, and voices of our diversity to all levels of organizations and society.

When people respect each other and value differences, they can work together more amicably which results in greater productivity. Multicultural leadership encourages synergy, innovation, and resourcefulness.

This book provides the knowledge base to ignite and inspire a core of multicultural leaders. Transforming leadership into a multicultural model will take a dedicated cadre who recognize that diversity and inclusiveness are intrinsic to creating an authentic

MULTICULTURAL LEADERSHIP IS . . .

An inclusive approach and philosophy that incorporates the influences, practices, and values of diverse cultures in a respectful and productive manner. Multicultural leadership resonates with many cultures and encourages diverse people to actively engage, contribute, and tap their potential.

and equitable democracy. Our future economic well-being is tied to our ability to effectively engage and develop the potential of our culturally distinct world. To that end, this book explores eight principles that integrate the practices of communities of color into an inclusive and democratic leadership model.

Some readers may be wondering why we need to develop a multicultural leadership model. Didn't we just point out that diversity is politically correct and culturally desirable? Isn't America already a multicultural nation? On any given day, a person might have enchiladas for lunch, listen to jazz or hip hop, wear exquisite Navajo jewelry, watch *Oprah* on TV, and cap the evening off with a margarita. It is true that culturally, communities of color have greatly enriched America and that many gains were achieved by the civil rights movement. Today, we live in a smorgasbord society in which many enjoy the fruits of a cultural cornucopia. Nevertheless, within this kaleidoscope of diversity, mainstream American leadership has not integrated the rich practices of communities of color. Until a more inclusive form of leadership embodies our diverse society, a truly multicultural society will not be attained.

Infusing Salsa, Soul, and Spirit into American Leadership

THE CHALLENGE NOW is to spark people's interest in transforming leadership into an inclusive and multicultural form. We can ignite this by recognizing the vibrant flavors and gifts that American Indians, Latinos, and African Americans bring to leadership and by emphasizing multicultural leadership as a strategic advantage in our global community.

In the Hispanic tradition, someone embarking on a journey, a new venture, or a new stage of life asks for a *bendición* or blessing from her grandmother or other respected person. American Indians burn sage to purify the person with smoke. African Americans might sing a traditional hymn, followed by a communal prayer, and a collective, heartfelt *amen!* A coach's motivational talk to players, which gets them psyched up and ready to perform at their optimum is intended, in a similar way, to prepare them for a good outcome. Let our journey begin in an inspirational way by highlighting the energy, spiritual insights, experience, and effective leadership that American Indians, Blacks, and Latinos bring to America.

Pass the Salsa

As far back as I can remember, I would be lifted in my father's arms dancing to the salsa beats of quick, quick, pause; quick, quick, pause. Seven beats in all, because when it is repeated there is an empty space, like the zero that my Indian ancestors from Central America discovered. The salsa beat was a magnet. I could never resist the fusion music that blends African drums, American Indian rattles (maracas), Spanish guitars, Moorish sounds, and Caribbean rhythms. It is no coincidence that salsa is also the spicy, hot condiment giving food flavor and bringing zing to the palate. Salsa adds a little variety to the rice and beans that are an everyday staple in Latino cuisine.

Salsa is a great metaphor for diversity. Just as no two individuals are alike, every batch of salsa is *unico*. Each cook makes salsa in a particular way, with a little of this and a little of that.

 Salsa is a great metaphor for diversity. Just like no two individuals are alike, every batch of salsa is unico.

Traditional Latino cookbooks include in their recipes a guideline called *a gusto* (to your liking or taste), reflecting that you must be flexible and adaptable to tend to people's needs and preferences. This is one of diversity's golden rules.

Besides the fact that every salsa maker has a personal recipe, the size of the tomatoes and the strength of the onion, herbs, and spices change the taste. But the real wild card is the jalapeño peppers. Latinos know you approach jalapeños with *respeto*. You take a teensy little bite to determine whether it is mild, hot, or Ay Chihuahua! Just as no jalapeños are the same, each individual is a unique, one-of-a-kind design.

Salsa is now America's favorite condiment, having passed the more homogenized and sugar-laced ketchup in the early nineties. The salsa dance craze is sweeping the nation as young and old discover the pleasure of moving to the Latin beat. But salsa is more than a dance or a racy condiment. Salsa is a way of life. *Tener salsa en la vida* is to fully enjoy life, by treasuring family, relationships, work, and community. Salsa is the spice of life—the energy, vitality, and *gusto*! *Salsa en la vida* has been a key ingredient enabling Latinos to sustain themselves through the past five hundred years since the conquest of this hemisphere.

Putting the Gusto into Leadership

Latinos are invigorating American leadership. They have the highest participation in the labor market of any group that is tracked by the U.S. Census and are the fastest growing small business sector. Today, Latino U.S.A. has the eighth largest gross national product in the world.[10] Their core values include faith, family, hard work, honesty, sharing, inclusion, and cooperation. It could well be that Latinos will make their most significant contribution in the realignment of America's values. As Raul Yzaguirre surmises, "Latinos live America's core values of family and hard work. Instead of asking us to change our name and culture and to assimilate, Latinos should be saying 'you should become more like us.' We espouse an America that lives up to its values. America is the best country in the world—but it cannot become a true world leader unless it embraces all people. *America will become more American* when Latinos are fully integrated at all levels of our country."

In Thomas Friedman's masterful book, *The World Is Flat,* he surmises that the twenty-first century will be "more and more driven by a more diverse—non-Western, non-white—group of individuals . . . You are going to see every color of the human rainbow take part."[11] As a fusion culture and not a race, Latinos are white, red, black, brown, and yellow and all the mixtures in between. Over 80 percent speak some Spanish at home. (Spanish is the language spoken in the greatest number of countries in the world.) Latinos are a rainbow people. They are connected by language to twenty-three countries and are therefore a springboard to our global community.[12]

Latinos live America's core values of family and hard work. Instead of asking us to change our name and culture and to assimilate, Latinos should be saying "you should become more like us."

—Raul Yzaguirre

Within the United States the Latino landscape is also varied, containing a wealth of histories, backgrounds, and countries of origin. Sixty percent of Latinos are of Mexican descent. Puerto Ricans form the second largest group, comprising 10 percent. Cuban Americans are 3.4 percent. Latino diversity continues to expand. In the 2000 Census, almost 9 percent were of Central and South American descent, and there was a 96.9 percent increase in people reporting origins other than Mexican, Puerto Rican, or Cuban.[13]

An interesting fact is that the four million people living in mainland Puerto Rico are not included in the Census, even though they are U.S. citizens. Puerto Rico was invaded by the United States during the Spanish-American War in 1898 and has remained a Commonwealth. Despite over one hundred years of strong U.S. influence, Puerto Ricans are proud of their distinct culture, history, and language, which is enriched by the mixture of aboriginal, Spanish, and African peoples. Today, there are almost as many Puerto Ricans in the continental United States as on their beloved island.[14]

As will be seen in subsequent sections on the eight principles, Latino values and worldview align with those of cultures emphasizing collectivism, generosity, mutual help, extended family, and the common good. Latino leadership reflects a social and celebratory nature, a community-oriented centered approach, and a people-centered process. These qualities are becoming valued traits of twenty-first-century leadership. Latinos only emerged as an identifiable group in the last forty years. As a budding force, their influence and flavor have just begun putting the salsa into American leadership.

The African American Soul Sings

SOUL HAS BEEN DEPICTED as the immaterial essence or substance, the animating principle or actuating cause of life. Soul represents the immortal and permanent, the spirit, life, and vitality. The atrocities and dehumanization of slavery were rationalized, in part, by propagating the belief that Africans did not have a soul and were therefore less than human. This was reinforced by the Constitution's designation of the Black man as three-fifths of a person. Nevertheless, the African soul was resilient, rooted in an intense spiritual tradition birthed in ancient times on the continent where humans first evolved. Like the tradition of the indigenous people of the Americas, it is nature based and sustained by community ritual, song, and dance. *The struggle of African slaves is the struggle of a people who were literally fighting for the recognition of their souls.*

W. E. B. Du Bois, the first African American awarded a Ph.D. from Harvard, explored the philosophical, spiritual, and cultural dimensions of Black people's religion in his classic book, *The Souls of Black Folk*, written in 1903. Du Bois wove the sacred and the secular together, setting the stage for the advent of African American leadership, which would spring out of a spiritual foundation and address social injustice. The Black church had become the social, intellectual, and economic anchor of community life. A distinctive religion developed in which emotional release, communal refuge, and wailing against injustice were found. Out of the pain of slavery a unique spiritual music was born, which Du Bois called the "sorrow songs," designating them as "the greatest gift of the Negro people" and the only distinct "American music" form.[15]

Sorrow songs were the voice of an oppressed people, and yet, they are prayers that breathe hope, faith, and renewal. This vigorous spiritual musical tradition incorporated African aesthetics through call and response, melodic riffs, repetition and revision, and the integration of song and dance through foot stomping and clapping. It would evolve into a new gospel sound, eventually become rhythm and blues, and then be transmuted into soul music. These sounds are the lifeblood of much popular music today—jazz, rock and roll, and rap all spring from the gospel tradition.

Soul, which some attempted to deny Black people, bloomed into one of the essential features of their culture. Soul reflects a deep well of resilient hope, a spiritual family bonded by common hardship, and an emotional connection that forges community consciousness. Even physical sustenance became soul food—a delicious masterpiece born of adversity. Scraps from the slave master's table became tasty dishes of black-eyed peas, cornbread, sweet potato pie, catfish, or turnip greens seasoned with pigs' feet or ham hocks. The resilient and creative impulse that engendered soul food fed the spirit, not just the body.

Soul, which some attempted to deny Black people, bloomed into one of the essential features of their culture. Soul reflects a deep well of resilient hope, a spiritual brotherhood bonded by common hardship, and an emotional connection that forges community consciousness.

Soul music, soul food, soul brother—the concept of *soul* permeates African American culture. Soul represents a deep understanding that their spiritual wellspring sustained Black people through the trials and tribulations of slavery, racism, and oppression. When gospel music sang out about freedom, it was about liberty not only in heaven, but on the earth as well. The infusion of soul into all facets of life brought forth a unique form of spiritual activism in which Black leadership was ignited from the pulpits in the sermons of ministers. This tradition blossomed during the civil rights movement, infusing American leadership with a new moral fiber.

Furthermore, the African American adage "if it doesn't kill you, it will make you stronger" reflects a biological reality. Those who made it across the Atlantic and withstood the hardship of slavery brought a vitality, resilience, and spiritual strength. Combined with the mutual support of the slave quarters community, this strength enabled people to survive the traumas of their history. This collective focus evolved into an unshakable sense of community, which continues to be the basis for African American progress and leadership.

The Soul of Leadership

Dr. Jim Joseph, former U.S. ambassador to South Africa, explains the power of this form of leadership: "The initial group of African American leaders in the fifties and sixties were ministers. They were totally independent and had the freedom to act on the basis of their social conscience, without the threat of being terminated by some white-controlled structure. Their source of livelihood came from Black people and Black churches." The most prophetic voice to arise from the Black churches in the last century was that of Martin Luther King Jr. He poignantly challenged the materialistic and racist bent of the American culture: "We are prone to judge success by the index of our salaries or the size of our automobiles, rather than by the quality of our service and relationship to humanity."[16] King believed that Black spirituality and faith would bring a moral reawakening that would restore a sense of economic justice and social responsibility and would affirm the sacredness of life.

King built on a pervasive spiritual tradition that had nourished Black people for generations, allowing them to shed the residues of slavery and oppression without destructive bitterness or anger. He cultivated a scope of leadership that had at its core a belief in redemption and forgiveness of one's enemies. These may be said to represent the higher qualities of human consciousness or soul. It is ironic that the very soul qualities once denied Black people constitute one of the great legacies they are bequeathing to American leadership.

American Indian Leadership— Being in Right Relationship

A S THE SUN COMES UP each morning and as it sets in its resting place in the evening, the native peoples of the Americas give praise to the Great Spirit. They believe that all life flows from this one source—*the unifying life force*—that is present everywhere. The rivers, rocks, earth, plants, animals, and all people are made of this same spiritual essence. All life is related and sacred. Benny Shendo Jr., a young Jemez Pueblo leader who is also New Mexico's Secretary for Indian Affairs, reflects on this way of life: "I was taught we are spiritual people living in a spiritual world, walking the spiritual path, and there is a higher power."

This core spiritual belief defines the nature of relationships: human beings belong to one spiritual family. In the Lakota tradition, when people meet, they say *mitakuye oyasin* or "all my relatives." This ancient way of acknowledging each other, which is also followed by the Cherokee or Tsalagi people, contains the idea of kinship—of being family and thereby being responsible for one another.[17] The Mayan golden rule "I am another yourself" represents another universal way of reflecting the oneness of humanity. Within these traditions, everyone must be treated with the respect due a family member.

Seeing human relations in this way results in a circular view of the universe. Giving and sharing provide a way to nourish and regenerate oneself. In many tribes, people are respected not for how much they have, but for their generosity, how much they share and give away. This extends to sharing ideas, stories, and life experience, giving of one's time, and contributing one's talents to the well-being of individuals and the community.

The belief in the pervasiveness and continuity of spirit also unfolds a way of life that is collectively rather than individually oriented. Even the names of many tribes translate into

 The belief in the pervasiveness and continuity of spirit unfolds a way of life that is collectively rather than individually oriented. Even the names of many tribes translate into the people—*meaning that everyone belongs.*

the people—meaning that everyone belongs.[18] Central to Indian culture is the collective welfare and the need to ensure that the people or tribe continues for posterity. Their leadership forms, which have been on the earth for many generations, flow from this orientation.

The Spirit of Leadership

An eagle feather lifts the sweet grass smoke into the sky. A prayer of gratitude is offered. People ask for guidance and good outcomes. First, there is silence as people gather themselves, tune in to one another, and connect with the spiritual force that unites them. Then the meeting begins.

 Native American leadership is based on time-honored traditions, cultures, and religious beliefs, including an understanding of the relationships between human beings and the larger world. Tribes have a long-term view of things.

—John Echohawk, Pawnee

Prayers, rituals, celebrations, and ceremonies are ways that Indian leaders make the *spirit visible in everyday life* and bring a higher dimension to community endeavors. By acknowledging that everything comes from and is unified by the one life source, leaders remind people of their responsibility to one another. Offering a prayer to begin any endeavor, and expressing gratitude for all that has been given, reinforces this bond.

American Indian culture impels a leadership form that centers on communal responsibility, a concern for the welfare of *the people* or tribe, and stewardship for all life. As Benny Shendo notes, "In the other society, when a person is elected to office, he is responsible in a sense to the people who voted for him. But the eagles don't vote, the trees don't vote, the buffalo don't vote, the waters don't vote, the stars don't vote, so in the other society people don't understand the broader concept of what our overall responsibility in this world means. The only responsibility is to you as a voter, because you can vote me out tomorrow. The Jemez leader has to be responsible for the community, for the future, and for the natural world in which all people live." John Echohawk emphasizes this responsibility: "Native American leadership is based on time-honored traditions, cultures, and religious beliefs, including an understanding of the relationships between human beings and the larger world. Tribes have a long-term view of things."

Many authors today emphasize the spiritual dimension of leadership. Often, this refers to "working on oneself," developing better habits, improving one's character, or becoming a better person. This reflects the individualistic orientation of the dominant culture in which spirituality is a personal focus and endeavor. In the American Indian tradition, spirituality is the unifying factor infusing all aspects of one's life—one's relationships, responsibilities, community obligations, and connection to the natural world. American Indian spirituality demonstrates how centering on *collective* rather than *individual* advancement can lay the foundation for a society that places the community's welfare above individual gain. Like the Great Spirit—which is pervasive, life-generating, and timeless—American Indian leadership brings a spiritual foundation, which respects and benefits all life and ensures the continuity of future generations.

Clearly then, Latinos, Blacks, and American Indians are bringing wisdom, vitality, and vision to American leadership. So, let us begin our journey to infuse American leadership with *salsa, soul, and spirit*. The next section offers an overview of the eight principles that can be used as guideposts for leading from a multicultural orientation.

Eight Principles of Multicultural Leadership— An Overview

THE FIRST STEP in integrating the leadership practices of communities of color into an inclusive and multicultural form is exploring a number of core values that are keystones for these cultures. Values, explains Burt Nanus in *Visionary Leadership*, shape our assumptions about the future, provide the context within which issues and goals are identified, and set standards for people's behavior and actions.[19] Values also define the range of people's choices, identify what is good and desirable, and give definition to a society's culture. Leadership, therefore, reflects cultural values and societal norms.

Part One, A New Social Covenant, describes the value changes that are necessary to create an environment in which inclusive and multicultural leadership can thrive.

These three principles are

- *Sankofa*—Learn from the past

- *I* to *We*—From individualism to collective identity

- *Mi Casa Es Su Casa*—Developing a spirit of generosity

Many African Americans honor the symbol of *Sankofa,* a mythical bird with its feet firmly planted forward and its head looking backward. Coming from their West African ancestors, *Sankofa* means "Return, go back, seek, and retrieve." *Sankofa* urges us to reflect on and learn from the past. Expanding leadership into a multicultural form requires an understanding of how Eurocentric and hierarchical leadership became dominant in the first place. Beginning with the myths concerning the "settling of America," which deny the historical contributions of communities of color, we can seek new insights concerning the leadership practices of the diverse groups that shaped our country. Some of these practices, particularly those of American Indians, existed before Columbus landed in this hemisphere.

Building a pluralistic and equitable society requires a shift from today's emphasis on individualism to one in which people's mutual welfare and the social good come first. This change from an *I* to a *We* reference point alters one's orientation so that the collective welfare is now seen as central to one's own well-being. Blacks, Latinos, and American Indians are collective cultures who consider the family, tribe, or community before individual advancement. The shift from an *I* to a *We* orientation focuses leadership on community, service, and mutual advancement.

From a *We* perspective, the spirit of generosity can be nourished because people will understand that a collective point of reference is the foundation of a caring and just society. *Mi casa es su casa*—"my house is your house"—is used to denote the generosity found in communities of color, which is reciprocal, circular, and a way to nurture oneself and others. Generosity is one antidote to the rampant materialism that reinforces individualistic advancement over the common good. In communities of color, being generous is an expected leadership trait that is equated with integrity and garners respect. Collectively, generosity and sharing enabled these communities to survive when faced with scarcity and oppression.

Part Two, Leadership Styles in Communities of Color, speaks to three primary roles and functions that American Indians, Latinos, and African Americans assume.

These three principles are

- *A Leader Among Equals*—Community conferred leadership

- *Leaders as Guardians of Public Values*—A tradition of activism

- *Leaders as Community Stewards*—Working for the common good

A Leader Among Equals comes from the American Indian tradition in which leadership was rotated and shared. This principle levels the playing field and supports a distributed and circular form of leadership, which topples hierarchy and privilege. In communities of color, a leader's influence and authority comes from being part of and sanctioned by one's people. Conversely, to be perceived as someone who puts oneself above others will destroy one's credibility.

Because leaders represent people with unequal access to opportunities and benefit, they are responsible for addressing issues and institutions that barricade full participation. By articulating values such as pluralism, justice, and equality, leaders in communities of color beckon our society to live up to the *public values* on which our democracy was founded. During the civil rights movement, Black Americans brought leaders as guardians of the equitable society to the foreground. To accomplish this, leaders bring people together and inspire them to collective action.

As builders and guardians of community progress, *leaders as community stewards* nurture a network or legacy that continues to advance people. Community stewards foster group consensus, create a shared community vision, weave partnerships, and use culturally effective communication. Community servanthood redefines servant leadership as social responsibility and addressing the common welfare.

Part Three, Creating the Circle of Leadership, reflects the expansive view about the ways people are related that is integral to Black, Latino, and Indian cultures. They understand that each person's well-being is intimately tied with the well-being of others. Two principles embody these tendencies:

- *All My Relatives*—*La Familia,* the village the tribe

- *Gracias*—Gratitude, hope, and forgiveness

As noted earlier, the Lakota tribe's traditional greeting is "All my relatives." Contained in this is the idea of kinship, of being responsible for each other and living respectfully with all of life. This sense of global family and social responsibility is reflected in the seventh principle, *All My Relatives*. The belief that we are all connected opens the pathway to a collective way of life and repositions a leader's relationship with people as ongoing and reciprocal. Regardless of position, social class, or ranking, people should be treated as family.

Leadership in communities of color is grounded in *spiritual responsibility*: leaders attend to people's material and social needs, as well as provide inspiration and hope. Spirituality has flourished despite oppression and economic need because of several highly valued attributes: gratitude, faith, hope, and forgiveness. These attributes that serve as spiritual sustenance are expressed in the principle of *gracias*.

Gracias in Spanish means "thank you," but it also means "grace." *Webster's Dictionary* defines grace as "the influence or spirit of God operating in man; the condition of being in God's favor." It is an accepted belief that without God's grace people of color would not have survived. As a leadership principle, *gracias* signifies a deep-seated optimism, a focus on thankfulness rather than lack, and the ability to forgive and start fresh regardless of past transgressions or difficulties. *Gracias* offers another antidote to the materialism dividing our nation and prepares the way for a compassionate society in which taking care of people's needs is our highest priority.

The tradition of *gracias* has very old roots in America, going back to the first multicultural celebration, in which native people joined with settlers to express thanksgiving for their survival. This feast day is a beautiful model that illuminates the benefits of integrating practices from communities of color into mainstream society.

Part Four, Leadership for a Multicultural Age, is a call to action and an invitation to join the growing cadre of leaders who are crafting our global future. We will explore how the process of assimilation and the myth of the melting pot negated the cultures, languages, and histories of America's great diversity. Acculturation—the process through which people learn how to expand their repertoire and adapt to different cultural perspectives—is presented as a way to enhance one's ability to engage in our multicultural society.

Multicultural leadership also entails changing organizational structures so that diversity becomes part of the framework and the standard way of operating. This requires a shift from hierarchical pluralism, which dictates that people must conform to dominant cultural norms, to egalitarian pluralism, with values and norms that reflect a multicultural perspective. We will explore egalitarian pluralism as well as highlight a few corporations that are moving in this direction and are using the leadership principles from communities of color in their business practices.

As we near the end of our journey, we will acknowledge global pioneers who are embracing the mantle of social responsibility and exemplify the principle of leaders as guardians of public values and as community stewards. They serve as prototypes of how leaders can serve the collective good, joining with people of all nations and cultures to forge our multicultural future.

Like world music, which reflects the melodic creations and the upbeat sounds of our expansive global cultures, this book invites the reader to step into the world of diversity, become a multicultural leader, and join in the dance of our kaleidoscope world.

PART ONE

A New Social Covenant

 MERICA WAS FOUNDED on the values of rugged individualism and competition. The next three chapters review how these qualities fashioned a society in which people have a greater orientation toward the self rather than the collective good. In the spirit of *Sankofa,* which beckons us to reconcile our past with our present, we question the historical belief in individualism, which asserted that human nature was driven by self-interest, competition, and acquisition. Individualism replaced early collective and cooperative cultures and established a social covenant in which government or society was a safeguard against man's competitive and aggressive nature. In this worldview, leadership was the domain of the enlightened few, tended toward control, and was competitively oriented.

This view of human nature as self-centered and individualist is no longer suited to our world village, in which advances in technology and communication link us intricately together. In his visionary book, *One: The Art and Practice of Conscious Leadership,* Lance Secretan describes the idea of people being separate individuals as an antiquated concept: "We have become aware that the world is smaller, more interdependent, and integrated." He continues, "Community is growing in importance. The new reality is that we are one."[1] This, of course, is the basis for the indigenous worldview, which has been sustained in the collective identities of communities of color.

In response to this new environment, the old individualistic form of leadership has been shape-shifting into a cooperative, collaborative, and people-oriented form. It may be said that leadership is changing from an individualistic, self-centered orientation to a *We* or *other-centered* orientation. This shift is in alignment with leadership in communities of color, which must be other-centered because leaders derive their authority from the people they serve, so they rely on the people's support. Leaders are sanctioned by their communities by putting the collective welfare above self-interest.

Putting the common good first goes against the grain of individualism—*We* takes precedence over *I*. A deep sense of generosity, sharing, and reciprocity sustains this mutuality. Leadership in this context is not a vehicle for individual advancement, but instead is based on a collective orientation and responsibility.

The Principle *Mi Casa Es Su Casa* (my house is your house) expresses the profuse generosity in communities of color, in which wealth traditionally meant giving to others and assuming responsibility for community needs. To take more than one's share and to accumulate excessive wealth was a cultural anathema. This generous orientation encompasses a long-term perspective that includes the sustainability of future generations and the natural environment.

Today's interdependent and fragile world is calling for a new social covenant that is centered not on every man for himself, but on caring for each other and looking out for the mutual good. This covenant was envisioned by Martin Luther King Jr., who believed that other-centered men could build a society that would restore "dignity, equality, and freedom for people's spirit," a society in which "people everywhere can have three meals a day for their bodies, education, and culture for their minds." King appealed to our morality and conscience when he said, "What self-centered men have torn down, other-centered men can build up."[2]

An other-centered society would incorporate the core values of collectivism and generosity that emanate from communities of color. These values are the touchstones for multicultural leadership principles dedicated to building a benevolent and just society that upholds the well-being of all people.

In Search of Multicultural Excellence

MAINSTREAM BOOKS ON LEADERSHIP routinely emphasize organizations and companies that represent "the ideal." Books such as *Good to Great*, *Built to Last*, and *In Search of Excellence* put forth models that illuminate the possibilities when visionary leadership takes the helm. Authors do not spend much time with topics such as "In Search of Mediocrity" or "From Bad to Worse," although there are myriad examples of organizations that are middle-of-the-road and leaders who falter in their commitments. By stressing the ideal—the best of the best—and by having positive models to emulate, leaders and organizations expect to improve and move toward that vision.

Likewise, when Anglo values and cultural norms are discussed, the positive attributes are usually highlighted and even revered. Individualism is rarely discussed as a value that may lead to social isolation and personal discontent as one is constantly comparing oneself to others. Competition is seen as a positive force that brings out the best in people and organizations, not as a stance that sometimes rends the fabric of a mutually supportive society in which everyone is valued. Youth is venerated and in alignment with the new and improved mentality of today's marketplace; the youth cult is not presented as a dead-end street leading to a society with a short-term memory that disregards the wisdom of age and the lessons from the past.

Accordingly, in this book I will present African American, Indian, and Latino cultures from the *highest standards* of these communities. This is not to deny the inconsistencies and undesirable aspects present in all cultures. In communities of color, however, oppression, slavery, and colonization are historical traumas. Remnants of these difficult circumstances have resulted in higher rates of poverty, low self-esteem, and low educational levels. We must strive to separate the gifts and positive attributes in these communities from the residues of discrimination and oppression that manifest today as lower economic, educational, and social status.

The leaders whose voices resonate on these pages are some of the most talented and committed people who have guided communities of color in the past decades. They represent the ideal. Their values, approaches, and dedication have laid the foundation for multicultural leadership. Concentrating on the ideal is intended to call forth the best in communities of color and construct a mental model of a desirable future state. As these communities step forward, embracing the leadership principles described in this book, they will embark on a bold and worthy journey to build a world that honors our human potential and celebrates our great diversity.

For mainstream leaders, recognizing this ideal is an opportunity to incorporate the best practices from communities of color into their repertoire and to acknowledge their promise and potential. Young and emerging leaders of color will expand their understanding of the tremendous contribution our communities bring to America. I hope this inspires them to stay true to the values that have shaped their communities and to realize that their greatest contribution comes from being the architects of our multicultural future.

Sankofa—
Learn from the Past

ILLING OUT MY FIRST U.S. CENSUS FORM, I went back and forth, turning the form one way and then another, searching for a category that acknowledged my Latino roots. I felt a loud thud in my heart as I finally checked the Caucasian box. Latinos were not recognized as a group by the U.S. government until the 1980 Census. The need to be accepted for who you are is a very deep longing in all people, but particularly in communities of color, whose members have been relegated to a minority status and measured by a White ideal. As I filled out the form, I heard my grandmother's sweet voice, *"Aye mi jita, nunca olvides quien eres y de donde venistes."* ("Oh, my dearest little daughter, never forget who you are and where you came from.")

This notion of remembering your roots and staying connected to your ancestry is of biblical import in Black, Latino, and American Indian communities. Forgetting where you came from is known as *selling out*, becoming an Uncle Tom or an Oreo or a coconut (Black or Brown on the outside, but White on the inside). Staying connected to one's roots includes being in tune with the history and struggles of one's people. Communities of color relate to the past as the "wisdom teacher," the source from which culture flows.

Sankofa, the mythical bird from West Africa who looks backward, symbolizes the respect African Americans have for the insight and knowledge acquired from the past. *Sankofa* reminds us that our roots ground and nourish us, hold us firm when the winds of change howl, and offer perspective about what is lasting and significant. Although *Sankofa* rests on the foundation of the past, its feet are facing forward. This ancient symbol counsels us that the past is a pathway to understanding the present and creating a strong future. *Sankofa* invites us to bring forward the meaningful and useful—including the values and spiritual traditions passed from previous generations—to learn from experience, and to avoid the dead ends and pitfalls of history.[1] As the song that is considered the Black national anthem, "Lift Every Voice and Sing," proclaims: "Sing a song full of the faith that the dark past has taught us." The song also inspires hope, because despite past trials and tribulations, people survived and are now thriving.

Latinos connect to the past during *El Dia de los Muertos* by recognizing the gifts inherited from their *antepasados* and reflecting on the wisdom their ancestors have passed on. On this day, many Latinos compose an altar with pictures of their mother, father, *abuelos*, and other family members who have passed on. Surrounded by marigold flowers, flickering candles, and perhaps a mantle embroidered by their grandmother,

 Sankofa *is a mythical bird with its feet firmly planted forward and its head looking backward.* Sankofa *means return, go back, seek, and retrieve.* Sankofa *urges us to reflect on and learn from the past.*

they play old songs and tell stories about these relatives. Fried plantains, *arroz y frijoles*, rice pudding, or other special foods are made. Brandy, chocolate, strong coffee, and other delicious treats are left on altars so that those who came before know they are welcome, loved, and remembered. Latinos also take flowers and food to family burial plots, and thus the roots of the past are affirmed and strengthened.

American Indians believe their ancestors, the venerable ones, walk right alongside them and are accessible even though they have passed on to the spirit world. Prayers are made to the grandfathers and grandmothers, asking for their blessings and good counsel. The Navajos honor this connection each time they introduce themselves by referring to their heritage and lineage: "I am the grandson of . . . and the great grandson of . . ." Indian history, culture, morals, and values are passed on through the oral tradition in stories and fables that often enumerate the feats of those that came before. "Learn from the past," a slogan for the Native American College Fund, encapsulates the belief that by understanding history, people will not repeat past mistakes and can create a better future.

Through time-honored traditions, these cultures keep the past alive and accessible so it feeds the present. Since their history is a tale of conquest, cultural oppression, and racism, reclaiming and remedying the past is crucial to recovering power and wholeness. For many, this is not about times gone by, but their recent family history. Secretary of the U.S. Treasury Ana Escobedo Cabral grew up in a migrant family in the Santa Clara Valley, listening to the stories of her grandparents and great grandparents. She says, "I feel very fortunate that I lived with several generations. I learned about the struggles they endured—losing children to disease and hunger, coming across the Rio Grande, and walking all the way from Texas to California with no money and then working in the fields." Cabral believes this motivates her to improve the lives of others. "One thing that will always be culturally important is the connection to your own family history. Through that you'll understand people's pain, suffering, and struggle."

Healing the Past

IT MAY BE DIFFICULT for many people to understand why we need to reconcile the past in order to build a pluralistic society and fashion multicultural leadership. Yet the vestiges of the past and the inequities that existed for centuries continue to impede inclusiveness and equity. For example, imbedded racism, which has its roots in slavery, was evident in the television images of the destitute and homeless Black people after Hurricane Katrina ravaged New Orleans. Inequality has lingered long after emancipation. Similarly, five hundred years after the conquistadores slashed their way through this hemisphere, Latinos still struggle with being colonized people. An example of this discrimination is that Latino wages are actually falling even as their labor participation increases. They are working more and earning less.[2] Another is that Latino high school dropout rates hover at 40 percent, which is attributed to inadequate and poorly funded schools in high-density Latino neighborhoods.[3] By understanding the historical systems that continue this type of discrimination, Latinos can remain resolute and stay the course.

Indian lands were snatched from them *way back* during pioneer times. After the Indians were rounded up and confined to reservations, Christian ministers baptized them and banned many of their religious practices. Children were sent to boarding schools to learn the "White man's ways." Stripped of their spirituality and land, this great and noble people could have had their heritage wiped out like the bison that once grazed the open range. The movement to reinstate tribal lands took shape only in the 1960s when the first Indian lawyers examined the old treaties. The Indian's battle for tribal sovereignty and cultural preservation persists today.

These examples shed light on how history continues to affect people of color and the reconciliation that is needed to create a truly inclusive future. Understanding and healing the past can move people beyond the vestiges of oppression and old transgressions. The reconciliation movement in South Africa sheds light on how the past can be a force for change and new beginnings. After people had suffered under the cruelty of apartheid, leaders urged them to come forward and publicly acknowledge their grievances and transgressions so that the past could be healed and a new country could be born.

In practicing *Sankofa,* our starting point will be the genesis of America. The convergence of certain European philosophies drove the exodus across the Atlantic and made the settling of the western hemisphere a de facto conquest based on the oppression of indigenous people. These antecedents set in motion a leadership form that was exclusionary and denied the history and contributions of diverse people. For mainstream leaders, understanding the history that gave rise to ethnocentricity is perhaps the most difficult step in transforming leadership to an inclusive, multicultural form. *Sankofa* beckons us to look at the past courageously and to learn from history, and it assures us that this will generate the clarity and power to construct a better future.

 The convergence of certain European philosophies drove the exodus across the Atlantic and made the settling of the western hemisphere a de facto conquest based on the oppression of indigenous people.

History recounts the events of the past, but not from an objective frame of reference. Depending on who wrote it, a certain perspective is espoused. Women in the last century, for example, were enlightened by the realization that males wrote history and how this affected their current status, self-concept, and collective empowerment. *His*-story and not *her*-story revealed a past in which men were the great heroes and women's contributions were lost like etchings in the sand. Likewise, people of color know the prevailing history is also not *our-story*, but reflects instead an Anglo and European philosophy and worldview. Communities of color see history in a different light. Sharing this perspective can level the historical playing field. Constructing a future that integrates the perspectives of all Americans must start with an inclusive historical foundation.

Whitewashing the Settling of America

OKAY, I'LL ADMIT IT. I am "old school." I was raised in the 1950s, when the settling of America was presented in a romantic and adventurous way. "In fourteen-ninety-two," my classmates chorused, "Columbus sailed the ocean blue." I envisioned the first Pilgrims in their crisp white collars stepping off their boats, amazed at this vast and beautiful land, unspoiled and untamed. The first Thanksgiving was a wondrous feast with helpful Indians serving up hearty portions of squash and corn. My vivid child's imagination saw covered wagons forging across the rugged plains to settle the wild, wild West. American history at that time was written *of, by,* and *for* the people who conquered this land; it described what happened from their point of view. And I believed every word of it.

What kind of trauma do persons of color undergo when the reality of what really happened to their ancestors unfolds like a jarring nightmare in the dark night? I remember my grandmother admonishing me, "Don't wear your skirts too short, like I did." As a Central American Indian she blamed herself, and did not understand that the ravishing of young native girls was a tradition carried over from the conquistadores, who took what they wanted. In fact, the Mestizo or mixed race throughout Central and South America is the offspring of the forced integration between Indians and Spaniards. For Indian women, it didn't matter how long or short their skirts were.

The story of the settling of America is a cultural construct. The sugarcoating of history is a hard pill to swallow if it was your grandmother who was abused or your native soil that was lost. To build a multicultural nation, we must peer through a different looking glass. Are we going to refer to this as the *discovery and settling* of America or are we going to call it a *conquest, colonization, attempted genocide*? Was the land free or stolen? What really happened after Christopher Columbus set foot on the coast of San Salvador and the Pilgrims eagerly followed, landing at Plymouth Rock?

Looking at the past from this frame of reference may be disturbing, may be seen as irrelevant, or, worse, may create resistance. Contemporary American culture lives in the *ahora*—the present. Getting things done now is imperative! The past is tucked away, mythologized, and certainly not seen as the backdrop for the present. Others may claim, "This is old hat! Do we have to revisit the antecedents of racism, again? Haven't we done enough of this? Besides, it wasn't me!" The individualist nature of American culture makes it difficult to assume a collective understanding of or responsibility for how the past structures our current reality and affects us today. Cultural amnesia results, so people have no memory of the trials and tribulations of the past.

Can we go down a different road? Is it possible that, by getting right up in the face of historical whitewashing, we can heal the social disease that finds justifications for why one group is better than another? Can we uproot the mind-set that proclaimed that this hemisphere was here for the taking and its inhabitants were savages? When the past is reconstructed in the bright light of honesty—or at least when everyone's story is told—we can begin restructuring leadership from a Eurocentric form to one that's more diverse and inclusive. We can construct a new leadership covenant that reflects and respects the history and culture of all Americans.

Bueno; to do this, our story must start before the Pilgrims and conquistadores began their stressful journeys. We must understand that the estimates of the native population in the Americas in pre-Columbian times ranged from a low of 12.5 million to a high of 25 million. Central Mexico alone, it is conjectured, contained almost ten times the number of people in England at that time.[4]

So why did Columbus sail the ocean blue in 1492, and why did the inhabitants of this hemisphere stay home?

The cultures of the western hemisphere as we will explore later were rooted to their homelands, whereas Columbus's landing in America spurred an exodus among the greatest in history.

The European Exodus

BEGINNING IN THE SIXTEENTH CENTURY, religion, politics, and economics converged in Europe, setting forth a new worldview. It defined man's nature as acquisitive and competitive, supported the advent of capitalism, and provided a strong rationale—even a religious mandate—for conquering the Americas. The

Protestant reformation was in full swing. When Martin Luther, a devout Catholic priest and a purist by nature, nailed his ninety-five theses to the door of the Wittenberg Church, man's very relationship to God was turned upside down. A central facet of Protestantism was that the individual did not need an intermediary such as a priest, a saint, or even Santa Maria—the Holy Mother of God—to communicate or have direct contact with God. This was heresy to the Catholic Church, which for centuries had controlled the pipeline to the deity through their black-clad priests and holy saints.

Fueled by Calvinism which had spread across Europe, the Protestant ethic propagated industriousness, duty, hard work, progress, and the accumulation of wealth. This was a 180-degree turn from the partnership-oriented early cultures that had stressed sharing and living in harmony with nature. Furthermore, Protestantism ran a pretty tight ship. Rules, formal regulations, subduing of the "pleasures of life," self-control, and rationalism reigned. A diligent person would be working too hard to have time for such frivolities.

It was the entrée of economist Adam Smith's idea of capitalism in 1776, however, that hammered the nails into the coffin of the mutually assisting early cultures. Capitalism compelled individuals to go in search of personal wealth. As the free-market economy proliferated, the belief in self-interest took precedence over public welfare or social good. The individual was now unfettered from the need to consider the effects of his actions on the collective.[5] The free market economy, competition, and "survival of the fittest" replaced early communalism. Now the operating words were looking out for *numero uno*—every man for himself.

Political theorist and influential thinker Thomas Hobbes capped this off by espousing that the fundamental motivation of human nature was selfishness. Individuals, he believed, were in a perpetual struggle for advantage, power, and gain. Hobbes argued that society was simply a group of selfish individuals united together to maximize safety and protect themselves from one another. His social contract was based on human beings wanting a moral authority to safeguard them from their own selfish nature.[6] This is evidenced today in the mushrooming number of laws intended to contain and police human behavior.

The free market economy, competition, and "survival of the fittest" replaced early communalism. Now the operating words were looking out for numero uno—*every man for himself.*

One shift that altered humanity's entire cosmology was the Newtonian concept of the natural world as a machine to be engineered for humankind's benefit—a far cry from early societies in which the earth was considered a living being and humans a part of the intricate web of life. Hobbes and Newton provided a platform on which rugged individualism and materialism formed the matrix of the *individualistic* culture. Changing man's relationship to the earth from steward to subjugator also set the stage for an economic system that allowed the using up and abusing of natural and human resources.

Writing in the 1950s, historian Max Weber accurately described the Protestant ethic that holds that accumulating money is an expression of virtue as the seedbed for the capitalist economy. Its proponents reason that making money is an expression of virtue and one's purpose in life; thus, becoming wealthy is an end in itself—and even a moral imperative![7]

It is somewhat incongruous that while Adam Smith was writing about the benefits of free market politics, there were approximately 26 million peasants in Europe who were unemployed and starving. Famine was widespread. In France, this led to peasant revolts and the destruction of feudalism. People became more autonomous and separate, more in step with the Industrial Revolution, which lured them to factories in urban areas. When people migrated to the city, they became, of necessity, more self-reliant. In addition, the means of production were consolidated into fewer hands. This intensified inequality in the societies that replaced the collaborative orientation of agrarian communities.[8]

This Land Is My Land

The European exodus spanned almost four centuries. The conquest and colonization of the western hemisphere was fueled by the overpopulation and the broken promise of the Industrial Reveloution, which left many people earning meager wages and living in squalor. Armed with a strong Protestant work ethic, a competitive drive, and an individualist spirit, thousands made the long journey across the Atlantic seeking land, wealth, and prosperity. When the Europeans saw the expanse of the American frontier and its wealth of natural resources, it was *bonanza—all systems go!* As they saw it, their thirst for material gain, ordained by the Protestant god, was being fulfilled and sanctified by this new opportunity.

While their northern European counterparts came to homestead and profit, the Spanish conquest was shrouded as a holy crusade. The Catholic Church sent priests to save the souls of the heathen savages—which didn't exclude enslaving them and profiting from their forced labor. Unlike North America—which, despite the extensive inhabitation by thousands of native tribes, was essentially still a natural wilderness—the city of Tenochtitlán (now Mexico City) was larger than any city in Europe, with more inhabitants than London or Seville. Hernán Cortés found a radiant island metropolis laced with canals, with beautiful palaces and accumulated treasure.[9] Consequently, there was a different kind of exploitation. Mass quantities of gold and silver were plundered and sent to the Spanish crown.

In his eloquent book *The Rediscovery of North America*, Barry Lopez proposes that the conquest was from the outset a series of raids and irresponsible and criminal behavior, a spree the end of which was never visible. Timber, land, gold, precious ores, as well as indigenous people, were bountiful and there for the taking. He notes that the conquerors' belief in their imperial and unquestionable right, conferred by God, was supported by a belief in racial and cultural supremacy. Sanctioned by the state and the militia, and fueled by the Protestant ethic, the assumption that one is due wealth became justification for exploiting the land, water, and people.[10] This acquisitive mentality meant there would never be a time when one would say *Basta!* ("This is enough.") The new frontier was seen as boundless.

The indigenous cultures in America could not understand or withstand the avaricious and acquisitive behavior of their White conquerors. They had no frame of reference for dealing with a worldview so divergent from their own. Pre-Columbian cultures were tightly interwoven. The group took precedence over the individual. People shared what they had and cared for one another. Cooperation, not competition, nurtured the collective and group harmony. Many tribes had creation myths in which their homeland was bestowed by the Creator. Everyday life was punctuated with rituals and celebrations to mark the passing of the seasons. People strove to live in harmony with nature, which they regarded as sacred. These cultures honored the wisdom of their ancestors. The idea of getting on boats and crossing to another continent to find more land or resources was as foreign to them as the conquistadores on their large, swift, and powerful animals. They felt blessed to live in a place that was both beautiful and rich in the resources needed to sustain life. All that was needed was already here. Why would anyone leave one's family, tribe, the comfort of community, and the sacred land that contained the bones and stories of one's ancestors?

The clash between these two worldviews is illustrated by the story of Montezuma, the emperor of the Aztecs. Knowing the Spanish wanted gold, Montezuma took Hernán Cortés to his palace, where mounds of the precious substance were kept. He told Cortés, "Take what you want," thinking Cortés would be satisfied. The emperor did not realize that the lust for gold was endless and this would only whet the Spanish appetite. Similarly, the Indians who taught the Pilgrims to survive their first winter and shared Thanksgiving dinner with them could not fathom that their new neighbors would soon declare them savages, devastate them with war and introduced diseases, and gradually herd them onto reservations.

It is difficult to calculate the number of distinct tribes that existed before Columbus, but it is known there were over a thousand languages and cultures. In the western hemisphere, only three can be described as acquisitive—the Aztecs, Mayans, and Incas. Despite the fact that these cultures built empires that might be considered akin to the European model of expansion, they were also decentralized and, historical studies suggest, often preserved the cultures and languages of subjugated people. It is safe to suggest, then, that the cultures in the western hemisphere were overwhelmingly collective, lived in harmony with nature, and valued cooperation.

Perhaps it is fitting that this hemisphere bears the name of Amerigo Vespucci, the Florentine explorer, because he saw the western hemisphere as a utopian world: "The people live in agreement with nature. They have no property; instead all things are held in common." Without the concept of private property, there was no need for the strong tethers of the individualistic culture. "They live without a king and without any form of authority. Each one is his own master."[11]

Work and Individualism Become an American Ethos

WHEN I HAVE SHARED the preceding perspective on the "settling" of America with young college students of all races, they are usually captivated by the fact that they studied Thomas Hobbes, Adam Smith, and the Protestant Reformation, but never connected these to current-day issues of racism or exclusion in America. I realize some readers may not share these sentiments and will instead feel uncomfortable and unsettled by these revelations. It is important to remember that people of color have already studied history from a White perspective. To be successful, we have had to learn to think, speak, and act in ways that would be acceptable to the dominant culture. *Authentic diversity, however, can only happen on a two-way street*—understanding must go both ways. Looking at history from a different point of view and considering the reason why the past is so relevant to people of color can be the springboard for learning to lead from a multicultural orientation.

Another incentive for examining the past is "fast forwarding" to the present and taking into account how unfettered individualism, the Protestant work ethic, and capitalism may be impairing people's quality of life today! America may need a course adjustment. One benefit of multicultural perspectives is that they allow us to tap a wider range of choices and potential benefits. The next section, Principle 2, looks at the societal downsides that have resulted from the preeminence of the Protestant ethic and individualistic values. This sets the stage for discussing the benefits of balancing these values with the more communal ones that have supported and sustained communities of color.

The Frenchman Alexis de Tocqueville, in his astute observations of our young country in 1835, noted that the characteristic he most admired was our individualism. He clearly warned, however, that if individualism was not continually balanced by other habits that would reinforce the social context and fabric of community, it would inevitably lead to separation and division.[12] The respected sociologist Robert Bellah and his colleagues, in their book *Habits of the Heart,* argue that the time de Tocqueville warned of has come—unchecked individualism has led to emotional isolation and fragmentation.[13]

In his acclaimed book *Bowling Alone: The Collapse and Revival of American Community,* Harvard professor Robert Putnam identifies the phenomenon of withdrawal from community as both the cause and the result of larger social changes. As Americans become more isolated,

Alexis de Tocqueville clearly warned that if individualism was not continuously balanced by other habits that would reinforce the social context and fabric of community, it would inevitably lead to separation and division.

civic engagement, social involvement, and volunteerism are declining. Even entertaining at home, the all-American pastime, has dropped 45 percent since the mid-1970s. Putnam documents that nearly one in five Americans moves each year. This means that fully 20 percent are new arrivals who, it's been demonstrated, are less likely to vote, join civic organizations, or build lasting ties with neighbors. He surmises, "For people as for plants, frequent repotting disrupts roots systems."[14]

A survey conducted among first-year students by the University of California since the mid-1960s indicates that the trend of disengagement is continuing. Young students in the 1960s had a much greater interest in civic engagement than in making money. By the turn of century, these priorities had reversed. Seventy-five percent indicated that being well-off financially was their most important concern.[15]

As suburban sprawl widens the distances between people, we are losing familiar community meeting grounds and a sense of place. Putnam notes the increase in commuter time, estimating that every ten minutes spent in the car cuts civic engagement by 10 percent. Community connection points have been replaced by malls decked out with art and decorations, providing a festive air. People bustle around, shopping, drinking lattés, but the crowd is made up of strangers. These mass commercial spaces are designed not to connect us, but to move us from place to place or from store to store. We are in the presence of others, but the sense of belonging and community that was once the core of human identity is not being nurtured.

In 2006, researchers skeptical of Putnam's theory conducted a major national survey, only to find that although people are networking on the website www.myspace.com, text messaging on cell phones, and blogging at all hours, they are less up close and personal than they used to be. One-quarter of those responding indicated that they have no one with whom to discuss the most important personal issues of their lives. The researchers reported that in the past two decades, based on comparison data from national surveys conducted in 1985, the average number of close friends an individual has dropped from three to two. The survey provides powerful evidence that supports Putnam's research indicating that we are becoming increasing isolated even as cell phones, the Internet, and technology make us more interconnected.[16]

Balancing Individualism with Community Good

THE PROTESTANT ETHIC, which equated wealth with virtue coupled with capitalist economics, forged a country with unimaginable wealth. Through their industriousness, Americans became some of the richest people on the planet, boasting the fourth highest per-capita income in the world. Has the drive for materialism mutated into obsessive consumerism? The drive for more and more material consumption is apparent when we note that in 2005 the world's average per-capita income was $5,800[17]—and the average credit-card debt in the United States was over $8,000.[18]

The emphasis on industriousness also instilled a propensity for overworking. Americans are the most workaholic people in the industrial world, putting in *three hundred and fifty hours* (nine workweeks) more on the job each year than their European counterparts. According to the Families and Work Institute, the number of Americans who feel overworked is rising like a thermometer on a hot July day, from 28 percent in 2001 to 44 percent in 2004. It is difficult to enjoy the fruits of one's labors when working excessively; this also jeopardizes family life, community involvement, and health. Imagine how fulfilling life could be with nine weeks each year to enjoy family, travel, read and learn, take up a hobby, exercise, or engage in community service![19]

The emphasis on industriousness instilled a propensity for overworking. Americans are the most workaholic people in the industrial world, putting in three hundred and fifty hours (nine workweeks) more on the job each year than their European counterparts.

Does focusing on oneself and material acquisitions at least make us happy? Isn't materialism a fulfilling trip to nirvana? The book *From Me to We: Turning Self-Help on Its Head* by Craig and Marc Kielburger, two young brothers who are Canadian altruists, disputes the assumption that "*mo money equals mo happiness.*" Citing a 2003 poll of 1,500 Americans by the Roper Organization, they concluded that unless you are desperately poor and do not have basic necessities, money has little bearing on how happy you are. Seventy-four percent of those earning less than $25,000 a year reported that they were somewhat or very happy with their lives. Interestingly, among those with incomes of $50,000 or more, this dropped to 10 percent.[20]

The Roper study also found that "From this point on there was no discernible difference in overall happiness with friendships, standard of living, marriage, children, and appearance in incomes of $100,000 and more."[21] It was also noted that people who believe that money equals happiness are less satisfied with their self-esteem, friendships, and life overall. It seems that once North Americans reach a certain level of financial security, making more money does not directly affect their level of happiness.

In support of these findings, the Kielburgers cite the World Values Survey's assessment of life satisfaction, conducted in more than sixty-five countries between 1990 and 2000. The report indicates that the correlation between income and happiness rose at similar rates until an annual income of about $13,000 per person. After that point, having more money yielded little growth in self-reported happiness. Are Americans, who are some of the wealthiest people, the happiest people in the world? Hardly! The country with the highest number of happy citizens was Nigeria, followed by Mexico and Venezuela. Americans ranked sixteenth![22] Is this at least improving over time? Actually, it is worsening. In fact, the number of "very happy" people in the United States peaked in 1957. Even though Americans consume twice as much as they did in the 1950s, it has not made us happier.[23] *Apparently, we were happier when we had less stuff to worry about.*

Returning to a *We* Culture

The next section, Principle 2, continues in the tradition of *Sankofa* by reviewing the change from the first cultures that centered on *We* to the individualist or *I* culture. *Sankofa* reminds us that for most of human history, people lived in *We* or collective cultures, in which the collective superseded individual gain. The strong hold of the *I* culture in America has weakened the support systems and relationships that once existed in extended families and communities. An indication of this is that more than one out of four Americans now lives alone.

The highly respected author M. Scott Peck, after searching for the keys to human fulfillment in his classic best-seller *The Road Less Traveled*, turned his attention to the role community plays in people's sense of well-being. Peck found that people are thirsting for a sense of place and belonging. He envisioned a world in which a "soft individualism" acknowledges our *interdependence*. Rugged individualism demands that we always put our best foot forward, hide our weaknesses and insecurities, and put on a mask of self-sufficiency. This effort leaves people feeling exhausted, alone, and inadequate. Peck believed that humanity stands at the brink of annihilation if the bonds of community and interdependence are not rewoven. He prophetically stated, "In and through community lies the salvation of the world."[24]

This longing for community reflects the collectivism of early *We* cultures, which is still the essence of African American, Latino, and Indian people today. *We* satisfies our need to belong and have meaning in our lives. *We* values generosity and taking care of one another. Since collective cultures were the cradles of humankind, *We* is an intersection and connecting point that can bring people together. *We* means remembering that our collective efforts ensured our survival, and it holds the promise to our future existence.

Developing a *We* orientation, as found in communities of color, can be an antidote for healing much of the social malaise that unbridled individualism, overwork, and materialism have spawned. Thus, in the spirit of *Sankofa* in which we learn from the past, we can heed the good counsel given by de Tocqueville almost one hundred and seventy-five years ago—balancing individualism with collective good will reinforce the social context and fabric of community.[25]

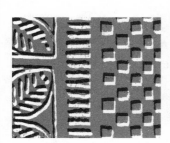

NEXT STEPS

**Reflecting On
and Applying
Principle One**

Sankofa—Learn from the Past

Honor your heritage that you may honor the heritage of others

When people immigrated to America, they were urged to cut ties to their homelands, forget their customs and language, and merge into the melting pot. Thus, homogeneity and a monocultural approach emerged. A multicultural perspective requires honoring the history and culture of all people. *To do this we must first honor our own heritage so we may appreciate the heritage of others.*

This exercise lays the foundation for leading from a multicultural perspective. It is a reflective piece that participants may want to think about and research. I have found that sharing in dyads followed by a group summary works best.

- What is the story of how your family "got here"?

- What are characteristics, strengths, values, and family traits you have inherited?

- How have they helped shape who you are today?

- What else would you like to know about your heritage and how can you find this out?

- Who in your family might shed light on your heritage and family traditions?

Connect to your collective history, extended family, and "tribe"

This exercise illustrates the American Indian connection with their ancestors and their understanding that a person has a lineage that provides wisdom, guidance, and energy. Introduce yourself, using the Navajo greeting that delineates your lineage. Groups can share this with one another and talk about the unique qualities of their ancestry. People who do not know the names and histories of their grandparents often begin to seek this out and reconnect to their cultural roots.

I am _____, the daughter/son of _____,

the great grandson/granddaughter of_____,

the great-great grandson/granddaughter of_____.

Discuss participants' feelings about connecting with their past and their roots. Did they experience the power of ancestry?

Seek out and learn from people with a different perspective on history

To create our multicultural future, all people's voices and perspectives must be welcome. History is not an objective narrative. Many people from communities of color have a different slant on historical events but have not shared this openly. A genuine dialogue on people's historical perspectives can be the first step in creating open communication and learning from one another.

The following guidelines for dialogue can assist with this process:

- Listen and speak without judgment

- Respect differences

- Reexamine all positions

- Search for strengths and values in the way others see things

- Explore common ground

- Focus on learning

- Release the need for outcomes

- Seek to walk in another's moccasins

 (NEXT STEPS I CONTINUED)

Recommended readings and resources

- *The Rediscovery of North America* by Barry Lopez (Vintage Books, 1990).

- *1491: New Revelations of the Americas Before Columbus* by Charles C. Mann (Knopf, 2005).

- *On Dialogue* by David Bohm (Routledge Classics, 1996).

PRINCIPLE 2

I to *We*—From Individualism to Collective Identity

I WAS BORN INTO a *We* culture in which seven people lived in a tiny house with one bathroom. There was no concept of private space—a person never went to his or her room; the whole house was common ground. A *We* culture meant my mother, Maria, dressed us up on Sundays and marched us to church, where we took up the whole pew. She watched over us like an eagle circling the morning sky. She only had to give us that look to scare us into perfect piety. *We cultures have a strong sense of belonging and sticking together.*

A *We* culture meant my mother hurried home from church, took off her black mantilla, and then cooked the Sunday chicken, which was carefully divided so that every other Sunday I got a leg. *We cultures share everything.* A *We* culture meant that on Saturday mornings everyone scrubbed doors, walls, and windows, shook rugs, took out the mattresses for a good airing, and washed down the sidewalks. *We cultures work together so everyone benefits.*

The preparation for a *We* orientation starts early in life. Latino babies are never left at home with a babysitter. At Sunday gatherings or *fiestas*, babies are passed around like precious treasures. People anxiously wait their turn to sing to the baby, pinch its cheeks, and make it laugh. Babies are called *preciosa* and told over and over how *linda* (pretty) they are! At parties, they are bounced from lap to lap. When the music starts, they are sashayed onto the dance floor and rocked to a ranchero or salsa beat. Latino babies get accustomed to people at an early age; that is how they become *We*. **We cultures center on people.**

One time when I had a bad tooth, my mother took me to the dentist, and then we went to see the movie *The African Queen*. It is a vivid memory, because it is the only time I remember one-on-one time with my mother. *We* meant I was never alone or just with another person. **We cultures are collective and relish togetherness.**

No one gets left out of a *We* culture. Uncle Huey showed up on a sweltering August day to the warm embrace of my father. He would spit brown tobacco off the front porch and aggravatingly clear his throat ten times a minute. His trousers hung off him like the laundry on my mother's clothesline. We pleaded with our Papí, "He is embarrassing, *pleeeze s*end him back home." This was to no avail. No matter how obnoxious he was, he was part of the *We*—he was my uncle. **We cultures are impeccably inclusive.**

For Latino Catholics, first Holy Communion is a solemn and festive day, one's first encounter with the heavenly host—a baby step into spiritual maturity. As the big day approached, I was worried. We didn't have any money and all the young girls would be kneeling before the holy altar in fancy white dresses. My mother took the precious cotton brought from Nicaragua out of the old trunk, she had been saving for herself. She measured me here and poked me there. She sewed late into the night after working all day, cooking the family dinner, and putting her children, us, to bed. A week later, she proudly held up a simple white dress with lace stitched around the collar, where she pinned a cotton flower bought at Woolworth. The other girls had store-bought dresses with lace and taffeta, but my dress was the most beautiful because no one else's Mom had sacrificed so much. **We cultures put benefiting the whole before the individual.**

I still can't imagine how my mother with her broken English figured all this out! Where did she find the money to do these things? It was her total dedication to the *We*, that unbroken promise that her family and children came first. *We* was all she knew. She passed on that sense of a family and culture of togetherness to me. *We* was embedded deep in my soul. I didn't understand it then, but it sustained me when I left my family to go to college and live in the strange land of the *I*'s. **In We cultures the I exists only in relationship to others, not as a separate entity.**

I and Individualism or *We* and Collectivism

ANTHROPOLOGISTS WHO study and categorize cultures make broad distinctions between collectivist or *We* cultures and those that are more individualistically or *I* oriented. American Indians, Latinos, and African Americans are considered collectivist cultures, whereas North Americans and western Europeans are considered individualistic. In *Managing Diversity: People Skills for a Multicultural Workplace*, Norma Carr-Ruffino comments that most of the world's cultures, as well as women in all societies, are collectivist.[1] This is understandable, as individualism is a historically new phenomenon that grew out of the Protestant ethic and European intellectualism. We should not look at collectivist or individualistic cultures as distinct categories, but rather recognize that in today's rapidly changing and interdependent world, cultures are blending aspects of both. For instance, to function successfully in dominant culture organizations, people of color have learned the individualistic orientation.

The previous principle, *Sankofa*, reviewed the roots of individualism; we will now take a closer look at collectivist or *We* cultures. Our goal is to understand the nuances of both orientations and to consider how these have influenced leadership. In this way, we can integrate the best of each viewpoint into a multicultural leadership model.

We should not look at collectivist or individualistic cultures as distinct categories, but rather recognize that in today's rapidly changing and interdependent world, cultures are blending aspects of both.

It is important to clarify that the term *collectivist* does not refer to today's political concept of socialism, but rather to an ancient, tried-and-true form of social organization. Collectivist *We* cultures have been on the earth for a very long time; their traditions and histories go back many generations. These cultures, therefore, are stable, with highly defined and specific rules, and they change more slowly than individualistic cultures. Collectivist cultures are usually portrayed as tightly woven and integrated. As noted previously, these cultures cherish group welfare, unity, and harmony. To maintain these, people behave politely, act in a socially desirable manner, and respect others. The family, community, or tribe takes precedence over the individual, whose identity flows from the collective. People work for group success before personal credit or gain.

Individualistic cultures, on the other hand, appeared relatively recently in history, and they are more loosely integrated. Change and risk taking are embraced. Individuals are *highly differentiated* from others. Self-identity and self-interest are keystones. To grow up means to become independent, autonomous, and responsible for one's own life. Individual freedom and choice are highly valued. In these cultures, individual needs supersede collective ones. This is not considered selfish. The individual serves society by living up to her or his potential. Achievement and getting things done take priority.

Whether a culture is individualistic or collective depends on the degree to which individuals' beliefs and actions are independent of those of the group. *We* cultures emphasize group opinions and actions, and they stress psychological closeness. Individual goals are integrated with those of the collective. Individualistic cultures, on the other hand, emphasize personal opinions. Being able to think for yourself signifies intelligence and competency. Competition with others is considered healthy, motivating, and beneficial. Calling attention to oneself or standing out from the group is a way to advance.

 Culture, the lens through which a group of individuals defines reality, has been described as collective programming. *Cultural determinism proposes that a person's values, beliefs, and worldview are riveted on this early conditioning.*

The extent of one's individualist or collectivist orientation determines how much control one assumes in life. The independent focus says, "To a very great extent, I control my life, determine my reality, choose my experiences, and shape my destiny. I am the captain of my own ship." Collectivist cultures are more in tune with natural cycles and believe in a life power that is external to them. These forces influence their lives. They also take into account what other people think, want, and need. These lessen individual freedom of choice.

People from collectivist cultures, therefore, have a greater belief that things happen to them. The Spanish language contains a passive tense in which innate objects or others assume responsibility: "The glass fell"; "The taxi left me"; "It didn't call my attention." Similar verbal constructs can be found in the Zulu and Xhosa languages as well as those of other African tribes.[2] This signifies an external source of control, which simply means there are many more factors than just what *I* want that must be consulted and considered.

Culture, the lens through which a group of individuals defines reality, has been described as *collective programming*. Cultural determinism proposes that a person's values, beliefs, and worldview are riveted on this early conditioning. Today's diverse society and global marketplace require leaders to free themselves of this type of conditioning in order to attain a broader cultural perspective and repertoire. The next section reviews early *We* cultures that have existed since prehistoric times. Considering these antecedents provides insights for understanding how leadership in Anglo society is different from leadership in communities of color.

Our First Culture Was a We Culture

BEFORE THERE WAS an *I* culture, *We* ensured our continued existence. Those who adhere to man's evolutionary heritage coming from anthropoids—the great apes—can witness even today their cooperation, strong sense of family, and mutual care. Genomics has confirmed that fully 99.4 percent of our DNA is similar to that of the anthropoids. Our genetic footprints follow their path. Much early human behavior was patterned on the great apes and their communal behavior.[3] Obviously, no "lone wolf" survived and evolved alone. In fact, the idea of the lone wolf is a misnomer because wolves are in fact wedded to their pack. Our immense journey has been a journey of *We*—a collective one. The long, dependent childhood we live through before we can live on our own means that someone fed us, cleaned us, and made sure we were safe, warm, and dry. **We *is the reason we are alive.***

Primitive times were brutal and treacherous, with wild terrains, hunger, predatory animals, and tempestuous weather. Early humans had to be constantly alert—ready to defend themselves or to take rapid flight and flee the threat. Alone, a person would die from the elements and a multitude of dangers. The tribe was the warm bear robe essential for protection. Whether for hunting, taking care of domesticated animals, raising children, planting or harvesting, or preparing medicinal and herbal remedies, the tribe brought people together for preservation, safety, comfort, ritual, and celebration.

Through tribal living, human beings developed complex and mutually beneficial ways of working together, including the differentiation of roles based on one's abilities or lineage—today, this is still the basis of organizational development. The herbalist, the potter, the fire keeper, the weaver, the warrior, the chief, the ruling council, and the hunting party, all first came into form when humans lived in tribes. Just as important, the tribe uncovered and explained the meaning of the universe and man's place in it. In times when the mysteries of life were stupefying, humans looked to the medicine man, the chief, or the wise woman to explain events in the natural world and provide guidance.

Tribes were the vehicles for a collective human identity or the sense of *We* to evolve. Even today, many tribes dress in identical clothes, wear their hair the same, adorn themselves similarly, and follow the daily rituals that give meaning to their lives. Contemporary American teenagers who long to belong cling to this tribal tendency by looking and acting *like, you know*, the same.

Individualistic cultures would have us believe that survival of the fittest was an every-man-for-himself instinct in a dog-eat-dog, competitive environment. In actuality, the collective lifted man to the top of the evolutionary pyramid. In her notable book *Calling the Circle,* visionary author Christina Baldwin uses the term *first culture* to refer to the time when humans lived in tribes or small communities in which everyone was needed and included and everyone belonged. Baldwin points out that human beings survived and thrived because of their ability to care for each other, work together, and help one another. *We* was our "competitive evolutionary edge" over other species. Survival of the fittest was a cooperative and reciprocal experience.[4]

 Human beings survived and thrived because of their ability to care for each other, work together, and help one another. We was our competitive evolutionary edge over other species. Survival of the fittest was a cooperative and reciprocal experience.

Riane Eisler's landmark work *The Chalice and the Blade* documents early societies across Europe, Asia, and the Americas in which people worked in partnership, living in harmony with nature. She notes that human survival was largely due to the cultivation of highly sophisticated ways of working together that included collaborative decision-making structures.

Eisler describes many Neolithic cultures as ones in which "social relations are primarily based on the principle of linking rather than ranking, [and] may best be described as a partnership model where both men and women worked together for the common good." First cultures by necessity were tight as a drum, and their foundation was *mutual assistance* and *loyalty.*[5]

To understand the deep groove that "the tribe" or collective existence has made in our memory banks, consider that humans have first appeared about 195,000 years ago.[6] For over 80 percent of this time span, humans lived in caves, surrounded by a tribe that provided protection, love, warmth, food, family, and a sense of identity.[7] Human beings are social animals; *We* have always lived in groups. Through our long evolutionary journey, our reliance on each other was linked directly with the need for survival—the strongest instinct we have. First cultures, therefore, are humanity's home base.

We Is the Tribe, Community, and *Familia*

The mutuality of early cultures has survived in its most vibrant forms among indigenous people and in Indian, Latino, and African American communities, in which sticking together has been a survival tactic. This is evident today in their collectivist orientation, which centers on the common good rather than on individual gain. As in early cultures, an individual is defined by one's group and relationships.

American Indian leadership, for instance, is based on a great deal of introspection and work on identity—both individually and collectively, for the two are intertwined. Individuals are like strands of straw making up a woven basket that is decorated with traditional designs and colors. The basket is the tribe, holding individuals in place and giving them a sense of unity, identity, and sustenance.

LaDonna Harris, president of Americans for Indian Opportunity, observes how this works: "In Native cultures, *strong personal identity and collective identity stand side by side.* A good tribal person must have self-worth, positive qualities and skills, and be as healthy as possible so they can contribute to the community. The collective is only as strong as the individuals who give it life." Benny Shendo Jr. concurs: "The tribe and community are central, then the extended family, the clan, and then perhaps the individual. Yet, people are secure in their personal identity. In the Anglo culture, individualism is stressed. The reality is you can be collective *and* still be an individual. You can be totally yourself, a real character, but you are yourself within this spectrum of community and tribe first."

 The reality is you can be collective and still be an individual. You can be totally yourself, a real character, but you are yourself within this spectrum of community and tribe first.

—Benny Shendo Jr., Jemez Pueblo

Shendo reflects on the collective identity: "For Native Americans, who you are depends on what tribe you belong to. Your rights, like the right to live on our lands, for example, come from your tribal membership. It's not about the individual. In all Indian cultures, the tribe is paramount because it's that community, that group of people who create the collective identity, the songs, traditions, and culture . . . When I meet Indian people, the first thing they say is 'what tribe are you?' That's how we establish our initial relationship, and it is a collective identity."

The first premise of the American Indians Ambassador Program reflects this point of view: "The strength of the Indian peoples, both collectively and individually, is the tribe. It is our culture, family, community, and tribe that define our role in society and our self-identity." Collective identity is in sharp contrast to individualism, which touts personal achievement and competition. There is no concept within any American Indian tribe of winning at the expense of others. [8]

Similarly, a core belief in the Hispanic culture is that other people come first. This drives a humanistic set of values that are other-centered rather than self-centered or individualistic. The Latino tendency toward collectivism is evident in the treasured value of *la familia,* which broadly refers to groups with a special affinity who provide assistance and support. Latinos cherish belonging, group benefit, mutuality, and reciprocity. Interdependency, cooperation, and mutual assistance are the norm. Unlike the Anglo emphasis on the nuclear family, the Latino *familia* is elastic and grows to include *padrinos* or *madrinas*—godparents for baptisms, weddings or confirmations, and *"tías"* or *"tíos"*—honorary aunts or uncles.

Then again, in Latino culture, while simply walking down the street with a close friend, a person may be suddenly introduced as a *compadre* or *comadre,* indicating that he or she is now considered family. Even sponsors for *quinceaneras* (a religious ceremony in which a young woman is presented to the community), wedding anniversaries, or baptisms become part of the family. Latinos have an open-door policy when it comes to *We.* The value of *bienvenido*—welcome and hospitality—implies an inclusiveness that makes for a dynamic and expanding family much like a tribe.

This tradition has roots in both the indigenous and the Spanish cultures that are the ancestry of Latinos. The large extended families in Spain ensured that a relative or close friend was contacted when a need arose. The Aztec culture was organized in multiple family groups who governed themselves and worked as a unit. The growing of crops, building of homes, trading, and caring for children were all based on a *We* orientation. This reflected the Aztec belief that human beings are related to one another and that what one does to another affects oneself. Today these tendencies can be found in the Latino values of helping one another and being of service.

African American ancestors came from tribal cultures that mirror a similar sense of connectedness, interdependence, and reciprocity. Dr. Jim Joseph, in his insightful book *Remaking America,* termed this the *cosmology of connectedness.* "The idea that a person cannot be fully understood apart from the community which determines his or her personhood was fundamental to the African view of moral duty and social obligation."[9]

African Americans carry on this collectivist tradition. Because the plight of slavery was a communal one, everyone suffered under the same yoke. Black people faced discrimination and racism by "sticking together." The *We* in the song "We Shall Overcome" indicates an understanding that solidarity is their source of strength and salvation. Indeed, since the practice of slavery tore families apart, African Americans don't know if someone is a blood relative or not, so they refer to each other as brother, sister, or cuz (cousin). When walking into a room, although Black people may not know each other, they recognize they are related through a common history, faith, and culture.

Dr. Joseph believes the large family patterns that Black people develop, which include step-parents, peer group members, community leaders, meeting brethren, teachers, and special friends, is also a legacy inherited from the African world. He surmises, "While the bonds of the extended family were severed by the massive transcontinental displacements that brought Africans to American shores, the spirit of community not only survived but took on new forms and meaning."[10]

 Black people faced discrimination and racism by "sticking together." The We *in the song "We Shall Overcome" indicates an understanding that solidarity is their source of strength and salvation.*

African Americans continue to have an immutable group identity. In 2005, Kanye West, the controversial rap singer, was chosen by news columnist Barbara Walters as one of the most fascinating people of the year. When asked to describe himself, his first word was *Black!*[11] Likewise, when I am working with African American youth, when I give them a sheet with the question "Who are you?" repeated ten times, for almost every teenager "Black" is the first choice. The White culture does not have that kind of central-ized identity with people of their race or color.

The highly developed sense of We—*community, extended family and tribe—has kept communities of color intact for the past five hundred years. That strong sense of* We *was their survival, hope for tomorrow, and anchor of mutual protection, support, and celebration.*

I Is Contained in *We*

I AND WE are not a dichotomy. The *I* is intrinsic to the *We* orientation—individuals must be strong for the collective to thrive. *We* do not have to choose one or the other. This concept of *both and* rather than *either or* is a thread that runs through collectiv-ist cultures. Because they are more tightly woven, there is a sense of wholeness in which many things, including differences, can exist at once. Just as the corn stalk grows tall on its own but only fully matures when many are planted and cross-fertilization occurs, the *I* is nourished in the rich soil that has been cultivated by the collective not just today, but for many previous generations.

The challenge is to balance communal good with individual gain—to reach the higher ground of interdependence. This implies a social imperative whereby personal gain cannot be shouldered at the expense of the common good. Today, the widening gap between the haves and have-nots and the stark social inequities that go with it indicate that the pendulum has swung too far in the *I* direction. Balancing individualism with collectivism may sound easy; however, it proposes a new *cultural equilibrium* that runs contrary to social conditioning and the historical antecedents of the dominant culture.

As previously noted, individualistic cultures are competitive and acquisitive. When these cultures clashed with collective ones, the *We* has always been relegated to the underdog position. Even today, individuals from collective cultures may feel exploited or ripped off when they sacrifice for the group or organization and are not recognized for their hard work or are passed up for promotion. The question is, how do we balance the *I* with the *We*? If we can accept that human beings have an innate drive for connect-edness and taking care of one another, then returning to a *We* perspective and a mutual sense of responsibility is a natural homecoming. Einstein once remarked that our sense of separateness was "a kind of optical illusion." To live in a mutually caring world, he continued, we must undertake a deliberate change in perspective. "Our task must be to free ourselves . . . by widening our circle of compassion to embrace all creatures and the whole of nature . . ."[12] Einstein's unified field theory runs contrary to our individualistic and autonomy-focused culture; it resonates instead with the holistic worldview of indigenous communities.

Shifting from an *I* to a *We* orientation implies an alteration in values whereby social responsibility and looking after the common good is embraced. Almost unanimously, across collective cultures, it is understood that the excessive accumulation of wealth or power by a few hinders the well-being of the society as a whole. For this reason, deep sharing is a cultural touchstone and wealth is defined as being able to give to others. Principle 3, *Mi Casa Su Casa*, explores how people in communities of color have passed this trait from one generation to another and are expected to treat each other with a generosity of spirit.

I to *We*—From Individualism to Collective Identity

Understanding our group or collective heritage lays the foundation for appreciating our diversity

Participants bring the oldest picture they have of their grandparents or *antepasados* and something that represents their culture. Each person shares the story reflected in the picture. (In the oral tradition of communities of color, people embellish, use flowery language, and use their imagination!) Their cultural gifts are also shared. These are placed on a table that has been draped with a nice cloth and decorated with flowers and even candles. People comment on what they have learned about each other's history and unique backgrounds. This exercise creates a cultural collage of people's backgrounds and family histories.

Create a collective history for your community or organization

Traditionally, people grew up in the same place, knew each other's families, and had a common history and values. Today we are a mobile society in which people from many origins and places live and work together. Building trust is a key leadership challenge when people are diverse and do not know each other, and when newcomers must be integrated into the organization. Creating a community or organizational timeline acknowledges individual experiences, discovers mutual history, and nurtures a common ground.

Step One: Preparing a community or organizational timeline

A long piece of paper with the words "Our History and Significant Milestones" is placed on the wall. The years are posted on top, starting with the organization's founding or the initial time period that has affected the group. Increments of five to ten years are posted, ending with the present year.

Step Two: Exploring our connections

People reflect on significant global or societal events that impacted their lives; important life decisions, achievements, or events; milestones or changes in the organization or community. What is each person's history with the organization? When did he or she become a member? If the history is not known, people who can remember this can be invited to share their memories, which provides an opportunity to thank and learn from early contributors or founders.

These are recorded individually and then similarities, differences, and unique perspectives are discussed in small groups. The groups then pare down their experiences to three to five significant ones that they would like to share with the large group or their community. (Record these on sticky notes so they can be posted on the timeline.)

Step Three: Integrating our experiences and acknowledging our history

People reflect on the trends and patterns they see on the timeline. The whole group discusses what they have learned about each other, the societal influences that have affected them, and the organizational or community changes. Understanding a company's beginnings and founding vision can inspire a sense of purpose and belonging.

Recommended readings and resources

- For more information on completing a timeline, see *Future Search: An Action Guide to Finding Common Ground in Organizations and Communities* by Marvin Weisbord and Sandra Janoff (Berrett-Koehler, 1995).

- *From Me to We: Turning Self-Help on Its Head* by Craig Kielburger and Marc Kielburger (Wiley, 2004)

PRINCIPLE 3

Mi Casa Es Su Casa—
A Spirit of Generosity

MY SISTER MARGARITA was thirteen when we arrived in Tampa, Florida. Since she was raised in Nicaragua, she is culturally more traditional than I am. When I was in my thirties, she was visiting when my next-door neighbor dropped by to meet her. He casually admired a handwoven poncho hanging on the wall. "Thank you," I smiled, remembering its origins. "I got it in Chile." When he left, my sister scolded me: "Have you forgotten everything you were taught? You were supposed to give him that poncho!"

This jogged my memory and I flashed back to a fiesta I had attended with her a few years previously, when she lived in Guatemala. The hostess had flung open the door and gave me a big *abrazo* (embrace)—even though I had never met her and hadn't "really" been invited. Somewhat stunned at her generous welcome, I managed to gasp, "What beautiful gold earrings!" "Here," she smiled, "you must have them—they're yours." She took them off and handed me the treasured gift without a moment's hesitation.

The Latino saying *Mi casa es su casa* reflects a sprawling sense of inclusiveness and generosity. It encapsulates a joy in sharing and implies "What I have is also yours." In collectivist cultures, possessions are more fluid and communal. People take pleasure in giving things away. This can present a cultural conundrum. As I jokingly explained to my sister, unless both cultures value reciprocity, when I say "*Mi casa es su casa*," they will have the deed to my house. Then where would I live? Look at what happened to Montezuma or the Indian tribal lands, or still happens in the U.S. tax system in which some rich people hire lawyers so they don't have to pay their fair share.

 The Latino saying Mi casa es su casa *reflects a sprawling sense of inclusiveness and generosity. It encapsulates a joy in sharing and implies "What I have is also yours."*

In collectivist *We* cultures, generosity is not a two-way street; rather, it is a busy intersection where everybody meets. A good illustration is the way strangers are always made to feel welcome. You can rest assured that this kindness will come back to you. Even though a particular individual many never be able to reciprocate, one day someone else will surely return the kindness. Unless they have experienced this contagious generosity, people from individualistic cultures may find it difficult to understand or to aspire to this level of sharing. From a *We* perspective, because the self emerges from the collective, generosity toward others is actually giving to oneself. *Cyclical reciprocity means people are continually giving to one another*. This is beautifully captured in the saying of the South African Pedi tribe, "Giving is to dish out for oneself."[1] Generosity is the glue that holds *We* cultures together. The community fiber would be torn if some were to take more than their share or to accumulate great wealth at the expense of others.

You Are Invited; Please RSVP

INDIGENOUS PEOPLES of the Americas had many community celebrations and festivals that honored the changes in nature, rites of passing, or special feats of individuals. Everybody was invited and shared what they had. This strengthened people's bonds and added to their trove of communal memories. In traditional African societies, there were open weddings to which the entire village was welcomed. People did not arrive empty-handed; in the spirit of generosity, they brought gifts, food, and drink. Inclusiveness and sharing are two quintessential values for collective culture. The *We* cannot thrive or continue to exist if people are excluded, take more than their share, or do not replenish the communal treasure chest.

Many years ago, when visiting friends in Spain, I relished their *dias de fiestas*—a one-week community party where all in attendance eat, drink, and dance together. The main streets are closed, and people promenade dressed in the traditional colors of red and white, which adds to their sense of camaraderie. *Dias de fiestas* are like a community vacation in which everyone is off at the same time. Every year a substantial part of the budget or public funds is set aside to pay for bands, parades, fireworks, and special

 From a We *perspective, because the self emerges from the collective, generosity towards others is actually giving to oneself.* Cyclical reciprocity means people are continually giving to one another.

events so that everyone can participate. Bread, sausages, wine, sardines, and coffee are also free on special days. Since each town has its own *dias de fiestas*, some of the folks attending have come from other places. *No importa*—if you are there, then you are welcome to share in the food and festivities.

Because of the high value placed on harmonious relationships and inclusiveness in collectivist cultures, its members may find the notion of RSVP—that some people would be invited and others excluded—to be a disconcerting concept. The Latino culture's elastic concept of *familia*, for instance, extends to an open door to special celebrations, meals, and *fiestas*. If Latinos are invited to a party and have friends or family visiting, it is good manners to bring them along. (It is not necessary to call ahead, although it is considered helpful.) The unexpected guests are not a problem, because of collective generosity. At a Latino *fiesta* or event, all who attend bring gifts, flowers, food, wine, special treats, and desserts to share with their hosts. This is something akin to the parable of the loaves and fishes in the New Testament, in which there is more food and drink at the end of the gathering than at the beginning.

Generosity is also evident in one of the Latino golden rules: if everyone contributes and pitches in, no one bears the burden and there will be more than enough to go around. At Mexican weddings, there is the tradition of pinning money on the bride's dress or paying to dance with the bride and groom. People line up, and it is great fun as one guest after another steps onto the dance floor for their short twirl with the honored couple. Sponsors for baptisms, weddings, and *quinceaneras* gladly pay for the dress, photographer, *banda,* cake, or bar. In the Anglo culture, it might be embarrassing to ask people to pay for things in this manner. For Latinos, it is an honor that strengthens ties as well as encourages sharing which is the heartbeat of the culture.

Latino hospitality is effusive. People always reserve the best for their guests, serving special food and treats. The Mexican saying *Hechalé agua al caldo* (put another cup of water in the soup) means that no matter how little a person has, there is always enough to go around. Being generous also means showing a genuine caring and concern for people's needs, listening, and giving of one's time. In traditional families, it is embarrassing to have more or to advance ahead of the group. Success is evidenced by one's ability to take care of others, assume greater financial responsibility, and by one's willingness to help with special needs. Having more means being able to give more.

Giveaways, Throws, and Potlatches

THE ANTECEDENTS of Latino generosity can be found in the indigenous culture of the Americas. In early Indian cultures, people often competed with each other to see who could give away the most. No one wanted to be seen as a person who had more than others. Giving was seen as a way to honor people and to strengthen collective ties. LaDonna Harris illustrates how this generosity is still structured in Indian cultures: "The emphasis is not on accumulation, but on sharing what a person has. Everything is reciprocal, so possessions are more fluid and shared. Things are redistributed. There are many formal mechanisms for redistribution. Giveaways, throws, and the potlatch ceremony are three of the methods that demonstrate how integral these values are to Indian culture."

In early Indian cultures, people often competed with each other to see who could give away the most. No one wanted to be seen as a person who had more than others. Giving was seen as a way to honor people and to strengthen collective ties.

A striking difference between a materialistic culture and one based on generosity can be seen in the birthday celebration. In Pueblo cultures, when someone has a birthday, instead of receiving gifts, the celebrator might give back to the community by having a *throw*. After buying food and gifts such as blankets and shawls, the person goes up on the roof and throws the stuff out to the community. The celebrator is recognizing that many of the good things that happened in her or his life are largely due to the care others have provided.

Indian cultures also emphasize achievement as a collective feat rather than just a personal one. In the mainstream culture, when someone graduates from college, people bring gifts to acknowledge this person's achievement. In the tradition of the Plains tribes, a person might have *giveaways* on such occasions. LaDonna explains, "A young Comanche woman might be recognized by her tribe when she graduates, with song, dance, and a ceremony. However, the young woman understands she didn't accomplish this by herself. Many people contributed. In return, she might have a *giveaway* to thank people. She would give them valuable things, like blankets, household goods, or jewelry."

The potlatch, at which people share prized and beautiful possessions, is another way material goods are redistributed. These offerings are placed in the center of a circle where people can admire them. After a thanksgiving is offered, people talk about what they brought and why they are worthy gifts. Slowly and deliberately, people go to the center and choose an object to take home with them. It is a joyous sharing and celebration; people leave with a treasured item given in generosity—"richer" than when they arrived.

 Redistribution ensures that no one accumulates so much wealth or material things that it sets that person above others, thereby disrupting the circle of relatedness so pivotal to Native American philosophy.

—LaDonna Harris, Comanche

LaDonna sees these forms of redistribution as ways in which communal societies keep different economic and social classes in balance: "There isn't as much ranking. People save up for giveaways for years. Redistribution ensures that no one accumulates so much wealth or material things that it sets that person above others, thereby disrupting the circle of relatedness so pivotal to Native American philosophy."

Dr. Joseph, describing American Indian tribes in his book *Remaking America*, admired this profuse generosity: "The early Indian tribe was by its very nature a benevolent community in which sharing was a primary virtue and selfishness a primary vice." He observed, "In the Native American tradition, wealth is generated for its distribution, not its accumulation. The good of the community takes precedence over the good of the individual . . . This produced economic as well as social benefits by distributing goods widely throughout the community."[2]

Sharing Is the Soul of Community

FROM THEIR AFRICAN ROOTS, Black people inherited a tradition whereby the concept of *the village* meant people regarded themselves as an ancestral group for whom land and livestock were tended to communally. There was little regard for individual ownership. The care and nurturing of children was everyone's responsibility. This same sentiment surfaced in the slave quarter communities that functioned as a familial group, with a shared lifestyle and common interests and problems. The hardships of slavery necessitated sticking together for mutual help. Solidarity and protecting one another sheltered people and fostered their survival.

Throughout slavery, African Americans demonstrated a deep sense of taking care of one another and sharing what little they had. Assisting others was a moral obligation that extended beyond the quarter community into a network of mutual aid that encompassed all slaves. The depth of generosity in early Black communities is particularly admirable considering that even in the face of need, lack, toil, and trouble, people shared whatever they had, not just in their own community but beyond, with others who were in need. Dr. Joseph believes the benevolent actions of slaves who cared for people who were sick and in need, whether they were White or Black, is reminiscent of tribal society. "The capacity to express sentiments of generosity for those outside the group, the ability to love the enemy is an African American trait . . . There were evidences of a *universal compassion* within the community of Africans in the Americas that embraced both the near and distant relative."[3]

This tendency remains essential to Black culture. When people succeed, they are expected to help others and to give back to the community. Based on their interviews with over a thousand Black leaders in corporate America, Ancella Livers and Keith

There is an overriding belief among African Americans that service to God is linked to service to humanity. Thus feeding the hungry, housing the homeless, and providing educational opportunities, social liberation and economic empowerment are viewed as part of the moral imperative of religious faith.

—Dr. Jim Joseph

Caver found a deep sense of responsibility, which was described as a *moral obligation* to help other African Americans succeed. This desire to assist others was reported by 95 percent of the people surveyed.[4] Moreover, the African American community does not just participate in philanthropy; it trumps other groups in its generosity. The *Chronicle of Philanthropy* reported a 2003 study that found African Americans who give to charity donate 25 percent more of their discretionary income than Whites.[5] Despite the fact that their economic rungs are substantially lower, giving and taking care of others is a long-time trend of the Black community. Their deep faith and Christian tradition, observes Joseph, reinforces this tradition. "There is an overriding belief among African Americans that service to God is linked to service to humanity. Thus feeding the hungry, housing the homeless, and providing educational opportunities, social liberation and economic empowerment are viewed as part of the *moral imperative* of religious faith."

Community Celebrations: Generosity in Action

IN ALL WE CULTURES, generosity strengthens the social bonds that hold people together. Sharing is not limited to material possessions alone; it includes listening, visiting, and spending time with people; story telling, singing, and dancing; participating in rituals and celebrations; and working for community advancement. There are many treasured ways that *We* cultures create a collective spirit in which sharing and generosity permeate the social fabric.

The African American adage "Make sure people are *singing from the same hymnal*" is a unique way to express the fact that people must have unity and like-mindedness before taking action. Singing is a spiritual tradition that reinforces Black people's emotional connections and often describes their common journey. This type of community sharing underscores the cultural pedigree that singing has as a way to lift people up during hard times and strengthen resolve during demonstrations or political tribulations. Singing helped to energize the civil rights movement.

This tradition reaches back to the African soil, for which Dr. Joseph identifies a quality he calls *homo festivus*: "The idea that individuals and communities have both a capacity and the need to celebrate life even in the midst of tragedy." [6] In Nelson Mandela's poignant autobiography, *Long Walk to Freedom*, he speaks to this quality as sustaining the South African freedom movement. He recounts the difficult years on Robbin Island doing physical labor in the limestone quarry: "Singing succeeded in turning our suffering into happiness. We sang revolutionary songs as we worked and we deliberated matters of national importance. Singing made us overcome the pain of the work we were doing." [7] Singing builds the collective sense of *We*, allowing people to support and share with one another even under dire need.

The many ceremonies, celebrations, and community traditions in American Indian tribes provide opportunities for deep sharing. Everyone brings food and gifts to share and offers to house people. At annual celebrations such as the powwow, dancers wear bright jingle dresses or fringed shawls passed down from their grandmothers. Drummers hammer out a primal beat and sing traditional songs. Each tribe has unique ways of gathering. In September, when autumn floats its cool air, the Comanche come from the four corners of the country to their land in Oklahoma for a "Comanche Fair." Through prayer, storytelling, recounting of tribal history, horseracing, games, and special ceremonies that recognize community achievements, the strands of the collective tribal basket are tightly woven.

For generations, the Jemez Pueblo have run over the blue sage hills where the river ambles by on the way to the plains. Benny Shendo Jr. explains how running is part of their ceremonial way of life and brings people together: "Everybody runs, from the young boys to the old men. It's not about competition or winning. You are racing for the people and everybody has a place and a responsibility. The literal translation of one of our races is, praying with the clouds or running with the clouds. So you are running to bring rain or moisture to the land and to benefit the people."

From both their own indigenous traditions and those of the gregarious Spanish, Latinos have inherited a love of music, dancing, and celebrations. *Gozar la vida* ("enjoy life") is a deep-rooted philosophy, which means sharing good times with family and friends. Supporting this value are consumer studies that show Latinos spend more money on food, entertainment, and music than other market segments.[8] Regardless of obstacles or limited economic resources, there is a belief that while life may be difficult, it should be enjoyed. "Canta No Llores"—"sing, don't cry"—is a much-loved traditional song reflecting this philosophy. The song coun-

 Since Latinos have the highest percentage of participation in the U.S. labor market of any subgroup, they are great contributors at work and have an admirable work ethic. This reflects their value of generosity. Work is an opportunity to give of their talents and contribute to the welfare of the group and organization.

sels people not to cry, but to sing. In this way they will make themselves happy. Imagine how this good counsel uplifts people when they are poor, work at menial and backbreaking jobs, or deal with the social obstacle of racism!

In her last popular song, the venerated Salsa singer Celia Cruz acknowledged this philosophy. She advised, *"Aye, no hay que llorar, porque la vida es un carnival"* ("there is no reason to cry, because life is a carnival"). In keeping with this spirit, Latinos will find any excuse to host a fiesta, a celebration given for visiting relatives, births, baptisms, birthdays, anniversaries, Holy Communion day, when a young girl reaches fifteen, for a new job, moving to a new place, a promotion, or a retirement. Although Anglos may also celebrate these types of life events, for the Latinos' large extended family, which is not just blood related but more like a tribe, the fiesta is not a small intimate dinner but a community celebration. Furthermore, *bienvenidos* or welcome signifies the pervasive hospitality of the Latino culture and makes for an open-door policy that makes people feel at home. Just as their American Indian relatives do at their celebratory events, everyone contributes; the fiesta is an opportunity to share.

Since Latinos have the highest percentage of participation in the U.S. labor market of any subgroup, they are great contributors at work and have an admirable work ethic. This reflects their value of generosity. Work is an opportunity to give of their talents and contribute to the welfare of the group and organization. Latinos strive to balance working, taking time for people, spending time with their families, and enjoying life through fiestas and celebrations. This philosophy is woven into their religious practices and was upheld by César Chávez in the "Farm Workers Prayer": "Bring forth song and celebration, so that the Spirit will be alive among us."[9]

Generosity Benefits You and Others

BY ENUMERATING THE BENEFITS of building a benevolent society that values generosity and mutual care, leaders from communities of color can help people remember why it is better to give than to receive. Although many people give this saying lip service, the actions of our materialistic culture indicate that people don't really believe it to be true. But wait: what if this is actually the case and communities of color who practice generosity are onto something? Not only did they survive more than five hundred years of racism and economic oppression, but they kept their values of faith and dedication to the collective good intact. Moreover, they are still singing, dancing, and celebrating every chance they get!

Perhaps it would be advantageous to look at why generosity is such a healthy prescription for nurturing community, cultivating relationships, and celebrating life.

 "Love" appears in The Descent of Man *some ninety-five times, whereas only two entries address the "law of mutual struggle," as Darwin termed it. Darwin argued that more crucial than this is the "law of mutual aid" and human solidarity.*

Let us start by revisiting the "survival of the fittest" theory—whereby the idea that human nature is competitive and acquisitive first got on the fast track. Earlier, we surmised that our ability to work together and to look out for one another is one of the reasons humans finished first in the evolutionary ascent. Interestingly enough, although the theory of the survival of the fittest is often mistakenly attributed to Darwin, his work supports a more cooperative view.[10] In fact, Darwin found in animals admirable examples of reciprocity, cooperation, and even love. In *Darwin's Lost Theory of Love*, author David Loye points out that "love" appears in *The Descent of Man* some ninety-five times, whereas only two entries address the "law of mutual struggle," as Darwin termed it. Darwin argued that more crucial than this is the "law of mutual aid" and human solidarity.[11]

Over a hundred years after Darwin, Jane Goodall, the renowned primatologist, observed similar behavior in chimpanzees, who aided the weak, shared their resources, showed great affection, and comforted those in need. Like these evolutionary predecessors, human beings are social by nature and have a profound longing for connection and community. Can it be that the individualistic and self-centered view of human nature proposed by our society has overshadowed our generous and communal spirit? Can love, reciprocity, cooperation and mutual aid, and generosity be the core of our true nature? It is important to recognize that the underpinning of any society is its concept of human nature. Modify this and, like toppling dominos, other concepts begin to fall.

In fact, as described previously, human beings evolved from early *We* cultures that were based on people take caring of and looking out for each other. *Being able to share and be generous was, indeed, a survival tactic.* When a hunter brought back game, the entire tribe partook. In this way, everyone would eat again when another had good fortune. The tribal fire gave warmth to all its members. In a crisis, the tribe would come together to provide for those in need. Traditional African societies followed in this tradition, and Indian tribes have never swerved from this communal pathway. Latino values of mutuality, cooperation, and generosity also mirror the collective values of early cultures.

Communities of color offer rich examples of the benefits of generosity and mutual aid, which are in alignment with the biblical example of the good Samaritan and the counsel to "love your neighbor." The New Testament warns against being greedy and cautions that wealth can damage one's soul (Matthew, Mark, and Luke all recorded Jesus' words: "It is easier for a camel to go through the eye of a needle than for a rich man to enter the kingdom of God.") The Bible encourages us to be generous and to assume social responsibility for others. "The American way," discerns Benedictine monk Thomas Keating, "is to first feel good about yourself and then feel good about others. But spiritual traditions say it's the other way around—that you develop a sense of goodness by *giving of yourself.*"[12] Perhaps it is better to give than to receive because we bring forth our higher self, connect with others, and infuse our communities with generosity.

The Generosity Gap

YET DESPITE all the religious mandates, much of mainstream America today is more concerned about personal accumulation than the welfare of their neighbors. The result is that the gap between the rich and the poor has become an immense chasm. Catastrophic events like Hurricane Katrina shockingly remind us of a growing poverty normally hidden from us by the major media. The number of people in the United States living below the poverty line recently hit 36 million, or 12.5 percent of the population—*an increase of more than a million in a single year.* America's poverty rate is the highest in the developed world and more than twice as high as those of most other industrialized countries.[13]

 Wages have not kept pace with the cost of living, except at the top. In 2002, CEOs made on average 241 times as much as the average worker; in the 1980s their earnings were only 45 times higher.

There is also a direct correlation between poverty and race: only 8 percent of Whites are poor, compared with 22 percent of Hispanics and nearly 25 percent of African Americans. Many experts report that the primary economic reason for the increase in poverty is *low wages for workers of all races.* Wages have not kept pace with the cost of living, except at the top. In 2002, CEOs made on average 241 times as much as the average worker; in the 1980s their earnings were only 45 times higher. Greed at the top has led to depressed salaries, the slashing of worker benefits, the loss of jobs, and the end of secure retirement. The value of the minimum wage has eroded since 1996.[14] Adjusted for inflation and the cost of living, it is actually lower than the $4.25 minimum wage of 1995.[15] Young students, facing soaring college costs, are graduating with an average debt of $19,000—an immense hardship in starting one's life. In this, the only developed country without government-sponsored medical care, 46 million Americans, or 15.7 percent of the population, were uninsured in 2004, including 8.3 million children.[16] Finally, the soaring cost of housing, powered by speculative investing, has placed this longtime "American dream" out of reach for many, and programs for affordable housing are woefully inadequate.

America's leadership crisis is that its rich resources, entrepreneurial nature, and business and capitalist acumen have unfortunately led to a national malaise. The individual greed of many of our leaders has overcome concern for the common good and for supporting a society in which people can meet their basic economic needs. A safe and sustainable society is not possible with our resources so unequally distributed. *Dealing with the social structures and revitalizing public morality so that an equitable and compassionate society can thrive is a critical leadership issue of our times.* Raul Yzaguirre urges us to follow a new course: "Embracing the Latino values of generosity and helping one another would heal many of the divisions in America. Latinos are taught not to take more than their share. Many of the social ills facing this country today are the result of an unequal distribution of resources. Perhaps the solution is for the rest of Americans to become more courteous, community-minded, and generous."

Connecting to the Purpose of Leadership

A S A PIVOTAL VALUE, *generosity* is a key leadership trait in communities of color. On a personal level, leaders give to community causes, help those in need, share their time and resources, recognize the contributions of others, and empower people. At the community level, these leaders focus on *collective sustainability* rather than individual gain or personal advancement. As we will explore more deeply in the next section, leadership that is committed to creating a more compassionate and equitable society implies generosity and more equitable distribution of resources.

This brings us to a critical juncture. Before looking at the next three leadership principles in communities of color, it would be wise to consider the purpose of leadership. Although there are many views on this, renowned leadership expert James MacGregor Burns aligns most closely with communities of color. Burns defined leadership as a *collective process* linked to *social change* with the purpose of enhancing the *well-being of human existence.* He added that leadership implies the ability to *mobilize people* and engage them in a process in which both leader and followers raise one another to *higher levels of motivation and morality.*[17]

Leaders in communities of color receive their legitimacy from the people they serve. They garner this respect by exhibiting a high level of morality, including being generous, honest, and humble, and by serving. As they model these behaviors, they lift up the morality of their followers and community as well. With limited resources, leaders must be adept at mobilizing people to address critical issues, including an examination of the social structures that limit equal participation.

The purpose of leadership in communities of color is in step with Burns's description—to promote the collective well-being by creating positive social change and securing equal opportunities through a collaborative process that develops and uplifts people. Dr. Antonia Pantoja, the great Puerto Rican activist, stated this well: "I want to live a life of commitment to the human community for the betterment of all people."

 Tribal leaders think long-term, considering the impact on future generations. . . . Tribal philosophy puts things into a holistic and visionary perspective.

—John Echohawk

Many believe that there is a crisis in American leadership today—a failure to provide the high moral ground and morality Burns describes as two key functions. If leaders are to enhance people's well-being, then surely they must nurture a social, political, and economic environment in which people can get their basic needs met, including decent housing, work, education, and health care. Inspired leadership implies societal guardianship. The emphasis on wealth accumulation by many corporate leaders and the lack of socially responsible action by government leaders has threatened the very mandate society has been given to take care of our own and to ensure prosperity for future generations.

Leaders are also guardians of the social contract whereby people willingly follow the rules, laws, and structure of society in return for the benefits received. When these begin to unravel, there is social disengagement, alienation, and increasing economic need, as well as more violence and crime. Statistics presented in the previous section indicated that civic participation is on the decline; people feel overworked and are withdrawing from community. Furthermore, America has more people in prison as a percentage of population than any other country, the greatest number of laws to follow, and the most lawyers. Is this an indication that the social contract is withering and people no longer see our society as providing the means to satisfy their basic needs? How does this reflect the spirit of generosity whereby leaders are stewards and responsible for tending to people's well-being?

Leadership in communities of color, as described in the subsequent section, offers a number of remedies that can heal these ills and reengage people in society. This is not to imply that all such leaders follow these high standards. There are, of course, those who have swerved from traditional ways, who may be more identified with the mainstream culture or focused on personal advancement rather than that of their community. As described previously, the leaders interviewed for this book represent the ideal and put forward the best practices from communities of color, which allow us to glean principles that help us realize the promise and potential of leading from this orientation.

Leadership That Reflects the Spirit of Generosity

THE IROQUOIS TRIBE's rule for leaders was that they should consider the impact of their decisions on their children, their children's children, and unto seven generations. The imperative that leaders are the guardians of future generations mandates that they be good stewards and includes a vision for a sustainable future. To ensure this, *one generation cannot take more than their share.* Safeguarding the prosperity of the community implies an expansive generosity that reaches beyond today and into the unforeseen future.

Adhering to the seventh-generation rule creates a different leadership perspective.

 The Iroquois tribe's rule for leaders was that they should consider the impact of their decisions on their children, their children's children, and unto seven generations. The imperative that leaders are the guardians of future generations mandates that they be good stewards and includes a vision for a sustainable future.

Our now-oriented society and results-driven leadership consumes resources and people without considering the ramifications. American Indian leadership, on the other hand, is based on ancient traditions that include continuity and stewardship. John Echohawk explains, "Tribal leaders don't see land as a piece of real estate to be bought or sold, but as their homeland where their people will remain for all time. The land has to sustain the people. Leaders are stewards of the land for their tribe."

Echohawk sees a sharp contrast with the way Anglo leaders think. "In the American way, land is bought and sold and its value is monetary. We look at our earth as our homeland. We need to take care of it so it will sustain us in perpetuity. Tribal leaders think long term, considering the impact on future generations. This view oftentimes gets lost in a busy America that thinks in short-term profit and gain. Tribal philosophy puts things into a holistic and visionary perspective." On most reservations, for example, one rarely finds rich individuals or entrepreneurs. The purpose of economic development is creating *community wealth*, not wealthy individuals.

Generosity, mutuality, and helping one another has held Blacks, Latinos, and Indians together through oppression and economic scarcity. These qualities continue nourishing and sustaining these communities today. Generosity runs contrary to a few accumulating so much excess wealth that the well-being of society is threatened. Generosity is the basis for a more compassionate and caring society—the rich soil from which a benevolent community can grow. Generosity is the antidote to the rampant materialism that reinforces individualistic gain over the common welfare.

The three leadership principles in communities of color that we'll explore in Part Two build on the tradition of *Sankofa.* They have emerged from a historical context that was fueled by the civil rights movement. The fourth principle, *a leader among equals*, reflects the *We* or collective orientation in which leadership is shared, rotated, and reciprocal. The fifth principle, *leaders as guardians of public values*, defines leaders as those who safeguard the values our country was founded on: justice, equality, and the common welfare. Leadership in this context has a moral imperative to exhibit social responsibility. The sixth principle, *leaders as community stewards*, builds people's capacity and ensures continued progress. Leaders serve people by encouraging their participation and nurturing empowerment. In this way, they foster a community of leaders and build the critical mass needed to create positive social change. These principles lay the foundation for a leadership model in which generosity and serving the common welfare is the nucleus of an equitable democracy.

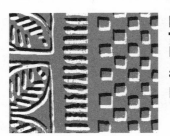

NEXT STEPS

Reflecting On and Applying Principle Three

Mi Casa Es Su Casa— Developing a Spirit of Generosity

Practicing sharing and developing a spirit of generosity

Imagine a culture in which people compete to give things away, a leader is respected because of his or her generosity, and material things are more fluid and shared! Think about giving as reciprocal and circular, with generosity meaning actually giving to oneself. The following exercises will infuse a spirit of generosity and giving.

Sponsor a *potlatch* in your organization, group, or family in which people each give away one really treasured item. Place these gifts in the middle of the room and have people gather in a circle to admire them. Each person talks about why his or her gift is special and valuable. People reflect on the gifts, and each chooses one to take home. This works well during the holidays or as an organizational celebration or team-building experience. Discussing the meaning and lessons from the potlatch can instill a new sense of sharing and mutual assistance in the organization and in teams.

On your next birthday or milestone (a promotion or graduation), announce that you are having a *giveaway* to recognize that your achievements have been possible only because of your family, coworkers, and friends who support (and put up with) you. Then be deliberate about buying gifts or mementos that are meaningful. Emphasize that this is not about them doing anything for you, but about your acknowledging the care and support they have already given that is responsible for your success.

Has someone admired something you own? The next time this happens, think about giving it to him or her. It might really *belong* to them. By so doing, you may put into motion the reciprocity that exists in communities of color, in which sharing of material things and gift giving are woven into the fabric of relationships.

How much of your income or the company's profits are set aside to benefit others? Following the example set by the Black community, do a generosity audit and make sharing a priority. Set a giving goal. This can infuse people and the organization with a higher purpose and sense of success. We have more than enough and can share our good fortune!

Conduct a life balance audit that includes looking at priorities and key values

At the Center for Creative Leadership, we would end programs with a goal-setting exercise in which participants set priorities based on what they had learned. Before doing this, we asked them to consider the following areas of their lives—career, family, self, and community—and to discern where they were spending their time and which needed tending. Mainstream culture emphasizes work, often at the expense of other areas in life including one's spiritual substance and relationships. Communities of color have different priorities. One benefit of a multicultural society is having more choices. Having a balanced life means being generous with oneself and others. Using a total of 100 points that represent how you spend your life energy and time, allocate them among the following six areas:

_____   _____   _____   _____   _____   _____

Personal   Family   Career   Community   Relationships   Spiritual sustenance

Based on your analysis, what did you learn about your life balance? What areas of your life need tending and where would you like to spend more of your energy? What is consuming too much of your time and energy? What specific and measurable goals would you like to set that will bring balance to your life? What compromises or adjustments will you have to make? Who can support you in making these changes?

Recommended readings and resources

- *Remaking America: How the Benevolent Traditions of Many Cultures Are Transforming Our National Life* by James A. Joseph (Jossey-Bass, 1995).

PART TWO

Leadership Styles in Communities of Color

WHETHER I OR WE IS CENTRAL to a society contours the shape of leadership. A *We* identity prompts a collective and people-centered view of leadership. Collective leadership by its very nature espouses the well-being of people as a whole, not just individuals. Anna Escobedo Cabral, who has led a number of national Hispanic initiatives, describes this commitment: "What motivates people in our community who are doing great work and leading efforts is that they are looking out for the collective. *The collective good drives them.*" Latino leadership, therefore, has a distinctly people-oriented flavor: leaders emerge from their community by addressing critical needs. Shared leadership is also a time-honored practice for American Indians, who espouse a circular approach and the rotation of leadership so that no one is elevated above others. *We* is the fountainhead from which their reciprocal and dispersed leadership flows. Just as identity is collective, so too the source of leadership is collective. A leader serves and is responsible to his or her community, tribe, and people.

African American Leadership, an extensive book by Ron Walters and Robert Smith, defines Black leadership as proceeding from the collective interests and concerns of people focusing on overcoming social, political, and economic impediments. To achieve this, Black leadership has relied on social rather than economic resources; this requires bringing people together and building coalitions. Walters and Smith speak to this *We* reference point: "Leadership derives its authority and legitimacy from the community from which it emerges."[1]

Mainstream leadership today is moving toward a *We* or collaborative form that resonates with communities of color. Like multicultural leadership, collaboration supports a reciprocal and dispersed style in which many people are prepared to participate and share responsibility. Looking at this shift to collaboration is a good starting point for examining the leadership principles in communities and seeing how these connect with today's emphasis on teamwork, partnerships, and shared responsibility.

The Shift to Collaborative Leadership

FOR GENERATIONS, the center point of mainstream American leadership was the *individual leader*. This fashioned a hierarchical leadership form, which was very effective in an assembly-line economy in which people followed orders and looked to the boss or supervisor for direction. In the last half of the twentieth century, the dynamics discussed in Principle 1—civil rights, globalization, changing demographics, democratic values, higher educational levels, and political awareness—that are transforming leadership into a multicultural form are also dismantling the hierarchical approach. These powerful social shifts are redefining leadership, from the domain of a few individuals to a more participatory and collaborative process that engages many people.

 In the complex and rapidly changing climate of the twenty-first century, individual leaders simply will not have the best answers or solutions. They must be able to encourage collaboration so that people generate creative solutions and ideas.

Collaborative leadership evolved as our economy changed from an industrial base to one driven by information, mass communications, technology, innovation, and the service industry. In this speed-driven environment, people must be able to think on their feet, solve problems quickly, and find innovative solutions. These shifting dynamics necessitate people's active participation, best thinking, and mutual responsibility for outcomes. In the complex and rapidly changing climate of the twenty-first century, individual leaders simply will not have the best answers or solutions. They must be able to encourage collabora-tion so that people generate creative solutions and ideas.

Based on a participatory and democratic form, collaborative leadership transforms the *I* orientation of hierarchal leadership to a group-centered or *We* orientation. Instead of supplying all the answers, the leader creates an environment that promotes working and learning together. Patricia Aburdene and John Naisbitt, internationally respected social forecasters, noted in their book *Megatrends 2000*: "The primary (leadership) chal-lenge will be to encourage the new, better educated work force to be committed, self-managing, life-long learners."[2]

Intrinsic to cultivating collaboration is nurturing people's potential and ability to work both autonomously and in teams. For this to occur, the leader must hand over the reins and have the confidence—as Peter Block, author of *Stewardship: Choosing Service over Self-Interest,* states—that "people have the knowledge and answers."[3] This again shifts the locus of control from the individual leader to the *We* or people served by the leader. In this way, teamwork, synergy, and group intelligence can surface.

Our changing demographics create a pressing leadership challenge: to foster col-laborative environments in which people of many backgrounds can work side by side in a creative and productive manner. Communities of color offer a rich foundation for building inclusive environments and respecting differences, which can take collabora-tion to a higher level by *encouraging equal access* and *urging the involvement of all the diverse segments.*

Collective and Collaborative Leadership

IN COMMUNITIES OF COLOR, leadership is both *collectivist* and *collaborative*. Because leaders identify with, arise from, and depend on their community for power and authority, leadership is collectivist in nature. Leaders are sanctioned by their com-munity and must be responsive and responsible to the people they serve. By identifying critical needs and interests and then working to address these, leaders stay connected to their people, whom they represent. Collectivist leadership springs from the *We* orienta-tion and therefore centers on what is good for the community, group, or organization.

Walters and Smith comment on how pivotal this approach is: "The primacy of the community or the Black collective is the basis of the internal democratic system of the

Black community and the ultimate basis too of the unity and accountability that are the source of its integrity." They also comment on the longevity of this approach: "The Black community has had a long history of attempting to fashion collective leadership, the origin of which might have officially begun on a national scale as early as the Negro Convention movement in the 1830s when Black men came together to address the urgent problems facing their people."[4]

Collaborative leadership speaks to a process or style in which people are encouraged to contribute and work together, particularly as teams, to achieve mutual goals. Leaders in communities of color have traditionally structured leadership as a collaborative process that supports participation. By working side by side with others, a leader is in tune with the community pulse and understands people's priorities. In addition, collaboration nurtures a network of leaders and sustains the web of relationships, which is the foundation of the *We* identity. A collaborative process also implies that leadership is rotated, distributed, and shared, which has been a mainstay in communities of color. The process of preparing many people to assume responsibility also increases ownership, nurtures continuity, and develops the critical mass to promote social change.[5]

The three principles we discuss examine how leadership in communities of color is structured around values that support collaboration and emphasize equal access. The first principle—*a leader among equals*—underscores shared leadership, in which the leader is not above others but remains part of the group. The principle of *leaders as guardians of public value* speaks to the mandate to transform the social structures that hinder people's full participation and to uphold values such as justice, equity, and the common good on which this country was founded. This drives an activist model of leadership.

Two prevalent cultural barriers that have obstructed equal participation are the *psychology of oppression* and *white privilege*. The psychology of oppression is the process by which people of color internalize the negative messages and beliefs about their race that exist in society and come to believe that they are true. The term white privilege describes the unspoken advantages and opportunities bestowed on people from the dominant culture in the United States. White privilege is not earned, but benefits people simply because of their race. A deeper understanding of white privilege and the psychology of oppression illuminates how exclusion and discrimination operate and form impediments to inclusive and multicultural leadership.

Both the psychology of oppression and white privilege operate at an unconscious level. Many people are thus unaware of how these social mechanisms operate in their personal lives, providing advantages to some and discriminating against others. On a societal level, these mechanisms reinforce White cultural dominance and institutional control while perpetuating the myth that equality has been achieved and democratic choice is equally available to all people.

Just as collaboration is a cherished tradition in communities of color, likewise the practice of leadership as *service* is fundamental. The principle of *leaders as community stewards* defines leaders as builders and guardians of community progress who nurture a network or legacy. This concept expands Robert Greenleaf's work, as described in *The Servant as Leader*, from an individual focus to one that serves communities and society.[6] Since Greenleaf's concepts are in close alignment with the leadership in com-

 The Black community has had a long history of attempting to fashion collective leadership, the origin of which might have officially begun on a national scale as early as the Negro Convention movement in the 1830s when Black men came together to address the urgent problems facing their people.

—Ron Walters
and Robert Smith

munities of color, a deeper look at his work is included in the discussion of Principle 6. Communities of color have much to share and teach regarding the practical application of collaborative and servant leadership. The three principles we will explore in this part offer valuable insights and knowledge that can be guideposts for leading from these orientations, restructuring leadership to embrace a higher social responsibility and to reflect our multicultural nation.

PRINCIPLE 4

A Leader Among Equals—
Community-Conferred Leadership

ARRIVING IN DENVER in 1971, armed with a master's degree in social work from the University of Wisconsin, I started working in the *barrios* with low-income Hispanic women. At that time, Brown America was in an Anglo no-man's-land—a group unrecognized by the U.S. census and barely visible to the mainstream culture. After a number of years of working in the barrios, I was convinced Latinas were on an economic dead-end street and that the way to empowerment was innovative programs, which built on our cultural strengths.

As I was mulling this over, the local Mennonite minister called to say, "There is a group of Hispanic Head Start mothers who want to talk about services for Latina women. They see that their children are learning, and they want to learn too!" Thus, a conversation began between a group of community grassroots women and Latina professionals that culminated in our starting a small women's center in the basement of the Mennonite Church. It was christened "Mi Casa" to reflect its role as a place Latinas could call their own and find cultural validation. Mi Casa provided employment and educational services that assisted women to acquire the skills to become economically self-sufficient.

Although I had spent many years working in the community, I had never led an organization and wasn't really sure how to do this. Yet I was impassioned about the need to build the first Latina service organization in Colorado. Anna Escobedo Cabral observes that this has been a traditional pathway: "I think a lot of Latino leaders see a problem, and they work hard to find a solution, and as a result they are put in a position of leadership to make change happen. However, it is not about them seeking that position. Rather it is about addressing some unmet need."

I stayed for the first ten years, during which we developed key programs, bought our own facility, and established a national reputation for our work in empowering Latinas. Key to Mi Casa's success was building a community of supporters and a committed staff and designating a group of "founding mothers" who were involved during the formative years of the organization. When resources are scarce and people power is critical, collective leadership—in which many contribute and have ownership—is indispensable. Creating a network disperses leadership and shares responsibility. This approach, which we called *la familia,* was in step with leading from a *We* or collective orientation.

> *There is this basic value that whatever you do, you do for the community and the family. It is not about you as an individual. Yes, it is important to do well, but because it will enable others to do well. Even in the midst of dire circumstances, people will say, "let me see if I can help."*
>
> —Anna Escobedo Cabral

Leading from a Collective Orientation

THE INDIVIDUALISTIC-COLLECTIVIST cultural continuum explored in the previous principles has a profound impact on leadership. When people succeed in a collectivist culture, they share their good fortune. Cabral believes this quality is inherent in Latino leadership: "There is this basic value that whatever you do, you do for the community and the family. It is not about you as an individual. Yes, it is important to do well, but because it will enable others to do well. Even in the midst of dire circumstances, people will say, 'let me see if I can help.'"

In collectivist cultures, a leader's authority comes from the group. Leaders are expected to reflect the group's behavior and values. By listening and gathering people's opinions, the leader integrates the group wisdom. The leader must find unanimity within the group *first*, and then act in concert with it. Like a battery, leaders charge people up, facilitate their working together, and assist them in solving problems. Through empowering others, a community of leaders evolves. Standing out too far from others or calling too much attention to oneself can damage the group cohesion that is central to collectivist cultures.

In an individualistic culture, *I* become a leader because of my personal initiative, accomplishments, and competence as well as my winning personality. *I* have a can-do attitude—a take-action personality. By my calling attention to myself—my accomplishments and skills—people believe *I* am competent and they are comfortable following me. Unanimity or group consensus *follows* the leader's decisions. The leader strives for self-mastery—as *I* become empowered, *I* can empower others. As *I* learn, *I* teach others. Leaders maintain status by remaining youthful, vigorous, attractive, and able. Seniority is secondary to performance. In contrast, the status of a collectivist leader increases as he or she becomes older and acquires seniority and experience.[1]

We cultures acknowledge that the community has nurtured and invested in a person. In individualistic cultures, there is a belief that *I made it on my own*. Bennie Shendo explains the distinction: "In some cultures people believe you achieve alone. I can never think that way." When he speaks to young Indians, he emphasizes the need to honor one's collective inheritance: "Understand that your success is not yours alone, it's due to your family, tribe, and community and it's because of the people that have gone before you that have prayed for you to be here."

Ada Deer, a Menominee who is the director of Indian programs at the University of Wisconsin at Madison, reflects on how the leaders in her tribe safeguarded the col-

 When I was growing up it, wasn't Me— *it was* We, *the family and tribe. Later, I understood that we wouldn't have survived as a people if our leaders didn't have that sense of obligation and responsibility to the tribe.*

—Ada Deer, Menominee

lective: "When I was growing up, it wasn't *Me*—it was *We,* the family and tribe. Later, I understood that we wouldn't have survived as a people if our leaders didn't have that sense of obligation and responsibility to the tribe." Dr. Pantoja saw this as an inherent condition of living in community: "I am interdependent. I was nurtured to be who I am and am responsible and accountable to a community of others."

This brief overview provides a glimpse of how these two cultural points of reference influence leadership. Our next section explores how the concept of leaders among equals is used in communities of color to empower people and ensure continuity. The following dynamics promote this concept: (1) authority comes from the group, which takes precedence over the individual leader; (2) leaders are chosen because of their character, including honesty, humility, and generosity; (3) leaders inspire people to identify with them by setting an example; (4) a leader serves something greater than her- or himself—the mission, cause, or well-being of the community comes first; and (5) a leader plays by the rules.

Leadership Is Conferred by the Tribe

IN MANY TRIBES, it is not culturally correct to say, "I am a leader." Leadership is externally conferred by people who recognize a person's abilities, talents, or vision and know how this benefits the community. LaDonna Harris explains how this operates in the Comanche and Iroquois tribes: "A leader was simply someone people followed. The Comanche didn't elect leaders. If a person had admirable qualities—generosity, sharing, responsibility to self and others—people would follow him. In fact, in the Iroquois Nation, a person will not be tapped as a leader if he expresses the desire to be in charge. In a communal society, a person is valued by what they can contribute to their community. Since everyone can contribute, leadership is rotated depending on the task or function at hand, and therefore, is much more distributed."

John Echohawk did not seek out the work, responsibility, or the high expectations of leadership. As early as junior high, however, friends and classmates told him, "You need to do this. You should do this. You should do this for us [the American Indian community]." Reluctantly, he accepted his election to leadership positions, including senior class president. Similarly, in law school, people wanted him to run for the Student Bar Association. He wasn't ambitious, but he acquiesced and served as president his senior year. Since John was the one of the first graduates of the Native American Law Program, when the Native American Rights Fund opened a central-western location in the 1970s, he was asked to become the executive director. "They were saying, 'We need you to do this.' I had to go along with it. If a person is asked to serve the community or tribe, it is his responsibility to comply. Even though it would be easy to say no, you can't, because you would be disappointing people and letting them down."

This sense of leadership as community responsibility is also evident in the Jemez Pueblo, who live on their ancestral lands outside of Albuquerque, New Mexico. The Jemez have been there since before the Spanish arrived, before this was New Mexico, before this was America. Their leadership forms follow ancient traditions. In the Jemez Pueblo, a person does not aspire to be a leader. Their traditional governing body, called the *cacique*, is a group that represents the various clans and religious leaders. The *cacique* is rooted in prehistoric times; it is charged with choosing leaders based on the qualities needed by the tribe. The *cacique* is responsible for maintaining tribal spiritual and cultural traditions.[2]

 For us in Jemez, we are leaders among equals ... at some point you are called and given certain responsibilities as a leader. People respect that. But, when your time is done, you are among equals again.

—Benny Shendo Jr.,
Jemez Pueblo

Benny Shendo Jr. was appointed the council's second lieutenant governor at a fairly young age. "I wasn't trying to be the leader. Since we don't have elections, at some point your name will be called and you won't refuse. When the *cacique* decides you are ready, you are ready! Obviously, certain situations call for a particular type of leadership." After Benny completed his council term, he returned to his role as an ordinary tribal member: "So now I'm among equals. I'm just a common man in the community. Other people will tell me what do . . . For us in Jemez, we are *leaders among equals* . . . at some point you are called and given certain responsibilities as a leader. People respect that. But, when your time is done, you are among equals again. I can't really say I'm better than you, because in a year or two, I'm going to be an ordinary tribal person again. So leadership rotates and no one is elevated above others." These types of practices promote a leadership form in which equity and reciprocity are the norm.

Personalismo—A Leader's Character and Example

IN THE LATINO CULTURE, people identify and work with a leader because of *personalismo*—people's respect for the leader as a person. Approaching leadership in terms of *personalismo*—the importance of one's reputation or character—has deep implications and points to a crucial question: What kind of person are you and how do you treat others? No matter how "important" a leader becomes, she or he must be willing to do the hard work needed for community progress. Leaders are expected to roll up their sleeves, stuff envelopes, clean up, cook, and serve food. Any type of elitism or projection that one is above a certain task will destroy a leader's credibility. Leaders also earn respect by being accessible and generously giving of their resources and talents. They work hand in hand with people, leading not just by words but also by actions.

Personalismo implies that leadership centers on character. The saying *mi palabra es la ley* (my word is law) emphasizes the importance of honesty as a leadership trait. Leaders must do what they say they are going to do. Following through establishes a leader's track record and credibility. In a survey of over three thousand Latinos, the National Community for Latino Leadership (NCLL) found that the quality most valued in Latino leaders was keeping one's word and delivering on one's promises.[3] Yzaguirre further explains these tendencies: "There is a lot of inconsistency with leaders today who articulate American values but don't live them. Latinos are living them every day. As a culture we believe that you do what you say you are going to do."

Latinos expect their leaders to accomplish *extraordinary* things while remaining *ordinary* people. In collectivist cultures, a leader must embody his or her community and never forget "where he or she came from." César Chávez, who is regarded as the most respected Latino leader of the last century, was passionate about improving life for farm workers. Latinos saw him living simply, making personal sacrifices, taking risks in demonstrations, and working side by side with people. Because he publicly demonstrated his values and never set himself above others, people followed him and took up the banner of the farm workers' plight. The *New York Times* in 1969 commented on Chávez's dedication to remaining one of the people: "He still lives on the $5.00 a week all union workers receive, and he invariably dresses in the same gray work pants and plaid wool shirt."[4]

Federico Peña, the former mayor of Denver, kept his campaign promises. He launched Denver International Airport and the new Convention Center. A major league baseball team, the Rockies, and Coors Field were negotiated under his watch. Denver's downtown was reenergized. Since few minority- and woman-owned businesses could qualify for city contracts, he took the lead in passing an ordinance that required large contractors to subcontract 30 percent of the work with minority- and woman-owned businesses. Finally, a great city values the arts: Peña started the city's Public Art Council and was a key supporter in the campaign to redesign the Denver Center for the Performing Arts, which today is second only to Lincoln Center in New York for performances, theatre space, and attendance. Peña's amazing political follow-through heeds the Hispanic mandate that *leaders keep their word*. He learned this value from his parents: "Consistent with my own upbringing was that your word is your bond."

Peña's slogan when he ran for mayor of Denver was "Imagine a great city!" One of his goals was to clean up the city's air. He launched his campaign by riding the city bus to work. Leading by example, Peña got people's attention concerning the critical importance of air quality to their health and Denver's future. By actually doing what he asks others to do, Peña led by example. Thus, people identified with him and believed they could do likewise.

Setting an Inspiring Example

PERSONALISMO RESONATES with a valued trait in the Black community—being known as one of the people who "walk their talk." African Americans value authenticity, genuineness, and being "real." A leader must therefore speak the truth, communicating with sincerity and conviction. The expression "Tell it like it is" underscores this importance. This trait is similar to the way in which Latino leaders relate to and reflect their community.

In the Black community, although uniqueness and personal style are celebrated, self-expression is considered a way to enhance collectivism—unlike the usual American individualism that separates one from the group. It's analogous to a jazz group playing different interpretations—the individual musician has to be in harmony with and contribute to the music of the group. When the piano player takes the lead, he spontaneously adds his own interpretation and style. He may even go off on his own, but he is always in sync with the group. The other musicians back him up, appreciate his improvisations, and egg him on. Their responses spark greater creativity in his playing. When he finishes, the sax player may take the lead, starting an improvisation that builds on the previous one. This differs from the kind of individualism in which a person sets herself apart, may point out how she is more adept, and may not necessarily enhance the group. To separate oneself, or act as if one is better or above others, would run contrary to nurturing group identity, which is a key function of Black leadership.

A Black leader's influence and authority come from *being part* of the community and people's identification with the leader. Historically, leadership emerged from the mutual interest and concerns of Black people. Since people are the collective force for getting things done, attaining the moral authority to lead requires earning people's trust and respect. A leader must be known as a person who cares about and serves others. Because Black leaders depend on the respect of their followers to sanction their authority, their credibility depends on their ability to model the highest qualities of leadership.

 In the Anglo community, it is not necessarily about the community ratifying a leader, but rather, "I am going to go out, and I am going to take this position of congressman or senator; as a result, I'm a leader now . . . it's mostly "this is my personal ambition."

—Anna Escobedo Cabral

Anna Escobedo Cabral, who served as the executive staff director for the U.S. Senate Republican Task Force on Hispanic Affairs, observes how this differs for mainstream leaders: "In the Anglo community, it is not necessarily about the community ratifying a leader, but rather, 'I am going to go out, and I am going to take this position of congressman or senator; as a result, I'm a leader now . . . ' And it's not about whether you can do it well, or not do it well, it's mostly 'this is my personal ambition.'"

In this scenario, somebody from *outside the group* might be promoted or elected to a position or be in charge. The leader, therefore, might not understand the issues people face or know the right solution or direction to take. When leadership is self-directed and self-initiated, the bond with followers may or may not exist. Furthermore, when leadership is shrouded in status and position, a socioeconomic distance can develop that disconnects leaders from people. Many leaders and politicians in America today are disengaged from real people's lives because of this phenomenon.

Leadership in communities of color has to be an *inside job*. An outsider would hinder people's identification with their leader, go against the grain of leaders among equals, reinforce people's minority status, and dampen their belief that they have the same potential as the leader. Fortunately, leaders usually come from similar backgrounds, so people can identify with them. By sharing their common histories, they strengthen their connection with people. Dr. Lea Williams, in her examination of Black leadership, observes this tendency: "Generally, black leaders, even though they tend to come from the black middle class, have experienced the same racial discrimination as working-class blacks, which forms a bond of kinship."[5]

Most people of color have similar stories. Raul Yzaguirre grew up in the poor area of the Rio Grande Valley in South Texas. His grandmother talked about the "race wars," in which the Texas Rangers systemically beat up and killed Mexican-Americans. His grandfather, who worked two jobs to support the family, was almost lynched for being on the street after dark. Restaurants had signs in the windows: "No Mexicans and No Dogs!"

Dr. Antonia Pantoja was born in a slum in old San Juan, Puerto Rico, to an unwed mother and was raised in Barrio Obrero, a worker housing community located on the outskirts of the island's capitol. When she immigrated to New York, Pantoja worked in factories; she remembers that these jobs, and traveling long hours back and forth, "consumed all my working hours." However, she gained "direct experience with the problems that Puerto Rican immigrants suffered."[6] When one's leader shares experiences such as overcoming discrimination and adversity, a natural bonding occurs.

Serving Something Greater

FOR THE INDIVIDUAL LEADER, the emphasis on equality in leadership can present a dilemma. On one hand, leadership implies being proactive, assuming responsibility, and taking charge. On the other hand, leaders are expected to remain part of the group and not stand out from others. Cabral's observation that leadership springs from the desire to address an unmet need speaks to this dilemma: "César Chávez was working in the fields and saw people who were being badly mistreated and needed someone to advocate for them. He rose to the occasion, and it was very difficult. He wasn't educated in leadership techniques, he learned these afterwards. But that wasn't his goal—to name himself as the leader of the farm workers and assume a position of power. He was really addressing a tremendous unmet need in a specific population that really needed help."

By putting the issue, the cause, and people's needs *first*, leaders actually serve something greater than they are and lessen their self-importance. Cabral continues, "Latino leaders think about the broader good and are not so focused on individual success, but rather, how do we achieve success for the larger community?" This again shifts the focus from the individual leader to the people he or she serves.

Dr. Pantoja believes that to achieve this, leaders must answer a pivotal question. "You have to ask yourself, am I a leader that is going to be accountable to my people, to the community from whence I came? If you decided to be that kind of leader, then your skills, energy, and endurance are for the well-being of your community."[7] Leaders who positively affirm their dedication to serve the collective advancement also serve by treating all people equally and with respect.

Personalismo refers to the character of the individual leader, how that person relates to the community and treats others; it is the measure of the leader's credibility and effectiveness. Yzaguirre sums up this concept: "Latinos treasure values such as hard work and faith, which can be found in many cultures. But there is also a sense of humility, modesty, and courtesy that means a truly complete human being, a successful person, is one who treats the shoe-shine boy and the maid with the same kind of dignity that he affords the president or CEO."

Federico Peña was noted for this quality. "My parents taught me to treat everyone equally and fairly. The best times I had at City Hall were talking to the janitors and city workers. Today, they come up to me and say, 'I'll never forget, you always talked to me in the elevators. Or you always talked to me when I was sweeping the halls.' The way I looked at it, we were all working together."

Playing by the Rules

TRADITIONAL LEADERSHIP TODAY, particularly in corporate America, is associated with fat salaries and mega bonuses, the big office, corporate jets, special parking places, and the numerous privileges that come with being in the top echelon. These types of perks create elitism that runs contrary to the principle of a leader among equals and results in an economic and social chasm between leaders and followers.

There also seems to be an unwritten agreement that leaders are above the rules and can even break the law and get away with it. If, through legal measures or by nature of their position, they can garner more than their share, then this is considered part of the entitlement of leadership.

Given that leaders in communities of color are followed because of their good character and are expected to lead by example, setting oneself up with the traditional types of privileges would mean one was not acting as a leader among equals. When leaders play by the same rules as their followers, it levels the playing field and boosts their credibility with followers. Raul Yzaguirre reflects on how this operates: "You have to work as hard as they do, or harder, and *with* them. You've got to be fair. You've got to say, 'These are the rules. I will abide by them.' You need to be willing to sacrifice if you are going to ask people to sacrifice. When I was president of the National Council of La Raza, I once mortgaged my house to make the payroll."

Peña believes this is integral to leadership. "Integrity and honesty is not just following up on commitments you made, but there is a way of doing it. There are people who get things done, but the process they use is full of corruption, bribery, and questionable tactics. I never did that. People would suggest, 'Why don't you give the contract to someone who supported you?' Or they would remind me, 'That person worked against you on your campaign. Why on earth are you giving them a contract?' I would say, 'I don't play that way. I represent all the people in Denver. I am not going to have a list of preferred contractors that are just my supporters. That is not right—it is not ethical.'"

 When leaders are consistent and treat everybody the same, when everyone knows what the rules are, and the leaders follow their own rules, *people will follow the leader to the end of the earth, because they believe and have confidence in him.*

—Federico Peña

Many people believe that politics equals payback and the pork-barrel model of you scratch my back, I'll scratch yours. Peña set a different standard: "I was raised to play by the rules. This means being evenhanded; not having preferences based on color, or friendship, or political support; and not paying people off. When people look at leaders, whether in companies or any field, they want to know if they are going to be treated fairly. If a leader plays favorites, then that person's power is gone. When leaders are consistent and treat everybody the same, when everyone knows what the rules are, and *the leaders follow their own rules*, people will follow the leader to the end of the earth, because they believe and have confidence in him."

If leaders assume they have special privileges, a favored status, or their own rules, they create hierarchy and perpetuate the subservient social status that already exists for people in communities of color. This stance runs contrary to empowering and actively engaging people. When access to resources and influence is limited, people's support and involvement are indispensable. Building the critical mass and collective force needed to promote social change is only possible if people are willing to walk side by side with the leader on the lengthy journey of bringing equal opportunity and economic advancement to their communities.

Leadership in communities of color has emerged from a long tradition of social activism. In the next section, exploring the principle of *leaders as guardians of public values*, we will

 I had to find the way to be an agent of change, working in partnership with the community of which I was a member. I had learned that we could work collectively to find solutions to our own problems. I knew we possessed courage and stamina.

—Dr. Antonia Pantoja

examine this tradition, which emphasizes the role of the leader as one who inspires people to believe in themselves, overcome the obstacles of discrimination, and uphold our democratic values. As we will discover in principle six, *Leaders as Community Stewards*, the power for change and transformation depends on the preparation and involvement of a critical mass of people. Power in communities of color authentically and realistically is people power. Walters and Smith describe this approach: "One of the most important resources has been human power, and this has required a concentration on the tactics and strategy of mass leadership, designed to effectively target the power of Blacks as a group to certain social objectives."[8]

As a young leader, Antonia Pantoja recognized that power in the Puerto Rican community had its genesis in its people. "I had to find the way to be an agent of change, working in partnership with the community of which I was a member. I had learned that we could work collectively to find solutions to our own problems. I knew we possessed courage and stamina."[9]

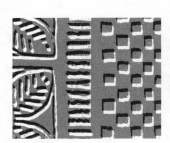

NEXT STEPS

Reflecting On and Applying Principle Four

A Leader among Equals

The first part of this book emphasized enhancing your personal understanding of collective or *We* cultures and the benefits of incorporating values from communities of color into our society. This part focuses on applying the leadership principles from these communities into your leadership style and into your organization.

Collective leadership

What differences have you discerned between leaders who come from an individualistic orientation and those who spring from a collective one?

- How could integrating practices from collective leadership increase your effectiveness?

A leader among equals

This kind of leadership centers on good character, honesty, humility, generosity, and keeping one's word. A key responsibility is treating everyone with fairness and consistency and following the rules.

- Have a discussion about these values—which ones would you like to emulate? How could these enhance the performance of your team or organization? Make individual and group commitments as to how you are going to treat one another to reflect these.

- Have people sign a group values and commitment promise and agree on periodic check-ins to see how folks are doing.

Leveling the playing field

Many organizations today practice collaborative leadership and yet have hierarchical management structures and reward individual performance. Consider how the practices of a leader among equals can level the playing field and instill an authentic collective and collaborative spirit in organizations.

- What specific steps can your organization take to ensure that leadership is rotated and distributed?

A greater purpose

A leader among equals focuses on the common good. His or her skills, energy, and endurance are for the well-being of the people they serve. Leaders who serve a greater purpose lessen their self-importance.

- What is the greater purpose that you serve?

Recommended readings and resources

- *African American Leadership* by Ronald W. Walters and Robert C. Smith (State University of New York Press, 1999).

- *Leadership Without Easy Answers* by Ronald A. Heifetz (Belknap Press, 1994)..

PRINCIPLE 5

Leaders as Guardians of Public Values— A Tradition of Activism

MI CASA WAS A CULTURAL BRIDGE, an oasis, and it worked! Thirty years later, Mi Casa continues to be a buzzing beehive serving thousands of women each year. Service organizations alone, however, cannot stem the tide of social, economic, and educational disparity that continues to bring women to Mi Casa's doors. Communities of color are caught in a crossfire. Providing services to ameliorate the difficult conditions in which many people live drains the resources needed to tackle the underlying causes of why these conditions exist in the first place.

In my early years with Mi Casa, I began to realize that breaking through this quandary would require a core of competent and committed leaders that could address these root causes. But leadership development is a Cadillac in a community in which people need bus fare and gas money. Getting a job, finishing high school, and learning English are economic necessities; leadership development, a luxury! Where would the money to train and groom this new cadre of leaders come from?

As I was mulling over this question, the phone rang. Frank Solis, community affairs director for the Coors Brewing Company, who knew about my work with Mi Casa, was on the line talking about a national leadership program for Hispanic women that Coors wanted to initiate. "Would you be interested in helping us get this program off the ground?" he asked.

I rolled my eyes upward, thanking Our Lady of Guadalupe. "Listo!" I said. " I'm ready! Vamanos!" Thus began my long and inspiring journey of learning and teaching leadership.

In designing the curriculum for what became the National Hispana Leadership Institute (NHLI), I assessed mainstream leadership models and found, not surprisingly, that they did not address or directly integrate the needs of Hispanics or other communities of color. In these communities, leadership springs from a collective orientation in which people have to be inspired to work together to solve mutual concerns. This can be difficult because resources are often scarce and people must prepare for the long haul. Some problems may not be resolved in their lifetime, so small successes are important. As people become confident, they can begin tackling the root causes and social structures that perpetuate the inequitable economic conditions that exist.

At the same time, leaders in communities of color need to master skills as taught by mainstream programs. The NHLI curriculum combined the good information and savvy approaches of these programs with an emphasis on community leadership, social action, and public policy change. The program was four weeks long. Two weeks emphasized Latino leadership, critical issues facing our community, and learning how to affect social and public policy change at the national level. One week was at Harvard's John F. Kennedy Center on Government, and another week was at the prestigious Center for Creative Leadership, where the women learned executive leadership. These mutually beneficial partnerships, now entering their twentieth year, demonstrate how diversity enriches and benefits all partners.

During this time, I was fortunate to spend time with Dr. Antonia Pantoja and discuss her founding of ASPIRA (to aspire), the first Puerto Rican leadership and advancement program started in 1961. ASPIRA brought youth together to study their history and culture, to learn skills to survive in school, and to choose areas of work or professions. The long-term goal was to help the community get out of the "firefighting" position and develop leaders who would attack the root causes of problems. Thus, youth practiced leadership skills by working on community problems. "The whole purpose of leadership," Pantoja explained, "is to exercise one's power, knowledge, and access to change those aspects of society that are inequitable."[1] Combining services dealing with immediate issues, while providing the leadership and knowledge to develop long-term solutions, has become a trademark of effective Latino programs.

Upholding Public Values

THE EMPHASIS on leadership as community action is in step with the philosophy espoused by Dr. Jim Joseph: "Leadership must address the barriers that perpetuate inequity and economic discrepancy." Joseph believes that to accomplish this, communities of color must assume a macro view of leadership that concerns itself with the public values and institutions that underscore racism and discrimination. He explains, "Even as a young boy, I always wondered why what was wrong and right focused on the rules and behavior of what individuals should do. Yet, as I grew up in the segregated south, where the doors of political institutions and social organizations were closed to Black people, I began to question why ethics concerned itself with individual behavior *but not how institutions acted*. I witnessed how institutions and society mistreated Black people. So, since my childhood, I have been concerned about *public values* rather than just private virtues."

In keeping with the societal emphasis on individualism, many Americans are preoccupied with private virtues—the microethics of personal behavior and morality. Black leaders have had an expanded approach. Dr. Joseph continues his observations: "We had to be concerned with the behavior of systems and institutions, or macroethics that focused on public morality and community values. Because those systems and institutions oppressed the freedom of our citizens, our leaders have focused on *public values* and *institutional ethics*. Historically, an African American leader emerged because he or she was concerned with the macroethics of large systems and institutions as well as the microethics or private virtues of individuals."

Early Black leaders saw the need to realign America with its democratic values and repositioned the compass of leadership to responsibility for the public good. Joseph summarizes this point: "In a segregated society, there was *intentional underdevelopment* that expressed itself *in* and was held in place *by* social institutions. Black leaders strove to humanize and sensitize these institutions in order to improve the lives of their people ... [and to] incorporate the concept of our common humanity and open the doors to people of all colors, cultures and religions."

Because of these efforts, Dr. Joseph designates Black leaders as *guardians of public values.* "Our country's founders talked about justice and forming a more perfect union, so community was a high public value. African Americans are very concerned about community and justice. The Constitution promoted the common good and the general welfare. African Americans aspire to create a better life not only for their own people but to establish a society that cares for all people." Enlightened Black leadership has cultivated this sense of social responsibility among all of America's people: "Oppressed people have to be concerned with justice because injustice is what holds them hostage. To change this, they have to reignite the spirit of justice in the general society so that their oppression begins to grate at the community conscience. Martin Luther King Jr. did this. Our founding fathers during our nation's formation did this as well. They rallied people to seek 'justice for all' as a public value."

Morals and ethics in the Black community incorporate *what is good for the whole*, not just individual behavior or private virtues. This commitment is integral to the way leadership developed. Dr. Joseph explains, "The initial group of Black leaders came from the religious tradition: Martin Luther King Jr., Jesse Jackson, and Hosea Williams were ministers first and then evolved into civil rights leaders. They came with a moral conscience that went beyond the notion of individual salvation to look at institutions that were barring Black people from equal participation here on earth. They appealed to our nation's conscience and tried to exercise power that was moral power ... a new awareness and commitment to public values—a return to the fundamental principles this country was founded on."

 The initial group of Black leaders came from the religious tradition ... They appealed to our nation's conscience and tried to exercise power that was moral power ... a new awareness and commitment to public values—a return to the fundamental principles this country was founded on.

—Dr. Jim Joseph

A Tradition of Activism and Active Citizenship

ACTIVE CITIZENSHIP is the lifeblood of a healthy and responsive democracy. The civil rights movement rekindled the flame of citizen involvement as a public value. A new social activism was born that revitalized America. Joseph explains, "It is not just individuals who have a responsibility to get involved, help change things and make a difference, but it is also Black churches and organizations. The whole tradition of activism, of 'voting with your feet,' is a legacy that drives the Black community. Without this, African Americans would have remained economic slaves in the segregated South. Again, this is a basic American value—active citizenship should be cherished in democracy."

The shaping of leadership as social activism was a natural evolution for collective cultures, in which protecting and sustaining the *We* is the heart of a leader's responsibility. This emphasis on responsibility to the collective is one of the sharp distinctions from the mainstream American leadership, in which there is a strong focus on developing the individual and managing organizations. Addressing the public welfare, societal institutions, or community involvement is not integral to this approach. In fact, public service usually pertains only to those in government or elected office. Concern with growing local capacity and augmenting citizen participation is usually designated as community leadership. In contrast, *leadership in communities of color is inherently a public responsibility to bring people together to address and change the social and economic conditions that affect their lives.*

This makes sense when considering that people of color are classified as minorities and do not share equitably in the American harvest. Leaders must challenge the social structures that keep people in lower-paying jobs, poorly funded schools, and dilapidated housing and receiving limited health care. Pressing social and economic needs drive a leadership form that challenges the status quo. Dr. Pantoja describes this approach: "The role of a leader is the role of advocacy. The purpose of leadership is to exercise one's power, knowledge, and access, to change the oppressive and destructive situations in society."[2] In her book, *Servants of the People: The 1960s Legacy of African American Leadership*, Dr. Lea Williams describes lack of political equality, inadequate economic opportunity, racial segregation, and societal violence against the Black community as the genesis of a leadership form whose goals are social reform and the redistribution of power and resources. She further explains that because these goals are viewed as antithetical to the status quo, Black leaders must be advocates battling against the resistance of the dominant society.[3]

When African Americans took up the banner of civil rights, American Indians and Latinos followed suit. This is evident in the following section's review of Indian activism, which targeted tribal preservation to protect their traditions and safeguard their cultural values. American Indian sovereignty is a model that has far-reaching implications for rebuilding our sense of community, promoting human coexistence, and supporting global harmony.

Tribal Sovereignty: A Model for Collective and Tribal Identity

Preserving tribal identities has been a long and arduous struggle, which required fighting the federal government's assimilation and termination policies. Without this resistance, American Indians would be as extinct as the tall-grass prairies of the Midwestern plains. From 1880 until 1934, when the Indian Reorganization Act was passed, minimal efforts were made to help tribes govern themselves. In 1970, the Indian Self-Determination Act was approved, which strengthened Indian autonomy. The Bureau of Indian Affairs changed direction; it went from managing Indian affairs to helping Indians manage their own affairs.

At the same time, the American Indian rights movement and a new breed of activists began to emerge. Educated and articulate, these leaders were able to navigate the American mainstream while following the drumbeat of their cultural traditions. Depending on the needs of their tribes, they would assume many roles: from warrior to peacemaker, from listener to consensus builder, from the holder of traditional ways to the innovator of new paths. Their ongoing legal battles won back rights that had been guaranteed by the treaties with the federal government—and renewed American Indian pride and identity.

 The shaping of leadership as social activism was a natural evolution for collective cultures, in which protecting and sustaining the We is the heart of a leader's responsibility. This emphasis on responsibility to the collective is one of the sharp distinctions from the mainstream American leadership.

These legal victories established sovereignty that recognizes tribes as nations and self-governing legal entities. American Indian sovereignty and tribal identity make a unique contribution to our multicultural nation by demonstrating how different cultural groups can function and retain substantial autonomy within one system or institution. In other parts of the world, different groups exist within one country, yet unlike American Indians they have no legal protection. LaDonna Harris explains, "Tribal governments are protected under the courts and the Constitution and in Congress. This premise anchors our leadership model—*tribal governments are sovereign units of government, and integral parts of the U.S. federal system of government, with the right and power to determine their own futures.*"

 Preserving and honoring cultural traditions and integrating these into a multicultural mosaic is a key function of leadership in a diverse society.

Ethnocentric thought and the pull for assimilation pose questions as to whether people can be Americans *and* still stay connected to their race, culture, country of origin, or ethnic group. When people are referred to as Native-Americans, African-Americans, or Hispanic-Americans, they may be seen as hyphenated people in a cultural no-man's-land. However, the renowned Chicano columnist Ruben Salazar saw that hyphen as a *bridge*, a cultural crossroads that connects two worlds and allows a person to bring forth the best from each one. Ethnocentricity blinds people to the benefits, customs, traditions, and languages of our rich cultural mosaic. This runs contrary to our world economy and the global village in which people with cultural adaptability and flexibility have a competitive advantage.

The task of preserving and honoring cultural traditions and integrating these into a multicultural mosaic is a key function of leadership in a diverse society. American Indian tribal sovereignty illustrates that people can be loyal and contributing members of more than one group. Just as America is enriched by the over five hundred tribes in our country, our nation can be strengthened by the many colors, races, religions, and cultures that compose our diverse society.

The desire to be part of a "tribe" is a timeless phenomenon dating back to early *We* cultures. Many people today have a heartfelt need for community, to belong and to be valued by others. LaDonna Harris passionately observes, "Perhaps these are the times to '*retribalize*' America. Not in the way politicians talk about—going back to family values—but by rebuilding our sense of community, mutual responsibility, and inter-dependency." American Indian tribes are a viable model for seeding and sustaining a renewed sense of community.

LaDonna believes there are also global ramifications:

> Across the globe, the Kurds, Northern Ireland, the Balkans, and parts of the Middle East and Asia are seeking political and cultural autonomy. They want their place in the sun and are saying, "We have a culture and want to keep it." Meanwhile, many Americans and Europeans see this as negative and label it "Balkanization." Tribal sovereignty is a five-hundred-year-old model for groups seeking cultural and political autonomy within a national system. As tribal and ethnic strife becomes the focus of unrest on every continent, Tribal America has a unique contribution to offer. We are part of the structure of federalism and co-exist within the federal government. Through this system, we have maintained over 500 different cultural groups or tribes. The idea of individual governments within a larger system of government is quite exceptional.

La Causa—The Cause

Unlike American Indians, who have distinct tribal identities and are recognized as sovereign nations, Latinos have seen their identity emerging only since the 1960s. As part of a fusion culture that spans many nationalities, Latinos are not a race but an ethnic group bound together by the Spanish language, colonization, the Catholic Church, and common values that stem from both their Spanish and indigenous roots. Latino leaders, therefore, are challenged to forge a shared identity, vision, and purpose from a conglomerate of people who are joined together like *pico de gallo*—a Latino condiment that includes bite-size pieces of many spicy ingredients.

To achieve this shared identity, Latino leaders must be consensus builders and community organizers, weaving social and political unity from the diverse Latino subgroups. Like the ancient Incas, who built suspension bridges across mountain canyons by braiding straw pieces into massive ropes, Latino leaders must integrate the many critical issues that touch people's lives and motivate people to work together to address these. In this way, they grow people's capacity to engage in concerted and collective action.

DISTINGUISHING RACE, ETHNICITY, AND CULTURE

Historically, the debate on race has been an intellectual roller-coaster ride, from race being *the* distinguishing human characteristic to race being seen as essentially a *social construct* and *generally self-defined*. This is not to say there are not differences based on skin color, facial features, and complexion, but a Black person in America might be classified as *colored* or *mulatto* in other countries. The U.S. Census currently defines six racial categories: Asian, American Indian and Alaskan Natives, White, Black, Hawaiian and Pacific Islanders, and Hispanic (also classified as an ethnic group). Furthermore, the Census identifies sixty-three possible racial combinations. Need I say more about race as a social construct?

Certainly there are genetically determined traits, and scientists can identify a propensity to certain diseases based on such traits. However, most scientists today, concur that human beings share a similar genetic profile and that race differences constitute less than 5 percent of genetic variations.*

The most significant differences in human beings come from the rich and varied cultural groups that have evolved over centuries. Cultural groups share a common ancestry, language, customs, religion, and historical experiences. Racial groups generally share these characteristics, and therefore, in addition to a common race, they have strong cultural ties. In this book, the term *ethnicity* is used interchangeably with *culture*. Ethnic groups have a complex set of distinctive characteristics that set them apart; these are often associated with a geographic region or nationality. (Jewish people and Greeks are examples.) However, since ethnic groups also share a common culture and heritage, they are also cultural groups.

---

* For additional information and references to race, ethnicity, and culture, see Vincent Sarich and Frank Miele, *Race: The Reality of Human Differences* (Boulder, CO: Westview Press, 2004), and I. Hannaford, *Race: The History of an Idea in the West* (Baltimore: Johns Hopkins University Press, 1996).

Yzaguirre reflects on this challenge: "In community organizing, when people are asked to take something on, there is no concrete reward. They have to be motivated, not ordered around. It just won't happen without inspired leadership: being able to encourage folks to take on perhaps an impossible task, against what might seem like insurmountable odds, is the ultimate leadership task."

Leaders also have to inspire people to believe in themselves. Yzaguirre has successfully used this technique. "Oppressed people have been taught they can't get things done—it's impossible and going to end in failure. They have to be convinced they will succeed and *can* do it! So the first step—the ultimate, all-important step—is to build their faith in themselves. Latino leaders' effectiveness depends almost entirely on their ability to work with people and engage them in community issues."

In community organizing, when people are asked to take something on, there is no concrete reward. They have to be motivated, not ordered around. It just won't happen without inspired leadership: being able to encourage folks to take on perhaps an impossible task, against what might seem like insurmountable odds, is the ultimate leadership task.

—Raul Yzaguirre

A point of cohesion for Latino leaders is that they are united by a concept known as *La Causa*—the cause—which recognizes leaders as *advocates* for justice and equal opportunity. La Causa answers the question "Leadership for what?" Leadership is fighting for La Causa—for uplifting people and continuing the movement toward economic and social progress. Like African Americans, Latinos have a tradition of call and response. For Latinos, the call is *"Que viva"* (long live), and the response is the cherished quality. A traditional call for Latino leaders is *"Que viva la Causa!"* César Chávez understood the significance of this connecting point: "In the movement for social justice, our love for one another is sustained by the love of La Causa." La Causa offers an emotional bond that regenerates leaders in the difficult work of social change, which will continue for generations.

When she served on San Antonio's City Council, Maria Antonietta Berrizobal would use the metaphor that she was in the middle of a whole stream of people that began with her ancestors and included the many, many leaders of her time. This stream flowed into the future and would continue when she was gone. "I do my part," she would say, "and others do theirs. Eventually we will make the current so strong that it will sweep away the old and bring in the new." The belief that they are part of a long-term social movement—La Causa—sustains Latino leaders.

Based on their dedication to change social and economic conditions, Latino leaders emphasize service, community organizing, and giving back to benefit the whole. This concept of *community servanthood* speaks of a collective and collaborative vision of leadership that stands in sharp contrast to individualistic and hierarchical leadership. Anna Escobedo Cabral has seen this tendency in her extended work with Latino leaders. "Our ultimate motivation is a concern for the people we serve."

Understanding the Barriers of Exclusion

CIVIL RIGHTS, La Causa, and American Indian sovereignty are three distinct pathways that illustrate how leaders in communities of color tackle the barriers that keep their people from full participation and access. In addition, leaders must deal with the harsh reality that people of color have been defined as "minorities," which means they are marginalized, especially in terms of power and the decision-making structures of society. *Minority* is a recent socioeconomic term and something of a euphemism for people who have historically been in subservient or oppressed positions. Leading people who have been classified as minorities presents distinct challenges.

 Based on their dedication to change social and economic conditions, Latino leaders emphasize service, community organizing, and giving back to benefit the whole. This concept of community servanthood *speaks of a collective and collaborative vision of leadership that stands in sharp contrast to individualistic and hierarchical leadership.*

Minorities are on the outskirts of the dominant culture. On the periphery, they are always seen in reference to and measured by dominant norms and standards. In the United States, this means White culture is presented as the *ideal*, the standard, innately superior. Anglos are the top dogs; their norms rule. The media, school systems, and society reinforce the message that White is superior. Historically, as this subliminally seeps into the minds of young people in communities of color, it has diminished their self-worth, both individually and collectively. They begin to believe that success means cloning the behavior and thinking patterns of the White society and distancing themselves from their own group. Yet, no matter how hard they try, they will never totally fit in. The psychological pain of rejecting oneself and one's own group, together with the confused identity that results, was termed the *psychology of oppression* by the perceptive Brazilian thinker Pablo Freire.[4]

The Psychology of Oppression

Freire observed that as social mechanisms bombard the oppressed with negative messages and stereotypes about themselves, they begin to believe these to be true and to *internalize* them. Once this occurs, they are held hostage by their own minds. They begin to collude with the system that keeps them "in their place." This has had a number of ramifications for people of color, including (1) a lack of confidence in others of their race, (2) the exclusion of those who succeed as "not being like us," and (3) the whitewashing of minority talent, in which people of color disregard their own culture and emulate White people in order to succeed. The psychology of the oppressed is externally reinforced by social stratification, whereby members of White society reap disproportionate economic benefits, have a higher standard of living, and enjoy greater opportunity.

 Minorities are on the outskirts of the dominant culture. On the periphery, they are always seen in reference to and measured by dominant norms and standards. In the United States, this means White culture is presented as the ideal, the standard, innately superior.

From an individualistic orientation, a lack of success or the feelings that one cannot measure up could be attributed to one's personal lack of initiative or abilities. However, when an entire culture or race cannot compete equitably and must battle the obstacles of discrimination, this becomes *systemic oppression*. Dealing with oppression, people's lack of belief in their abilities, and the cold facts of discrimination is a central charge of leadership programs in communities of color.

In the Ambassadors' Program, LaDonna Harris defines the psychology of oppression as both a personal and a leadership problem. On the personal level, if a young Indian's teachers never look like him, the books he reads are written by people of other races, and the doctors and nurses who attend to his health are always Anglos, he may conclude not only that *he* is not smart but that American Indians in general are not smart. The young boy has thereby internalized the stereotype of "dumb Indian," believes it about himself, and projects this onto all Indian people.

 Because of the inherent nature of racism, whereby African Americans internalized negative stereotypes and were stripped of their identity, they still go through cycles of wanting to escape their history and culture, and then recognizing that this is who they are and coming back. Dealing with these differences—the separation, the internalized oppression, and the healing—continues to be a major challenge African American leaders shoulder today.

—Dr. Jim Joseph

LaDonna sees this internalization of oppression as a collective and leadership problem, which can manifest as Indian people putting each other down. "If one's reference group is believed to be inferior, then one must separate from them to feel worthwhile and emphasize that one is better than or not like them. Historically, in Indian society this lack of support was not accepted and was considered disrespectful. A person could never be a leader if she was going to put that kind of stigma on her own people. The people who felt offended also had a problem because they believed they were made to feel inferior. However, they allowed that person to put them down and diminish their ability. The Ambassador Program looks at all these different tenets of internalized oppression to help people let go of negative stereotypes."

Dr. Joseph clarifies how internalized oppression affects Black people: "Because of the inherent nature of racism, whereby African Americans internalized negative stereotypes and were stripped of their identity, they still go through cycles of wanting to escape their history and culture, and then recognizing that this is who they are and coming back. Dealing with these differences—the separation, the internalized oppression, and the healing—continues to be a major challenge African American leaders shoulder today."

Andrew Young, civil rights activitist, relates that Black people have had to make cultural adjustments to oppression. He cites the old blues song, "Been Down So Long, Gettin' Up Don't Cross My Mind." "What many observers have described as apathy," he laments, "is often just a protective attitude that is necessary for survival, like that of the dog who gets kicked all the time and just moves out of the way whenever someone comes along."

The National Hispana Leadership Institute's initial training considered how the psychology of oppression is evidenced when successful Latina women do not support one another. For a Latina, garnering a good education, learning to maneuver through Anglo institutions, and developing the skills and talents to surface as a leader is a rare feat. As Latinas become successful, the distance between them and their barrio neighbors often widens. In the Latino community, one way in which the psychology of oppression can be detected is by the expression of *envidia* (envy). *Envidia* is attributing negative qualities to successful people; for example, "She thinks she is better than others" or "She has sold out." This isolates successful people and causes them great consternation. *Envidia* is also present in other communities of color and stems from the psychology of oppression in which one's negative self-worth is further exacerbated by other people's success.

We cultures also want people to stay with the group. To achieve, a person of color has to adapt and learn the success strategies of the White culture. Fitting in means learning the dominant culture's language, characteristics, and ways of thinking, and dressing as members of the dominant culture do. A psychological gap can open between oneself and one's family and community. There is also an authentic fear that the person venturing out will be harmed or rejected and, despite gargantuan efforts, will not be successful.

THE CRAB SYNDROME

Dark waves rustled like palm fronds on the coastal inlet. About four feet from shore, the boy in cut-off jeans flashed his spotlight into the black waters. Blinded, the crabs froze; one by one they were thrown into the bucket on the sandy beach. Slowly, the biggest crab began to climb out of the bucket. Strong and resilient, in a few minutes he would be free! Then he felt the sharp claws of the other crabs pulling him back. "Don't leave us. It is dangerous out there, and besides, we need you, and it is dark and cold in here." The big crab fell back, and though he tried to crawl out, he never outwitted the other crabs. So finally he held back, comforting them through the long night. Besides, he would be all alone if he escaped from the bucket, and he did not know what dangers awaited him outside.

My parents wanted to protect me; they struggled with my decision to leave home to attend college. They were also afraid that once I left, I would not come back. This tendency to hold onto people for safekeeping, which sometimes prevents them from leaving, is commonly know as the *crab syndrome* by many people in communities of color.

Leaders in communities of color must uncover how the internalization of the psychology of oppression has affected them personally. They must help people become aware of how *envidia*, the crab syndrome, and the lack of support for others can impede the progress of the community as a whole. LaDonna sees this as pivotal to American Indian leadership: "To integrate her identity and power, a leader needs to recognize the personal effects of oppression and release the bitterness and anger. *This can only be done through group introspection. Otherwise, the person keeps on internalizing, and believes he is the only one with the problem, or that the problem is inherent to his group*. By letting go of old, ingrained and limiting concepts, leaders in communities of color can embrace their power. Thus, they can fully contribute to their culture and society at large and help others do likewise."

Yzaguirre concurs; he believes that Latino leaders must work to transform both the internal and external effects of oppression. "These may be more subtle than in the old days when signs in Texas said 'No Mexicans and No Dogs,' but the prejudice and misconceptions are still there. The challenge is to keep reinforcing the positive aspects of the culture so Latinos take pride in their identity and, at the same time, to constantly emphasize to the dominant community the benefits Latinos are bringing to America and the contributions they will make in the future."

The Benefits of White Privilege

Just as people of color have to stand outside of their social conditioning to understand the psychology of oppression, White people who have benefited from an advantaged position in society must do likewise. Only by becoming aware of how society is structured to perpetuate the dominance of some groups and to limit access for others will leaders be able to create the framework for the just and equal society in which diversity can flourish. Multicultural leadership must be underscored by a deep sensitivity to how social institutions have built walls of separation between people of different backgrounds and to the mental constructs that have buttressed these walls.

The benefits that White people enjoy just by nature of their color was discussed at length in 1988 by Peggy McIntosh, a graduate student in women's studies at Wellesley College. McIntosh pondered the fact that men did not recognize that they were at an advantage in society, even though they were able to grant that women were at a disadvantage. She presumed that *this lack of awareness protected male privilege from being full recognized, diminished, or ended.* (If you are unaware of something, or do not recognize that it exists, you cannot address it.) Perceptively, she surmised that if men had an unearned advantage over women, the existence of such a social hierarchy would point to a similar dynamic existing between the races. Therefore, she determined that White people would have comparable advantages over people who were not of their race. She termed this benefit *White privilege.*

White privilege, similar to the male advantage, is unconscious and invisible. Like the air around us, it cannot be seen or touched, even though it is pervasive and always present. Because historically many Whites have not identified as a culture or group, it is logical, therefore, that they are unconscious of their advantages or privileges. McIntosh defines White privilege as "an invisible package of unearned assets which I can count on cashing in each day, but about which I was 'meant' to remain oblivious." Being born White gives people "an invisible weightless knapsack of special provisions, assurances, tools, maps, guides, cookbook, passports, visas, clothes, compass, emergency gear, and blank checks."[5]

These provisions are *societal assets* that provide White people with an unfair advantage over other groups. Furthermore, this advantage is embedded in institutions, creating a society of unearned entitlement in which Whites have a favored status. When Whites acknowledge privilege, they will recognize that many doors have been opened for them through no virtues or special talents of their own. The lack of awareness of White privilege perpetuates the myth that *democratic choice is equally available to all,*

 To integrate her identity and power, a leader needs to recognize the personal effects of oppression and release the bitterness and anger. This can only be done through group introspection. Otherwise, the person keeps on internalizing, and believes she or he is the only one with the problem, or that the problem is inherent to the group.

—LaDonna Harris

which supports the individualistic stance of meritocracy—that people make it based on their talent and hard work. Dismantling these myths is fundamental to supporting authentic democracy and to creating a multicultural society in which the assets of all people can be realized. The many societal shifts that are occurring, due in large part to our changing demographics, challenges White leaders to become aware of their privileged position and actively embrace a new model of social equity that taps the potential of our culturally diverse world.

Rekindling American Activism

WHITE PRIVILEGE, notes McIntosh, "may confer power, but it does not confer moral strength." In fact, she notes that those who have survived oppression and succeeded despite these obstacles have much to teach others.[6] Her observations ring true when considering the legacy of civil rights. In his autobiography, *An Easy Burden: The Civil Rights Movement and the Transformation of America*, Andrew Young sees the nonviolent approach used during the civil rights movement and practiced during the Birmingham demonstrations as a deeply spiritual and rational process that sought to heal rather than defeat the oppressor. The healing process, he noted, went both ways.

 The need for moral strength and public morality is a pressing and urgent leadership issue today. Our country flounders with unethical government officials and greed-driven corporate leaders. The call to serve the greater good and to embrace the public values America was founded on is the basis of leadership in communities of color and offers a needed antidote.

"The oppressed must be transformed, too. They must learn to value and respect themselves, to understand the ways they support an oppressive system, and they must learn to forgive those who have hurt them. In the process of citizenship schooling, the boycott, and demonstrations, people grew in understanding, and gained a sense of their own worth, power, and dignity. In the end, Birmingham and its citizens, black and white, were transformed to the greater good of all involved."[7]

Young believes that the civil rights movement focused the country on a specific moral agenda. He observes, "The work of Martin Luther King Jr. was to interpret the moral dilemma of America to White America and to the rest of the world. Black people already understood this."[8] America's moral dilemma is that our society speaks the language of equality but does not incorporate the founding values of justice, equality, and the common good into our institutions or social structures. The civil rights movement aimed to restore America's public morality. King believed this would redeem the soul of America.

Today, more than fifty years later, the need for moral strength and public morality remains a pressing and urgent leadership issue. Our country flounders with unethical government officials and greed-driven corporate leaders. The call to serve the greater good and to embrace the public values America was founded on is the basis of leadership in communities of color and offers a needed antidote. Standing with millions of people during the "We Are American" march in 2006, which highlighted the plight of immigrants, former Denver mayor Federico Peña urged Americans to embrace our country's higher values. "I believe a great people live by their moral and ethical principles. I believe that a great nation earns respect when it shows compassion and decency."[9]

As leaders in communities of color advocate for a society that is equal and just, White leaders are challenged to examine the roots of privilege, which sustains inequities in American society; to ponder the loss of potential this causes; and to realize how this damages both the privileged and the underprivileged. These reflections will bring leadership to a higher ground—one on which the well-being of all Americans is seen as intricately linked. Martin Luther King Jr., who epitomized an expansive compassion for humankind, understood these connections: "We are caught in an inescapable network of mutuality—tied in a single garment of destiny."[10] He also understood the social ramifications of our interrelatedness: "Injustice anywhere is a threat to justice everywhere."[11]

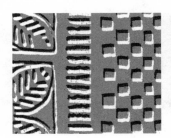

NEXT STEPS

**Reflecting On
and Applying
Principle Five**

Leaders as Guardians of Public Values— A Tradition of Activism

Leaders as guardians of public values

As guardians of public values, leaders assume a higher level of public responsibility and accountability that focuses on the common good. This broadens the work of leadership from individuals and organizations to addressing societal values and institutional ethics.

- Why is a key function of leadership in a democracy safeguarding public values such as justice, equity, and the common good? Do leaders in a democracy have an imperative to promote active citizenship and address the barriers that perpetuate inequity and economic discrepancy?

How would our communities, organizations, and nation benefit if leaders functioned as guardians of the public good? Is this a prerequisite for building our multicultural society?

The psychology of oppression and white privilege

These social mechanisms function at an unconscious level, providing advantages to some people and limiting access to others. Understanding these sheds light on how discrimination operates on a personal and institutional level. A group discussion is most effective, as people may be unaware of how these two mechanism have influenced their lives and can gain perspective only by sharing with others.

- What is White privilege? Have you had any personal experience with how it operates? How does White privilege reinforce cultural dominance and construct barriers to meritocracy and equal access? What are the advantages White people derive from their race and color?

The psychology of oppression describes the internal process whereby people who are not part of the dominant culture collude with the negative stereotypes and limitations placed on them by society. Shedding these requires group introspection so that individuals understand oppression as an external mechanism.

- Using dialogue techniques, have a group discussion on how discrimination is systemic and institutionalized and how this has affected people both in the group and in society as a whole.

- Describe any early experiences you might have had with discrimination. Share any insights or observations about how discrimination has occurred in other people's lives. Listen carefully and allow people to disclose any negative feelings associated with these experiences.

Preserving and honoring cultural traditions

A key function of leadership in a diverse society is to preserve and honor cultural traditions and integrate them into a multicultural mosaic. Tribal sovereignty offers a model for cultural and political autonomy within a national system. Latinos reflect a diverse cultural group and represent many races and countries of origin. African Americans treasure individuality, yet have an unshakable sense of community and a strong collective identity.

- What lessons do communities of color offer that point the way to respecting differences and honoring the cultural integrity of a multiplicity of groups? (American Indians have over five hundred tribes.) How can this begin transforming the cultural conformity and ethnocentric tendencies that historically shaped the United States?

Recommended readings and resources

- *Managing Diversity: People Skills for a Multicultural Workplace* by Norma Carr-Ruffino (International Thomson Publishing, 1996).

PRINCIPLE 6

Leaders as Community Stewards—Working for the Common Goal

N 1999, I INVITED a group of established Latina leaders to talk about the need for additional reinforcements, particularly young women, who could continue carrying the leadership torch. We realized that our hands-on, long-term experience advocating for Hispanic issues had made us seasoned leaders. A great part of our success was due to our mutual support, network, and ability to work together. Quite frankly, we weren't getting any younger, and we wanted to establish a legacy that would ensure our community's continued progress. Thus was born the Circle of Latina Leadership (CLL), an intergenerational program that prepares emerging leaders in their twenties and thirties to guide the future of Denver's Hispanic community.

To date, over eighty young women have completed the program, which spans a year and a half. A key component is mentoring by knowledgeable Latinas with experience in the issues and areas the young leaders want to influence. The participants also complete a Community Action Project in which they practice and strengthen their leader-

116

ship skills. Vital to their success has been connecting to a community of leaders, which includes the young women, mentors, board members, and other influentials. CLL'S mission, "To prepare the next generation of Latina leaders," cultivates continuity, underscores collectivity, and emphasizes leadership as service.

This seeding of leadership and building of a community of leaders is essential when a group's advancement depends on people power and collective resources. Reciprocal and shared leadership requires a pool of qualified people, as does the practice of a leader among equals. Collaboration and participatory leadership are long-established traditions in collective cultures, encouraging many people to get involved and assume greater responsibility. Values that emphasize sharing, generosity, and mutuality generate a leadership process that centers on serving and being a good steward of one's community. Community stewardship is the cornerstone of the Circle of Latina Leadership.

Leadership as Service

THE CONCEPT OF LEADERSHIP as service was brought to the foreground by Robert Greenleaf in 1970. His modest pamphlet, entitled *The Servant as Leader*, set the stage for the collaborative and participatory process to emerge, whereby leadership was not the hierarchical domain of the privileged few but entailed delegating responsibility, sharing benefits, and developing people. A philosophical and reflective man, Greenleaf surmised that the hierarchical leadership approach he had witnessed in his career at AT&T did not nurture other people's leadership skills and, in fact, did not develop the higher capacities of the leader either.

Greenleaf began reflecting on *why* a person aspired to lead. Unconsciously, he had tapped into an ancient American Indian stream of thought in which a person's intention—the *why*—was the central core from which all other actions flowed. In an individualist-oriented society, people are taught that the *why* is generated by self-interest. Leadership, for instance, is a prize people aspire to capture that brings privilege, status, position, glitz, and financial rewards. Greenleaf concluded that these types of leaders did not have a lasting influence on society or the people they led.

Looking at great leaders of the last century who had a substantial impact—Nelson Mandela, Martin Luther King Jr., Susan B. Anthony, and César Chávez—one can agree with Greenleaf that these leaders were not motivated by self-interest, personal influence,

Greenleaf tapped into the old forms of indigenous and tribal leadership and then brought it forth into a modern context.

—Dr. Jim Joseph

or power. In fact, they were sometimes enlisted through the pleas of their followers or drawn to leadership to address the injustices of their time. They accepted the mantle of leadership to serve the people, communities, and ideals they sought to further. This, concluded Greenleaf, was the distinction that set them on the path of what he termed *servant leadership*. They sought to *serve first* and then made the *conscious choice* to lead.

Once a leader was on this path, the litmus test of whether the leader remained a faithful steward was the effect on followers. Did they become *freer, more autonomous,* and *more capable of serving others?* In other words, did the leader empower people? Greenleaf added another caveat, which was a revolutionary departure from the hierarchical leadership of previous times: What was the effect on the less fortunate members of society? This connection to social good and the well-being of those in need repositioned leadership, bringing it back to the beliefs of indigenous people, and put forth a model that is closely aligned with communities of color. As Dr. Joseph observed, "Greenleaf tapped into the old forms of indigenous and tribal leadership and then brought it forth into a modern context."

Serving Society and the Greater Good

Greenleaf also defined servant leaders as affirmative builders of a better society. At first, he observed this phenomenon as largely person to person. Later, he urged large institutions to assume the responsibility of creating the good society. Greenleaf did not emphasize the social change movements, such as civil rights and women's liberation, that were surfacing during his life. Yet he described the times he lived in as follows: "The late twentieth century will be seen as revolutionary because, in this period, large numbers of influential men and women have come seriously to grips with the issue of power and authority." He saw a clear mandate for these times: "*making power legitimate for the public good . . . as an ethical imperative.*"[1] Greenleaf therefore recognized the underlying power shift that the movements of his time were advocating.

If Greenleaf were alive today, he might note that many people within the dominant culture have not heeded his call to transfer power for the public good. In fact, Dr. Joseph observes a shift in the opposite direction: "Today the dominant society has moved away from communal responsibility and concentrates instead on individual values. This approach blinds people to institutional racism and other social ills. It negates the mutual responsibility leaders have to create institutions that support the good society based on the values this country was founded on."

Fortunately, Greenleaf would observe, in communities of color, the blossoming of leadership is strategically engaged in "making power legitimate for the public good." Servant leadership is deeply anchored in Black, American Indian, and Latino cultures that center on community responsibility, the public welfare, and addressing the social structures that hinder people's progress. Antonia Pantoja was passionate about lifting up the Puerto Rican community. "I felt I was called to do something about the situation of the people I belonged to. That was not an option. I had a responsibility to contribute to my people."[2] Because Black, Latino, and American Indian leaders, like Pantoja, derive their power from the communities they serve and are accountable to them, they may well be described as community stewards. They are therefore expanding the focus and scope of servant leader to *community servanthood and stewardship.*

Today the dominant society has moved away from communal responsibility and concentrates instead on individual values. This approach blinds people to institutional racism and other social ills. It negates the mutual responsibility leaders have to create institutions that support the good society based on the values this country was founded on.

—Dr. Jim Joseph

Community Servanthood

COMMUNITY SERVANTHOOD repositions the responsibility of leadership to one of serving the collective. Federico Peña describes this emphasis: "The way I saw it was that I was a servant. I didn't become mayor because I was great, but because people voted for me. So I was there to serve them and the Denver community." Raul Yzaguirre describes this type of leadership as community empowerment. "Part of what I do is to educate Latinos, help them understand the larger issues, why things are the way they are, and what we can do to change that by working together." This resonates with the survey conducted by the NCLL that found that Latinos wanted *community centered and community serving leaders.*[3]

This concept of *Community Servanthood* is based on involving many people, sharing power, and benefiting others. Leaders, therefore, are like good stewards who build community capacity and group empowerment. Dr. Pantoja was an early pioneer with Puerto Rican immigrants who came to New York City. She reflected on this challenge in her autobiography, *Memoir of a Visionary*: "I had to find a way to become an agent of change working in partnership with the community. I learned that we could work collectively to find solutions to our own problems."[4]

John White, in his perceptive book *Black Leadership in America,* identifies community progress as a key component. "From colonial times to the present, Black leaders in America have developed and utilized their distinctive personal qualities in attempts to improve (or eliminate) the inferior caste status of African Americans. Their shared concern has been to improve the conditions of blacks through economic, educational, political, and psychological progress."[5] This progress was propelled forward by the formation of Black organizations in the 1960s.

Dr. Lea Williams documents that organizations such as the Southern Christian Leadership Conference and the Student Nonviolent Coordinating Committee "attempted to absorb the energy of the black masses to further an agenda of Black political and economic power." She goes on to say that these groups "had the potential to create social change through their mutual interaction." Their emphasis was breaking the chains of segregation and moving the Black community forward. The leaders who shepherded these organizations, she declares in the title of her book, were "*servants of the people.*"[6]

Thurgood Marshall, Fannie Lou Hamer, and Fredrick Patterson were part of the cadre of inspired leaders who left their imprints as servants of the people in the 1960s. Dr. Joseph believes they were united by their values that pointed them in the direction of community service: "Values such as a concern for fellow human beings, a keen sense of justice, an emphasis on the common good, not just individual attainment, sharing and interdependence are intricate parts of African American leadership and are the public values that shape individual behavior." These values are also the foundation for authentic servant leadership that goes beyond individuals and institutions to build the just and loving society that Greenleaf envisioned.

Leadership as community servanthood is central to American Indian culture. LaDonna Harris's working definition of leadership is "a communal responsibility with a concern for the welfare of the 'people' or tribe and then sharing the work that needs to be done based on skills and abilities. Leadership is seen as shared responsibility and promoting people's well-being." Similarly, the Jemez Pueblo's first principle of leadership, as described by Benny Shendo Jr., is "responsibility and serving the community." Consequently, he observes, people are willing to place their communities in their leader's hands.

 [Leadership is] a communal responsibility with a concern for the welfare of the "people" or tribe and then sharing the work that needs to be done based on skills and abilities. Leadership [is] shared responsibility and promoting people's well-being.

—LaDonna Harris

"There is profound trust in our leaders, a deep belief that they will always put people first." He notes that leaders are guided by the question "What's best for the people, for our community, for our way of life?"

Community stewardship prompts leadership that concentrates on building people's capacity. Leaders grow their communities by engaging people in the following practices: (1) encouraging participation and building consensus, (2) creating a community of leaders, (3) generating a shared vision, (4) using culturally effective communication, and (5) weaving partnerships and connections.

Encouraging Participation and Building Consensus

The Native American Council nurtures full participation, consensus building, and respect for each individual's opinion. The Council, which in many tribes is their governing body, protects the well-being of its community, honors diverse opinions, and achieves shared ownership. Only after much listening, interchange, and reflection does a collective answer or solution surface. Benny Shendo Jr. clarifies how this operates in the Jemez Pueblo. "Our decision-making is not about majority vote, but around consensus building. Are people comfortable, do they understand enough about it? If this decision is made, will the community move forward? If a decision is not made, how will this affect the community?"

Conflict occurred when voting was imposed on tribes that traditionally had made decisions and governed by inclusion, listening, and consensus. Since voting was contrary to long-established customs, a great deal of internal dispute resulted. The Comanche, for example, have a very flat society in which hierarchical leadership does not exist in a traditional sense. Representative government created elitism and hierarchy. When people were elected, they were elevated above the rest of the tribe.

The American belief that only democratic voting can ensure equal participation runs contrary to many indigenous forms and traditional cultures in which *building consensus, integrating people's needs, and strengthening the collective is the goal.* In democratic systems, voting signifies that the majority rules. In some instances 49 percent of the group might not agree with the other 51 percent, and rarely is there unanimity. In collectivist cultures, in which relationships are lifelong and ongoing, this would weaken the community fabric. The havoc that can ensue is evident in the political divisions in America today. Building consensus and integrating everyone's opinions takes time and a great deal of patience and dialogue! Encouraging everyone's participation may seem cumbersome. However, it is a surefire way to garner the collective wisdom and to secure the commitment of all involved.

Federico Peña exemplified these qualities: "When I was mayor, I always invited people to participate and to be part of the solution. There was a great deal of community involvement. People would say, 'Why is the mayor putting together another task force?' Well, I understood that you get things done by involving people and working as a community. Now people reflect back and say, 'By having that task force, you saved fifteen years.' When people become part of the effort, they want to support the effort and then they are helping to shape their destiny."

Creating a Community of Leaders

Creating a community of leaders grows other people's capacities and builds the critical mass needed to promote social change. Walters and Smith note that an impressively large number of talented individuals and organizations concerned with fundamental systemic change have flourished in the Black community. They observe, "The leadership of a minority within a majority has implied the use of strategies of leverage and coalition rather than outright power."[7] Through the process of growing a community of leaders, many are prepared to carry the cause or issue forward.

Martin Luther King Jr. had a creative way to cultivate this process. He always surrounded himself with a community of dedicated leaders. Some were seasoned, such as Ralph Abernathy, Hosea Williams, and A. Phillip Randolph. Others were young activists, like Andrew Young, who later became the mayor of Atlanta and ambassador to the United Nations. Congressman John Lewis was only fifteen when he met King. The young and fiery Jesse Jackson later served as a voice for the movement for many years. King had a practice of seeding and nurturing a circle of leadership around him. Young recalls, "We were really and truly a very close band of brothers. When Martin died, we felt a responsibility to live up to the moral legacy he established and to carry his mantle."[8] Thus, the legacy of African American leadership was secured.

Andrew Young continues King's tradition of growing new leadership. When he was mayor of Atlanta, he appointed Shirley Franklin as the first African American woman to serve as city manager of a large American city. Franklin guided the development of Hartsfield International Airport and served as the senior vice-president of the Olympic Games when they were held in Atlanta. Never having held public office, in 2001 she was elected in a landslide victory as the first Black woman mayor of a major urban area and was selected in 2005 by *Time* magazine as one of the five best American mayors.[9] Franklin follows in the footsteps of Young and Maynard Jackson, who was Atlanta's first Black mayor. The commitment to continuing the legacy of leadership is evident when noting that for over thirty years Atlanta, one of the most vibrant and multicultural cities in America, has elected Black mayors.

 We were really and truly a very close band of brothers. When Martin died, we felt a responsibility to live up to the moral legacy he established and to carry his mantle.

—Andrew Young

American Indians nurture a national network of leaders through a distinctive leadership program that is designed around their cultural dynamics. Started in 1970 by LaDonna Harris and renowned Indian leaders who saw the need to guide future generations, the American Indians for Opportunity Ambassador Program has served over 150 emerging tribal leaders. To ensure continuity, the founding board continues to shepherd the organization and remains active more than thirty years later. This sense of longevity is in harmony with honoring the elders and lifelong service to tribe and community. The program encourages participants to weave their traditional tribal values into today's contemporary reality—thus adapting to change while fostering a firm sense of cultural identity. The core cultural values shared across native tribes are the bedrock of the integrated and dedicated national community the Ambassadors Program has nurtured.

Perhaps no one has left a greater legacy of leaders who are following in her footsteps than Dr. Antonia Pantoja and ASPIRA, which is now the third-largest nonprofit serving the Latino community. ASPIRA has trained five generations of Puerto Rican leaders. *Aspirantes* (those who aspire), as graduates are called, are the leadership force behind Puerto Rican advancement and have been imbued with a leadership spirit that centers around challenging the obstacles that limit their community.

The enlightened leadership writer and activist John Gardner believed that the highly volatile issues of our times will require "a whole army of leaders." He also predicted that a very different model of leadership, unlike the hierarchal leadership of the past, would emerge in the future. "I can't emphasize strongly enough that we're at a historic moment. The next America is going to be forged at the grassroots. It is going to emerge from the communities of our great nation."[10] Leaders in communities of color have heeded Gardner's call. They are actively engaged in preparing this force, in which many can contribute to leadership for the public good. In recognition of this alignment, Raul Yzaguirre and Dr. Antonia Pantoja have both been recipients of the John Gardner Leadership Award given by the Independent Sector, the premier meeting ground for leaders in the nonprofit, charitable, foundations, and corporate–giving sector who seek to advance the common good in America and around the world.

Embracing a Shared Vision

As community stewards, leaders are dedicated to serving people, a movement, a cause, and a greater purpose. To accomplish this, they must be able to set the course toward a destination that represents real progress for their communities. A crucial step in setting this course is synthesizing a compelling and shared community vision. Such a vision must be grounded in people's collective experience, reflect their mutual concerns and wisdom, and reach for a better and more rewarding future. A shared vision articulates possibilities and opportunities. Connecting with people's aspirations, a shared vision magnetizes, providing a focal point for people's skills, talents, and resources. With that vision assuring them that their efforts will make a difference, people are willing to assume a higher degree of risk and make greater sacrifices.

In communities of color, leaders follow the wisdom of *Sankofa* as *keepers of cultural memory*. They integrate history and the lessons of the past with the compelling needs of today. Dr. Lea Williams reviewed Black leadership, beginning with the historical antecedents during reconstruction in the deeply segregated south over 150 years ago. She was able to trace the evolution of leadership from a time when Black leaders were controlled and threatened by the White power structure to the activist period of civil rights. Thus, Black leaders were able to build on the "the proud legacy we inherited" and to reaffirm people's faith and pride in the progress that had been made.[11]

Multicultural leaders must also be *trustees* of their community's future and guardians of future generations. They must articulate what could be, point the way for collective advancement, and actively engage people in finding solutions. Yzaguirre sees this as a primary function: "Leaders need to think big, but it is the little success that builds people's self-confidence. Having both a long-term vision and building sequential steps, *paso a paso,* keeps people moving and motivated. As people succeed, their vision of what is possible to accomplish becomes wider and more expansive."

Leaders in communities of color, therefore, are the link between the past, present, and future. They promote a sense of continuity and wholeness. Cabral offers her observations on this process: "Leaders in our community have a really good sense of the past and how it relates to the present. However, they know that in the end, they have to address the challenges the community is facing *today* and be concerned with the impact on the future. Our past guides us. It is important to know the struggles our community has faced, but we cannot live in the past. The challenge is to make sure the community is evolving and creating a better future."

In communities of color, leaders follow the wisdom of Sankofa *as keepers of cultural memory . . . they are the* link *between the past, present, and future, promoting a sense of continuity and wholeness.*

Servant leaders, according to Greenleaf, are guided by an overarching, prophetic, and transforming vision. For community servants, this vision must spring from the people. Cabral sees the leader's gift as being able to carefully conceive and articulate this vision. "Latino leaders take a comprehensive viewpoint. How do I forge a vision? How do I find solutions that respect everyone's contribution and take us in the right direction?" Perhaps the best example of a collective vision is King's "I have a dream" speech, made during the 1963 March on Washington. Starting with the public values of the American creed "that all men are created equal," King mobilized an entire generation to see equality and justice as the fulfillment of our country's greatness.

Integrating a community vision requires listening to different points of view, communicating in an open, give-and-take fashion, and welcoming new ideas. The leader helps people build consensus, clarify goals, and work together. Similar to a midwife who guides and nurtures the birthing process, a leader assists in the emergence of a shared and energizing vision. Leaders also communicate in culturally adept styles so people can relate and respond to their message. Leaders then become *spokespersons*, communicating the vision with passion and conviction.

Using Culturally Effective Communication

In collectivist cultures, communication is the heartbeat that nourishes relationships and sustains community. By listening patiently to people's voices and ideas, the leader ensures that everyone is on the same page and ready to lend their resources and energies. This reverberates with the African American adage—to accomplish things together, people must be *singing from the same hymnal*. Although there are intersections in the way Blacks, Latinos, and American Indians communicate, there are also clear distinctions. Leaders from these communities are keenly aware of culturally effective ways of communicating with their people. Three practices warrant special consideration: (1) call and response, (2) it takes as long as it takes, and (3) *cariño* (fondness or affection) and charisma. Using these practices can expand a leader's repertoire and enhance his or her ability to communicate in diverse contexts.

Call and Response. Perhaps because of the indigenous roots of communities of color, in which information was passed on through stories rather than in writing, there is a long history of cherishing the oral tradition. Lively and animated conversation and gestures are highly regarded, not only to pass on information but also as a way of entertaining people and nurturing relationships. Simply put, talking (and listening) reinforces the *We* and strengthens community. In communities of color there is much more tolerance for lengthy discourse, the use of metaphors, and flowery language. Communities of color relish leaders who are *storytellers* and gifted speakers who can unite people through language.

African American leaders stay connected to their communities through the special language form of call-and-response patterns. The familiar "Do you hear what I am saying?" asks for validation that the leader is on track. When people respond "I heard that," this creates reciprocity that builds on each other's verbal contributions. Similar to the collaborative nature of jazz, in which musicians are inspired by each other's contributions, call and response creates a collective and interactive communication process. Unlike Anglo communication, in which it is considered polite for one person to speak at a time and ideas to build sequentially, African American conversation zigzags from person to person. People "piggyback" on each other's contributions, creating a stimulating collective conversation and fusion of ideas.

African Americans have expressive communication patterns that include emotional intensity, colorful language, and an assertive style. People also connect through a feeling mode in which there is a high level of comfort with and skill at expressing emotions. Language is a powerful tool for African American leaders to stay in touch with their people, energize events and activities, and reinforce shared community goals.

Traditionally, the prophetic African American pastor used religion to deal with the oppression of everyday life. Dr. Joseph describes how they communicated this: "The ministers were very conceptual, painting pictures with beautiful words and phrases about life as it *could be*, not life as it was. They spoke about what a person had to do to be saved in this life. The slave masters and masters of segregation thought that they were preaching about an afterlife, but they were shaping people to be competitive and to deal with the realities of this life." He continues, "Slaves came together to worship and used the language of religion, whereas allegedly they were sometimes plotting an escape. The Promised Land for the Slave Master was by and by when he got to heaven. The Promised Land for the slaves was the possibility to change their life circumstances. It has always been *both* this life and the hereafter."

From the pulpit to the halls of Congress, Black leaders use inspired oratory to connect with and motivate people. Jesse Jackson, Andrew Young, and Congressman John Lewis used their skills as ordained ministers to follow the tradition of weaving spiritual practice with community activism and service. Senator Barack Obama, perhaps one of the most moving orators of our times, is bringing this gift to a new generation of Black leaders.

It Takes as Long as It Takes. Indian leaders spend plenty of time talking about things. Benny Shendo Jr. observes, "Council meetings can last three hours or all night. Time is irrelevant." John Echohawk relates that when people gather to make decisions, "It takes as long as it takes to talk things through. Regular kinds of agendas don't work. There can be a list of discussion items, but exactly how long that will take is secondary. Primary is that everyone has the chance to give their opinion and everyone's opinion is respected. It may take longer for people to agree, but once they come together, there is a melding

My natural tendency is to listen first, to reflect on what people are saying, and to discern the meaning behind this. Then I can see the common ground and the unifying themes. Sometimes this makes Anglo people uncomfortable, but really listening is what I do first.

—John Echohawk

of different ideas. Through talking, these are refined and the best solutions surface."

This traditional approach follows the tribal consensus form of governing and implies a great deal of listening. As John Echohawk perceptively observes, "When I am a part of a group that is non-native, I am usually quiet and spend a great amount of time listening and watching. I really want to know what other people think about an issue before I offer my opinion. I have been told that sometimes I am not seen as a leader in these situations. In the Anglo community, a leader takes charge and makes his ideas known first. My natural tendency is to listen first, to reflect on what people are saying and to discern the meaning behind this. Then I can see the common ground and the unifying themes. Sometimes this makes Anglo people uncomfortable, but *really listening is what I do first.*"

Deep listening is an ancient tradition that enabled the chief or leader to bring the community consensus together. Nelson Mandela credits the regent or head of his tribe as modeling this form of leadership: "He would open the meeting by thanking everyone for coming and explaining why he had summoned them. From that point on, he would not utter another word until the meeting was nearing its end . . . His purpose was to sum up what had been said and form some consensus among the diverse opinions." One of the most wise and respected people of our generation, Mandela followed this precept. "As a leader, I have always endeavored to listen to what each and every person in a discussion had to say before venturing my own opinion."[12]

Andrew Young notes that King had a similar habit of bringing people together and asking them to discuss an issue. He would not say anything, but would listen intently to everyone. After considering the counsel of others, King would spend time in reflection and prayer before making a decision.

Cariño and Charisma. Latinos love *charlando*—chatting about ideas, interests, dreams, plans, and possibilities. Being able to keep people engaged is a great asset and part of being *simpatico.* When a Latino enters or leaves a room, the polite thing to do is to go around the room talking and "connecting" with each person there. (This can include an *abrazo*, a pat on the back, or a kiss on the cheek.) Before and after any gathering or meeting, a social window must be open to allow people to share and communicate one on one.

Sharing feelings, self-expression, and *cariño* or showing affection are also cherished. The emotional connection between people and their leaders reflects these values. The Latinos surveyed by NCLL wanted their leaders to be *loving and kind and part of the family*.[13] In a world in which many feel isolated and alienated, expressing *cariño*—warmth and affection—is a special contribution Latino leaders make. They can demonstrate how truly caring for one's constituents and seeing them as *familia* holds people together during difficult times and makes the long journey more enjoyable.

Leadership experts James M. Kouzner and Barry Z. Posner, in *The Leadership Challenge*, identified leaders as people who "encourage the heart," providing the fuel that inspires and motivates.[14] Latino leaders bring this passion to their work—a fire ignited by their compassion, connection to their people, and commitment to improving the lives of future generations. Since many Latinos have traveled the path of social activism, their sense of urgency can be very different from that of leaders who are more traditional. The many needs and challenges in their community drive Latino leaders to want action *now*—not on a more comfortable timeline! This may lead to the perception that they are too emotional and pushy, and perhaps do not have "good manners" or know protocol.

In her review of key cultural dynamics, Norma Carr-Ruffino comments that Latinos have an idealistic bent. She identifies this with Don Quixote, who tilts at windmills, dreams the impossible dream, and even dies for a noble cause. Idealism is born in the Latino ability to dream and connect with the supernatural, which is intrinsic to their indigenous ancestry. Carr-Ruffino sees this as an integral part of the culture: "The spirit world lives alongside Latino Americans, particularly Mexican Americans, in their everyday lives."[15] The Latino tradition of *flor y canto* (flowers and music) is indicative of the tendency to combine the real with the mystical. Flowers symbolize truth, beauty, and authenticity. Music or song represents the higher ideals and noble aspirations.

In many cultures, flowers are given for special celebrations or as an expression of caring and regard. A Latino custom, *echando flores* or giving flowers, refers to using lavish praise, thanking people profusely, giving recognition, and sharing the credit.

Latino events are often characterized by the elaborate recognition of many people. In a people-centered culture, where leaders must have warm personal relations and be seen as never setting themselves above others, *echando flores* is an essential ability. Federico Peña is keenly aware of this valued trait. "A leader recognizes other people—the people who came before you, your parents, and the contributions of others. You don't take the credit. You make sure you recognize everybody else."

Passion, feelings, idealism, and a sense of urgency shed light on why *charisma* is so highly valued. Charisma is a special quality that gives a leader the ability to convey ideas with influence and power so that people are inspired and moved to action. In communities that experience times of doubt and difficulties, leaders who communicate with passion, inspire confidence, and assist people in weathering the storms are revered. Dr. Pantoja, who was charming, courageous, and *charismatic,* urged

> *One cannot have
> a lukewarm life.
> You have to live with passion!*
> —Dr. Antonia Pantoja

people to tap into this energy. "One cannot have a lukewarm life. You have to live with passion!"[16] Charisma, when put into service to one's community, persuades people to persevere and to channel their energies toward reaching their shared vision and dreams.

Weaving Partnerships and Connections

Encouraging participation, creating a community of leaders, generating a shared vision, and using culturally effective communication are all practices that assist leaders in weaving partnerships and connections. Leaders must also be shape-shifters, filling multiple roles—consensus builders, listeners, and spokespersons. Like a magnet, they draw the past, present, and future together so that a shared community vision arises. Leaders also represent their community *externally* by cultivating partnerships and accessing needed resources. Weaving these types of community connections requires leaders to be *cultural brokers* and *bridge builders*. One of the ways they accomplish this is to act as *translators* and *interpreters*. In American Indian communities, they also assume the role of *ambassadors*.

LaDonna Harris explains this term: "*Ambassador* is used instead of *leader* because it is more in harmony with the essence of Indian cultures. An ambassador represents his or her community as a messenger or spokesperson. Ambassadors are emissaries sent on 'missions' to voice tribal concerns to the greater society. Because tribes are sovereign nations, [ambassadors] function as diplomats, opening doors of understanding and interchange as well as conducting negotiations between nations—both other tribes and the dominant culture. Native American ambassadors are civil servants, helping their tribal government articulate the concerns of their people."

Another unique role, which is often assumed by educated young leaders in communities of color, is that of *cultural broker*. Benny Shendo Jr. understands how things operate in the dominant culture and knows how to position himself in this world. At the same time, he is clearly grounded in his family, tradition, and heritage. "People always say to me, you're able to bridge these two worlds very easily, you understand the system and how it works. But, you also understand what's important to us as native people and what our sovereign rights are. The charter school is an example of that. Here's my community wanting to have a school that teaches in our language and here's my understanding of how to get it done in the other world."

In their role as *translators* and *interpreters*, leaders ensure that the interests and concerns of their community are represented in mainstream culture. As a community interpreter, Benny conveyed to the outside world why the school was an important and unique cultural institution: "The Jemez is the only tribe on this whole earth that speaks our language. The school had been there for about 100 years and educated just about everybody in the tribe. So, this was not just about a school, it was about preserving a community and a way of life. It was about a sense of place and history. It was about one of the few people on earth who know their origins."

A *cultural broker* also identifies external resources, constituents, and institutional supporters. Benny had been the assistant dean of students and rector of the American Indian programs at Stanford and had held a similar job at the University of New Mexico. These entrées to educational communities provided a natural constituency to support the charter school. As a National Kellogg Fellow, he had connections with resources and contacts that could access funds to keep the Jemez School operational. "So when that moment came when there was a desperate situation in terms of our community, I had to call on just about everybody I knew that could some way help. And they did!"

As *bridge builders*, leaders forge partnerships and coalitions. One of the most successful examples is the Hispanic Association on Corporate Responsibility (HACR) started in 1986 by a group of Latino leaders, including Raul Yzaguirre. Realizing that one organization trying to influence corporate America would be like a voice crying in the wilderness, Yzaguirre brought together a coalition of the largest and most influential national Latino organizations to form HACR. Its mission was to monitor, assist, and prod corporate America to include Latinos on corporate boards, as employees, in their philanthropic practices, and in minority procurement at a level commensurate with Hispanic economic contributions. Twenty years later, HACR has established partnerships with over thirty of the largest American corporations and has made a strong business case for Hispanic inclusion.

As communities of color have developed power and influence, partnership and coalition building have greatly increased in scope. Just as the Black community took the lead in civil rights, leaders are forging new ground in building bridges across different sectors as well as using diverse strategies to achieve goals. At a forum of the Congressional Black Caucus, Jesse Jackson suggested that future success would depend on "some combination of registration, legislation, demonstration, and litigation."[17] The passing of the national Martin Luther King Jr. holiday is a good example of using multiple strategies and building diverse partnerships. Legislation was proposed for several years. National visibility increased with annual demonstrations. The Congressional Black Caucus mobilized mass support. Stevie Wonder popularized the cause with his rendition of the song "Happy Birthday to You," which celebrated the life and contributions of Dr. King. Through these strategies, momentum was built, and the legislation finally passed.[18]

The roles just described enable leaders to function as *community stewards* within the larger society and expand their community's influence. Building partnerships across sectors and with dominant culture organizations lays the groundwork for a multicultural approach to leadership. These partnerships showcase the mutual benefits that accrue when diverse groups work together. The partnerships that the National Hispana Leadership Institute forged with the Center for Creative Leadership and the John F. Kennedy School at Harvard University twenty years ago are prime examples. Harvard has substantially expanded the number of Latinas in the university's mid-career program who obtain master's degrees in public administration. The Center has had over four hundred Latinas attend their programs, which diversified the Center's classes and connected it with a new and growing market. Over ten thousand corporate executives have interacted with these high-level Latina leaders during these classes and thus had the opportunity to learn in a more inclusive and culturally dynamic environment.

Equality, Community, and Service

ART ONE OF THIS BOOK looked at three underlying social dynamics that are touchstones for communities of color: the integration of the past, a collectivist orientation, and a highly developed sense of generosity. The three principles in this part flow from those cultural dynamics and fashion leadership based on equity, strong communal values, and serving one's community. These principles transform the individualistic paradigm of leadership and instill a collective, collaborative, and people-oriented form. A circular, shared, and equitable perspective also replaces the traditional emphasis on hierarchical and power-centered leadership.

 A leader among equals adds a new dimension to collaborative, participatory, and team leadership. Not only is leadership shared, but rewards are more equitably distributed. Leaders are expected to set high standards and adhere to the same rules as followers; they are trusted to not take more than their share.

The principle of *a leader among equals* adds a new dimension to collaborative, participatory, and team leadership. Not only is leadership shared, but rewards are more equitably distributed. Leaders are expected to set high standards and adhere to the same rules as followers; they are trusted to not take more than their share. The result is an authentic collaborative environment in which people work together as equals to attain shared goals. In a truly collaborative environment, a *We* identity emerges and the spirit of generosity flourishes. When people feel like they are intricately connected, their motivation and commitment increases. This is the foundation for high-performing teams and transformational organizations.

The values of justice, equality, community, and citizen engagement espoused by *leaders as guardians of public values* are the keystones for collaborative environments and the inclusive society. The leadership context today is too narrowly defined, often referring to an individual or group that manages for results or strives to obtain a higher return for corporate investors. Leaders in communities of color embrace a broader perspective by integrating public dimensions and responsibilities. Leaders are actively engaged in creating the good and just society envisioned in the founding values of our country. The rekindling of active citizenship, as espoused by this principle, can infuse our democracy with a new vitality.

Leaders who function as community stewards serve the collective and use power for the public good. Serving people means growing their capacity and implies that everyone can contribute. This enables many leaders to develop and the principle of a leader among equals to be realized. Martin Luther King Jr. strove to infuse ordinary people with the power of service when he stated, "Everyone can be great because anyone can serve." When many serve, a community of leaders develops, and the critical mass needed to construct the good and equitable society is cultivated. This empowers many leaders and creates a legacy of leadership.

As we'll learn in Part Three, the final two principles, *All My Relatives* and *Gracias: Grace, Hope, and Forgiveness*, represent the spiritual essence of a collective worldview, which is the wellspring of leadership in communities of color. When people are truly seen as belonging to one family, then serving and sharing are a natural outcome. When family expands to community and to the greater society, then social responsibility becomes a way to care for one's own. *All my relatives* implies equality among people because the one spirit that permeates all life unites us.

 Leaders who function as community stewards *serve the collective and use power for the public good. Serving people means growing their capacity and implies that everyone can contribute.*

The qualities of *grace, hope,* and *forgiveness* ensure that spirituality is grounded in everyday behavior and action. These qualities sustained people of color through the dark night of oppression; nourished their values of generosity, community, and concern for the common good; and strengthened their belief in a better future. Leaders in communities of color demonstrate spirituality by upholding and living these qualities. In addition, *spiritual responsibility* means addressing the inequitable conditions of life, improving the lives of people, and increasing freedom and opportunity in society. Spirituality is working to alleviate social ills and bolster the communal good. Andrew Young recounts how this has been his daily philosophy: "I have always been taught it is my spiritual responsibility to feed the hungry, provide shelter to the homeless, comfort those in need and assist those who are less fortunate. This includes being dedicated to creating the benevolent society where all people are respected as children of God."

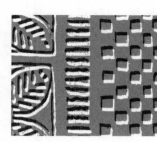

NEXT STEPS

Reflecting On and Applying Principle Six

Leaders as Community Stewards

Servant leadership

Reflect on two leaders: one whom you consider a servant leader and one a leader who attained position, power, and maybe wealth but, in your opinion, did not put people first or serve people's best interests.

- How do these leaders differ?

- What personal qualities do they have?

- What do you consider their long-term accomplishments or legacy?

- Who would you follow and why?

Community stewards

Community stewards derive their power to lead from the people they serve and are accountable to.

- How does this shape leadership in communities of color?

Community stewards build people's capacity and foster group empowerment. They are also *trustees* of their community's future and guardians of future generations.

- What are some of ways the leaders described in this book accomplish this?

 (NEXT STEPS 6 CONTINUED)

A shared community vision

A shared community vision is the collective aspirations of the group or the organization. Community stewards recognize that a shared vision promotes unity, continuity, and wholeness.

- Have a discussion concerning the shared aspirations of your community, group, or organization that builds on the collective history you shaped in Principle 1 and connects with the group values and commitments discussed previously. Based on your history, values, and mutual aspirations, develop a shared vision statement.

Weaving the collective wisdom

Stephen Covey, in his *Seven Habits of Highly Effective People*, identifies listening to understand as a key leadership trait. Many leaders in communities of color take this to a higher level by listening to everyone's ideas and ensuring that everyone in the group speaks before the leader ventures an opinion. In this capacity, the leader functions as a weaver, integrating people's ideas, discerning the group consensus, and bringing forth the collective wisdom.

- Discuss the power of this type of listening in identifying the common ground and in seeing unifying themes. In meetings or discussions, take turns assuming the role of leader as the weaver of ideas—the one who listens, waits until everyone has spoken, and then integrates the common themes.

The many roles of a leader

Leaders in communities of color assume many roles: cultural broker, translator and interpreter, bridge builder, ambassador, and spokesperson. These roles require the ability to be successful both in their own communities and in the dominant culture, and they require adaptability, flexibility, and the ability to engage different constituencies.

- How do these roles reflect the skills needed to lead in our diverse world?

- How could these be used in the environment in which you live and work, and in society as a whole?

Leadership lessons

What have you learned about leadership in American Indian, Latino, and Black communities that inspires you and that you would like to emulate?

- What is the unique role leaders in communities of color can play in building our diverse society and leading in a multicultural age?

Recommended readings and resources

- *Finding Your Voice* by Larraine Matusak (Jossey-Bass, 1997).

- *Memoir of a Visionary* by Antonia Pantoja (Arte Público Press, 2002).

- *The Servant as Leader* by Robert Greenleaf (The Greenleaf Center for Servant Leadership, 1970).

- *Servants of the People: The 1960s Legacy of African American Leadership* by Lea Williams (St. Martin's Press, 1998).

PART THREE

Creating the Circle of Leadership

ONG, LONG AGO, when the ancient ones were creating the magnificent structures of Stonehenge, they placed the monolithic stones in a circular form. Across the Northern Hemisphere, indigenous people constructed medicine wheels for ceremonies to connect to the power of life. On the continent of Africa, where human life first evolved, remnants of very old circles have withstood the ravages of time. And visitors walking the sacred valley of the Incas today can still find round stone formations in many places.

American Indians have traditionally used a circle for their councils and ceremonies. Likewise, people in tribal Africa would sit in a circle in the center of the village to discuss important community matters. In early times, women would gather in circles to honor the full moon. Since prehistoric times, in early *We* cultures, the circle has been the form used by our tribal ancestors as they gathered around the fire for warmth, protection, and the comfort of companionship. *The circle, which has no top or bottom, symbolizes equality.* All can see and hear each other. In the circle, everything is related and equal to everything else. There is nothing greater or smaller.

The African village, the American Indian tribal council, and the town meeting are all examples of cooperative circular structures in which the community considers important decisions. The African saying "One head does not a council make" underlies their very old tradition of tapping into the collective wisdom. The American Indian use of the "talking stick," which is passed around in a circle, gives everyone a chance to speak from the heart, so that a group perspective surfaces. The core Hispanic values of sharing, mutuality, cooperation, and community certainly imply a circular sense of all members being connected and taking care of one another.

The principle of *Sankofa* also evokes a more circular view, one in which the present flows out of the past and the future evolves out of a historical concept. Economic and social struggle in communities of color is centuries old. If people forget how much progress has been made, they may become cynical and think nothing ever changes. If they do not know their history, they will not understand how working together has been their salvation and safety net. Leaders in communities of color must keep the cultural memory alive—linking past, present, and future so a sense of continuity, wholeness, and hope for the future is nurtured. They must also build a circle of leaders in which everyone has the opportunity to lead and many people are involved. Thus, the community capacity continues evolving and a legacy of leadership is created.

The Continuity of Leadership

THE SEVENTH-GENERATION RULE of the Iroquois Indians—which states that leaders must always consider the effects of their actions on their children, their children's children, and so on unto seven generations—captures the long-term responsibility and stewardship of leadership. Each generation is entrusted with the care of subsequent ones and with continuing the *circle of leadership*. Leaders today can honor this rule by keeping their actions in alignment with the ongoing progress of their community, as well as by actively shepherding the next generation.

As noted previously, Martin Luther King Jr. abided by the seventh-generation rule by always surrounding himself with a cadre of dedicated leaders and by leaving a legacy people could follow. In this way, not only did the Black community keep on advancing after his death but also King's contributions continued reverberating and enhancing American society and the entire world. In a similar fashion, Dolores Huerta, who served as vice-president of the United Farm Workers of America, worked side by side with César Chávez. Huerta negotiated labor contracts and was a key strategist in the farm workers' movement. She continues this work today, decades after Chávez's death. When Raul Yzaguirre stepped down as president of the National Council of La Raza (NCLR) after more than thirty years, he had trained hundreds of leaders. Succession was securely in place as Janet Murgia, who had served on the NCLR board, took the helm. Similarly, Mayor Shirley Franklin continues the growth and progress made under the leadership of Andrew Young when he was mayor of Atlanta.

 The seventh-generation rule of the Iroquois Indians—which states that leaders must always consider the effects of their actions on their children, their children's children, and so on unto seven generations—captures the long-term responsibility and stewardship of leadership.

Historically, American Indian leadership has centered on a system of tribal governance in which elders or tribal members choose their leaders. Because leadership rotates, taking one's turn is an integral part of tribal membership. Indian leaders who function in mainstream society carry this sense of obligation and responsibility. Ada Deer, the first woman to serve as president of her tribal council, has remained engaged in her reservation in Northern Wisconsin for over fifty years, even though she directs the American Indian Studies Program at the University of Wisconsin at Madison. Benny Shendo Jr. left a job at Stanford University when he was asked to return to the Jemez Pueblo and help start the first charter school on an Indian reservation. Leadership is everyone's responsibility. By sharing and rotating power, the circle of leadership in Indian tribes remains strong.

The power of the circle is as old as humankind and centers on a very ancient belief that was essential to early *We* cultures—one of kinship, in which all people were connected. The seventh principle in this book, *All My Relatives,* recognizes the universal human family, which is being acknowledged today in the concept of our world village. Leaders who follow this ancient tradition treat people with the respect due a family member and see their role as creating a society in which everyone is valued and respected equally.

The final principle—*Gracias: Gratitude, Hope, and Forgiveness*—recognizes the spiritual attributes that have sustained communities of color and shaped leadership as spiritual responsibility to one's people. By focusing on thankfulness, communities of color were able to engender a deep-seated optimism despite economic need and discrimination. Thankfulness seeded generosity and reciprocity among people who sometimes had very little economic means or resources. The ability to forgive has allowed communities of color to heal the past and build new pathways of understanding. As evidenced in South Africa, forgiveness is pivotal to reconciliation and to creating a new spirit of community.

Reconciling the *past,* having gratitude for what one has *today,* and being optimistic for the *future* nourishes continuity and community integration. This supports the circle of leadership in which today's leaders shepherd future generations and honor the foundation laid by those who have come before.

PRINCIPLE 7

All My Relatives—
La Familia, the Village,
the Tribe

N THE CARIBBEAN COAST OF NICARAGUA, where my family lived for generations, the Mosquito Indians greet each other by putting their hands to their chests and saying "*Cupian kumi.*" ("We are one heart.") I was raised with this philosophy, an extensive and elastic concept of *familia,* which went way beyond blood or even distant kin. My Tío Cristobal lived on the banks of the Rio Coco, a dark chocolate stream that flowed into the Caribbean. For the holidays, he would butcher the ceremonial pig and send the word out along the river: "Anyone who does not have a place for Christmas is welcome in my home." Thus, many a salty sailor, a neighbor who had fallen into disfavor with his wife, or a traveler who could not make it home gratefully shared the Christmas meal and family festivities.

This spirit of taking in strangers and treating them like kin was one of my mother's trademarks, particularly when it came to little children. When I was a teenager, my older sisters financed a small addition to our home that was called Maria's nursery after my mother. My mother, patiently and with her "don't try any funny business" love, cared for hundreds of children who took over the whole house. Several *literally* became part of the family. They were *always* there, and it seemed their mothers had abandoned them.

I found out later that in fact they had! One child, who had been nicknamed Peewee by my father, had a mother who just didn't come back. Perhaps my mother should have called the welfare department, but instead she said, "They are like my children now. I can take good care of them." Peewee stayed the longest, but several other children also became part of the family. The funny part was that eventually the mothers would come back and be welcomed with open arms. Their children were fed, happy, and loved.

My mother's gift for caring for children that were not biologically her own was based on her expansive vision of *familia* and was integral to her spiritual beliefs. When she was dying, she said, "I am not afraid, because the children will open the gates of heaven for me." Her concept of *familia* and responsibility was to those around her, but it was wide enough to include the *universal connection* people have to one another. My mother absolutely believed that Peewee and all those children she cared for were her children, too.

This might seem strange, or like my mother was an exceptionally giving and spiritual woman (which she was). However, it is not that uncommon in collective cultures. Andrew Young remembers his grandmother having this same type of open-heartedness. "After informally adopting several children whom she raised along with her own, she was always taking in people throughout her life."[1] In communities of color, there is a willingness to take care of people who might be regarded as strangers in the mainstream culture. This widespread custom of treating people as relatives is a natural evolution of the *We* identity that is the heart of collective cultures. It reflects a spiritual understanding of the universal human connection.

Universal Kinship

UNIVERSAL KINSHIP—the concept that we belong to one human family—is the core of Christianity and the major world religions. When Jesus proclaimed "Our Father" at the beginning of the Lord's Prayer, he was affirming that people are spiritually one family. Dr. Lea Williams observed this same belief in Martin Luther King Jr. "He had studied theology, philosophy and the comparative religions of the world. King understood our common humanity and spoke a universal message of brotherhood."

The Cherokee or Tsalagi tradition in which people acknowledge each other as "all my relatives" and the Lakota greeting *Mitakuye oyasin*—"we are all related"—mirror this belief. *Huayucaltia*, the greeting of the Nahuatl Indians of Mexico, translates as "we are all brothers and kin." The Zulu word for community, *umphakati,* means "we are all together on the inside," indicating that all of us are essentially one and the same.[2] Many greetings of indigenous people speak to a connection that is *a priori*—a relationship that already exists based on the unity and similarities of being human.

Today the religious and cultural belief that people come from one family is being verified by science. A *New York Times* article in August 2000 declared, "DNA shows humans are all one race." Dr. Harold Freeman, the chief executive and director of surgery at North General Hospital in Manhattan and an expert on biology and race, noted, "If you ask what percentage of your genes is reflected in your external appearance, the basis by which we talk about race, the answer seems to be in the range of .01 percent." Dr. Craig Venter, head of the Celera Genomics Corporation in Rockville, Maryland, commented, "We all evolved in the last 100,000 years from the same small number of tribes that migrated out of Africa and colonized the world." Venter and scientists at the National Institutes of Health recently announced that they had put together a draft of the entire sequence of human genome. The researchers unanimously declared there is only one race—the human race.[3] This is not to deny the beauty or unique expressions that different races bring to humanity; however, our genetic commonalities as a human family are infinitely greater than those that separate us.

Quantum physics and system thinking also support the recognition that there is one human family. This vision of reality replaces the Newtonian concept of the world as a machine—which separates things into parts and segments—to one in which everything is connected and interrelated. Margaret Wheatley, in her groundbreaking work *Leadership and the New Science*, describes this as a holistic view in which the universe is a dynamic living energy and reflects a vast network of patterns. In this system-thinking approach, nothing exists independent of its relationship to something else, and everything is related. Quantum physics is in fact affirming the early beliefs of indigenous cultures whose worldview saw people as interconnected and as relatives.[4] In many different languages, this was expressed as "we are one planet and one people."

To understand the principle of *All My Relatives*, let us first look at how this manifests in communities of color and then consider the different ways these relationships expand to embrace a much wider circle. From this perspective, we can discern how treating people as relatives would transform leadership. We can also surmise how this would create a very different society—one that is more compassionate, equitable, and socially responsible.

The Kinship of Community

THROUGH THE PAST FIVE HUNDRED YEARS, communities of color have knitted together a strong and binding social netting. Even when people do not know each other, their common history and culture impart a deep feeling of togetherness. "*We* Shall Overcome" indicates the natural bonding and familiarity that comes from African Americans' recognition that their ancestors survived the same trials and common hardships. This facilitates the ability to identify with people not known personally.

There are nonverbal movements, lip gestures, unique nods of the heads, *abrazos*, and handshakes that Latinos, Blacks, and American Indians use to recognize and bond with people of their ethnic group or race that they do not know. The African American "high five" has now entered the mainstream and provides a glimpse of how easily people of color connect with one another. Latinos greet people with an *abrazo*, a full body embrace. Traditionally, they kissed one another on both cheeks. (In the Anglo culture, this type of intimacy is generally reserved for someone who is a close acquaintance or family member.) When American Indians meet, they first share their tribal backgrounds. Coming from cultures in which everything is related, they do this to honor each other's ancestry and acknowledge the historical connections between tribes.

The importance of acknowledging that *people are related* extends to leadership as well. Leaders are expected to treat people as family members. This is easier to understand when noting that leadership is not a position or a passing stage, but a lifelong commitment. Williams commends the longevity of service of the Black leaders she studied in the 1960s, whose average tenure was twenty-six years.[5] John Echohawk has been at the helm of the Native American Rights Fund since 1977. Raul Yzaguirre spent over thirty years building the National Council of La Raza into the largest and most influential Hispanic organization in America. Andrew Young is now in his seventies and has walked the road of community service for more than fifty years. Ada Deer is an elder who served as the first chairwoman of the Menominee Nation and continues her active involvement with her tribe in northern Wisconsin.

The enduring commitment of these leaders is held together by lifelong relationships based on a family or tribal model. The NCLL survey noted previously, indicating that Latinos wanted their leaders to be loving and kind and like part of the family, underscores the importance of this type of connection between leaders and people. Until she died at the age of eighty, Dr. Pantoja's devotion to her community was clothed in her deep sense of justice. "Somehow I learned that I belonged with my people and that I had a responsibility to contribute to them. I will participate in changing the situations of injustice and inequality that I encounter because they deny people their rights and destroy their potential."[6]

Somehow I learned that I belonged with my people and that I had a responsibility to contribute to them. I will participate in changing the situations of injustice and inequality that I encounter because they deny people their rights and destroy their potential.

—Dr. Antonia Pantoja

Relationships Carry Responsibility

IN THE MAINSTREAM SOCIETY, leaders may espouse Christian brotherhood and have good intentions regarding others. However, this does not mean that they see themselves as *responsible* for other people's well-being. The emphasis on individualism may even lead to people being blamed for bringing on their own plight. As Dr. Joseph has indicated, this posture allows leaders to be concerned with private virtues and individual behavior, but not with social accountability. The underlying social structures and institutions that perpetuate economic disparity and leave some people without basic necessities can be ignored. Much of the emphasis in U.S. politics today, in fact, concerns itself with people's individual lifestyles and choices and not with social responsibility.

Central to American Indian culture, on the other hand, is the belief that *relationship always carries responsibility.* Based on their circular, dynamic, and holistic view of the universe, everything is related through the One Great Spirit. The respect shown to the four-legged, the winged animals, things that crawl, trees, stones, and all living things flows from this belief. Connected by this Spirit, human beings are one family, with the

Earth as their mother and the Sun as their father. Because these relationships imply certain responsibilities, native people must take care of the Earth, live in harmony with the natural order, and treat each other as esteemed family members. Even the term *Great White Father*, which was used by native people to describe the top Anglo leader, is a relationship term—a form of respect that also implied a reciprocal obligation, although not necessarily the kind that exists between parent and child. There were some responsibilities Indians would assume and others that the Great White Father was expected to assume.

 Responsibility and obligation have a different connotation to Indian people. In Anglo society, it means have to, *but to Indians it means* want to. *Contributing to the welfare of others is an honor and part of our nature.*

—Ada Deer

Seeing people as relatives, as members of one big family, as one's community or village, presents a different model of how leaders relate to their followers. "American Indian leaders," reflects Ada Deer, "are entrusted to look out for and improve people's welfare. They have a sense of obligation and responsibility to the tribe. Responsibility and obligation have a different connotation to Indian people. In Anglo society, it means *have to*, but to Indians it means *want to*. Contributing to the welfare of others is an honor and part of our nature."

Benny Shendo Jr. describes the Jemez Pueblo, for whom this type of leadership exists, as "a community of mutual care where people see themselves as an extended tribal family. On the reservation, there are no homeless people. People always have a home. In our language we treat each other as brothers and sisters because spiritually we are all related." Seeing relationships as responsibility lays the foundation for leadership that assumes accountability for the social institutions that safeguard equity, the common welfare, and justice for all.

You Are a Person Because of Other People

Dr. Joseph describes the sense of kinship that exists among people in the African American community as the *cosmology of connectedness*. Inherited from their African roots, the cosmology of connectedness reflects the traditional belief in *ubuntu*, which signifies that interactions with others define a person's humanity. (A literal translation is "you are a person only because of other people.") *Ubuntu* manifests as people doing good through kindness and compassion to one another and to the entire community. When people practice *ubuntu,* they are recognizing the inner connection among people and acknowledging that their spirit and that of humanity are one.[7] This belief encourages people to treat others fairly and with respect and is the basis for leaders being one among equals.

Ubuntu emphasizes that a person is wrapped in the cloth of humanity—*my humanity is tied to your humanity.* Like a tribal drumbeat, *ubuntu* resonates across African cultures. It is not an ethereal spiritual concept of oneness, but a real day-to-day obligation to be sharing, open, and welcoming toward others. Since *ubuntu* signifies that the formation of one's identity and ongoing well-being depends on other people, it underscores the collective and the tribe.[8] The familiar saying "It takes a *village* to raise a child" reflects this and emphasizes the communal responsibility people have to all children.

The spirit of *ubuntu* nourished the unity of African slaves. When biological parents and families were ripped apart and sold to different owners, the community shared the role of mother and father. Dr. Joseph describes these relationships: "The [slave] quarter community addressed each other with familial titles and behaved towards one another as brothers and sisters with quasi-familial reciprocal obligations." He notes that this sense of responsibility for others extended to the *greater community* as well.[9] Dr. Lea Williams describes how this has continued to advance African Americans: "Our communities take care of one another. That has been our vision and salvation.

Our communities take care of one another. That has been our vision and salvation. It is what we must hold onto for our future well-being.

—Dr. Lea Williams

It is what we must hold onto for our future well-being." Seeing each other as related or as family continues to be a fundamental characteristic of Black leadership today.

La Raza Is Inclusive

A crucial difference between Latinos and either Blacks or American Indians is that there is no legal definition of what it means to be Latino. To be eligible for Bureau of Indian Affairs services, an Indian must be an enrolled member of a tribe recognized by the federal government. LaDonna explains, "Native Americans have blood *quantism* that was imposed by the treaties and Anglo colonialists, which means that a person must have legal proof of their blood line in order to be enrolled in a tribe." Many

Indians, however, recognize that a person's identity and sacred regard for the Indian worldview and way of life are the defining characteristics. LaDonna relates to a more mystical definition: "Blood runs the heart. The heart knows what it is."

African Americans have a more legally evasive identity. According to Dr. F. James Davis, author of *Who Is Black? One Nation's Definition*, the answer has been anyone with any known African Black ancestry. One of the mechanisms that made this a de facto proposition was what anthropologists refer to as the *hypo-descent rule*, which assigns racially mixed persons the status of the subordinate group. In the racist South, this was effectively the basis for the *one-drop rule*, which came to mean that anyone with any Black blood was considered Negro.[10]

Although the racial division in U.S. society imposed great burdens on Black people and American Indians and resulted in centuries of segregation, it also allowed for their cultures and communities to stay intact. Racial isolation nourished their identities and values and permitted their spiritual foundation to flourish.

Latinos, on the other hand, have only been recognized as a group since the 1980 U.S. Census, and there is still no set legal definition. In fact, Latinos are hybrids that come in many colors—black, brown, yellow, white, and red, as well as latté, mocha, chocolate, and many mixtures in between. It is paradoxical, then, that Latinos have a collective identity known as La Raza—"the race." *Que viva la raza* (long live the race) was a frequent slogan during the 1960s when César Chávez and Dolores Huerta were organizing the United Farm Workers, and it remains a rallying cry today. La Raza has a somewhat different connotation than race in English. La Raza is more of a *cultural identity magnet* that connotes a shared history and worldview and common values.

 My definition of Latino is anybody who wants to be a Latino, bienvenido—welcome to the family. This concept would revolutionize America's race consciousness.

—Raul Yzaguirre

As a fusion of different races and a blend of European and many indigenous cultures, Latinos embody a rich multicultural heritage. La Raza, therefore, does not signify racial exclusivity nor propose that one race is better than another. Inclusion is a historical reality and a heartfelt cultural value. Yzaguirre believes this inclusiveness is an open door that welcomes people to partake in the *Latinizmo* (the Latino cultural experience). "America needs a different paradigm of what it means to be Latino. The prototype of Native or African Americans, where your blood content defines who you are, does not work. Latinos are a culture, not a race. Inclusiveness and sharing are cherished values. My definition of Latino is anybody who wants to be a Latino—*bienvenido*—*welcome to the family.* This concept would revolutionize America's race consciousness."

 Because culture is learned, the important thing to realize is that people can develop affinities and sensitivities for a number of different cultures. Leaders can acquire multicultural competencies and work effectively with many different populations.

To explore Yzaguirre's concept in more depth, we could say that Latinos are a culture and culture is learned. There are many opportunities for people to become fluent in Spanish, live in a Latin country or *barrio*, adapt core cultural values, marry into the family, and even be taught to salsa with the best of them. Add to this Latino generosity, inclusiveness, the spirit of *bienvenidos,* and the desire to be *simpatico,* and people who are of like mind are welcomed into the culture. Sometimes it is difficult to discern whether people are born Latino or are simply "born-again Latinos"! With the growing demographics, influence, and emphasis on the international aspects of *Latinizmo,* many more people will be finding and enjoying their Latino affinity.

Yzaguirre is actually referring to an old tradition in communities of color. As mentioned earlier, Latinos designate people who become "like family" as *compadres* or *comadres, padrinos* or *padrinas.* American Indian and African tribes as well as other indigenous communities across the planet have ceremoniously initiated people into their tribes. Although these people were not born members, they exhibited—through their lives, special feats, loyalty, or marriage—their bond to the tribe. Today, people who have a special affinity with the American Indian culture are referred to as having an "Indian heart." Black families often adopt people who are not of their racial background but have strong and loyal ties to their family and race, and they may even refer to them as *brothers* and *sisters.*

Because culture is learned, the important thing to realize is that people can develop affinities and sensitivities for a number of different cultures. Leaders can acquire multicultural competencies and work effectively with many different populations. By incorporating the principles and practices described in this book, leaders can begin to expand their abilities to reach and connect with people from an increasing diversity of cultures.

A Society in Which People Are Relatives

IN COLLECTIVE CULTURES, again, *relationship always implies responsibility*. As described previously, leadership as social responsibility is founded on seeing relationships from a spiritual and universal perspective. When we accept the concept of the universal human family, then we are our brothers' and sisters' keepers. A society that regarded people as relatives would actively address the social and economic structures perpetuating inequities. As Ada Deer surmises, "Indian people see themselves as connected, as one community, and as relatives. If you don't see the human race that way, then you can take more than your share. You can be selfish. It is okay to take advantage of people. You see, it is a completely different way of looking at the world."

 Indian people see themselves as connected, as one community, and as relatives. If you don't see the human race that way, then you can take more than your share. You can be selfish. It is okay to take advantage of people. You see, it is a completely different way of looking at the world.

—Ada Deer

Dr. Joseph believes leaders must personally model the behaviors they aspire to see in society. "*Ubuntu,* where people are supposed to act with humaneness, compassion, and care, is an example of how *a private value can be reflected as a public value.* The private aspect is how individuals act towards each other and the public values are ensuring that the society is structured in such a way that people are cared for and treated humanely. Condoning and sanctioning the values of *ubuntu* would engender this type of society—one where leadership would tend to public values and social institutions."

When Andrew Young served as U.S. ambassador to the UN, he found in South Africa a model based on spiritual connectedness and the power of speaking the truth. "When the truth is spoken without judgment, but rather to point to the possibilities of a 'more excellent way of living' together as brothers and sisters, in spite of the differences of race, class, or creed, there is the potential of everyone accepting a new start. This is the way God deals with us as his children, and it is also the way we must learn to deal with each other."[11] Young believes this way of thinking brought reconciliation and understanding to South Africa and has the potential to heal the world.

César Chávez followed in this tradition. He not only embraced Latino and Filipino immigrants and farm workers but also spoke to neglected and marginalized people everywhere. He attracted people from across the country, including an ecumenical religious following, labor union support, and the respect of government officials. Finally, he led a national boycott against grape growers, inviting people everywhere to participate. Chávez cast his net very wide, reminding people that the same insecticides that were killing farm workers and their children presented a threat to all Americans, as the toxic residues persisted on produce. Like King, who described a dream for all God's children, leaders in communities of color must ensure that the table is wide enough to include all people of goodwill who are ready to build a society that will benefit the human family.

 Ubuntu, *where people are supposed to act with humaneness, compassion, and care, is an example of how a private value can be reflected as a public value. The private aspect is how individuals act towards each other and the public values are ensuring that the society is structured in such a way that people are cared for and treated humanely.*

—Dr. Jim Joseph

Living Simply So Others Can Simply Live

BECAUSE LEADERS IN COMMUNITIES OF COLOR are expected to set an example for others, many purposely live in a way that does not create social and economic disparities. I recall the first time I picked up my mentor, Bernie Valdez, at his home for our monthly lunch, where we just talked and ate. (In oral tradition cultures, knowledge is passed on through conversation and stories—food is also crucial.) Because he was a highly respected leader, I had unconsciously expected his house to reflect his stature in the community. Yet the man who would have the Bernie Valdez Colorado Hispanic Heritage Center and a public library named after him lived in a little house behind the Mile High Bronco stadium, the same house where he and Dora had raised their children. Just visiting his home reminded me why I was bothered by the contradictions I had seen in leaders in Washington and in corporations. Leadership as exemplified by Bernie Valdez was not having a big house or the trappings of wealth and influence. It was a lifelong commitment to live in your community, to serve your people, and to remain an ordinary person while accomplishing great things.

Andrew Young remembers a similar commitment from Martin Luther King Jr.: "Martin and Coretta King lived in an old wooden framed house near Ebenezer Baptist Church. There was nothing fashionable about his neighborhood, it was all but a slum. But Martin viewed living modestly as part of his commitment to social justice."[12] Likewise, César Chávez, who grew up in the migrant camps of California, continued to live humbly throughout his life, never making more than $6,000 a year.[13] King and Chávez studied deeply the philosophy of Mahatma Gandhi, who set the standard for living as modestly as one's followers did.

 When the truth is spoken without judgment, but rather to point to the possibilities of a "more excellent way of living" together as brothers and sisters, in spite of the differences of race, class, or creed, there is the potential of everyone accepting a new start.

—Andrew Young

Although these examples may seem absurd in our materialistic and profit-centered society, there are ethical and practical ways to accomplish a more equitable economic balance. A great economic disparity occurs when some people gobble up more than their share while others scarcely have enough to survive. Multicultural leadership implies a sense of generosity based on making a commitment to the collective *We* and accepting the responsibility for community stewardship. Part Four, Leading in a Multicultural World, examines how multicultural leadership principles can help individuals, organizations, and businesses reach a new equilibrium that can temper the growing materialism with a renewed sense of sharing and generosity.

Generosity Flows Naturally to One's Relatives

THERE IS A GROWING UNDERSTANDING TODAY that people are intricately connected and interdependent. The realization that we are all relatives is a crucial step in restoring the fragile and broken circle of life in which mutual care ensures the continuity of life. Leaders are challenged to bring together splintering groups who spar over resources, conflicting political and religious ideologies, and class and racial distinctions. In the competitive spirit of our country, resources are divided up and parceled out inequitably so that many do not partake of the American harvest. Evidence of this is the growing poverty rate: in 2003 over 3.59 million Americans lived below the poverty line,[14] and hunger rose by 43 percent between 1999 and 2005. Thirty-eight million Americans, including 14 million children, do not have enough to eat.[15] While the number is difficult to calculate, it is estimated that 3.5 million are homeless every year.[16] If society viewed people as relatives, with the generosity that this implies, the minimal bottom line would be that people would have basic necessities such as food to eat and a roof over their heads.

LaDonna Harris believes that rekindling the sense of kinship among people is crucial in today's conflict-ridden world: "If people on earth had this sense of family and responsibility toward one another, it would lay the foundation for world peace and human understanding." General Bob Neighbors, a truly warm and compassionate military leader who was one of my students at the Center for Creative Leadership, echoed this urgency. He was genuinely concerned about the escalating conflicts that were tearing apart prospects for a more peaceful world. "At any time on the planet some fifty conflicts are raging that are fueled by what people perceive as religious, political, or ethnic differences. Humanity is at a crossroads; we must find peaceful ways to assuage our perceived disagreements."

If people on earth had this sense of family and responsibility toward one another, it would lay the foundation for world peace and human understanding.

—LaDonna Harris

Almost fifty years ago, young President Kennedy voiced similar sentiments: "We can make the world safe for diversity. For in the final analysis, our most basic common link is that we all inhabit this small planet. We all breathe the same air. We all cherish our children's future and we are all mortal."[17] In other words, what unites us as humans is much stronger than what separates us. A visionary leader, Kennedy sensed that continuing global friction threatened our planet and its very existence. He recognized that our individual safety and well-being would be forever linked to our ability to tap into the shared human experience—the common ground that unites us all.

Like the sun that radiates warmth and light to all, the deep spiritual traditions of communities of color embrace the oneness, unity, and equality of all people. These traditions, in which people are seen as relatives, offer tried and true ways to create the world Martin Luther King Jr. envisioned in which all people had three meals a day, education, dignity, and freedom. It also engenders the potential, as LaDonna Harris has so wisely suggested, for world peace and human understanding.

Spirituality, Leadership, and Social Responsibility

BECAUSE IT IS A unifying and all-encompassing stream in communities of color, references to spirituality are interspersed throughout this book. The vibrant forms of spirituality embraced by these communities offer a renewed sense of our common humanity that is founded in our responsibility to one another and in our commitment to creating a society that cares for its people.

Many leaders in communities of color have sought not just to liberate the human spirit but to alleviate the harsh conditions many people encounter here on earth. Martin Luther King Jr., Andrew Young, Jesse Jackson, Adam Clayton Powell, and John Lewis were all ordained ministers. In Andrew Young's book, *An Easy Burden*, a chapter is entitled "The Lord Is with This Movement." Evidence of the integration of spirituality and social action is the pledge for nonviolence all demonstrators were required to sign during the early civil rights protests. Among these principles were:

- Meditate daily on the life and teachings of Jesus

- Walk and talk in the manner of love—for God is love

- Pray daily to be used by God in order that all men may be free

- Strive to be in good spiritual and bodily health[18]

Dr. Lea Williams described the inspired Black leaders who led the civil rights movement as *servants of the people.* She saw these leaders as being "sustained by and drawing strength from, an abiding faith—faith in God, faith in self and in others, faith in the vision and in the integrity of the cause." She notes the practical implications of this relating it to intuitive insight: "Faith plays a defining role because it assures the servant leader that even in the midst of fear and confusion, amid turmoil and uncertainty, appropriate actions and responses will somehow be revealed because they walk by faith and not sight."[19]

 The vibrant forms of spirituality embraced by these communities offer a renewed sense of our common humanity that is founded in our responsibility to one another and in our commitment to creating a society that cares for its people.

Spirituality is an electric current running through the Latino culture. Latinos acknowledge God's providence on a daily basis. The saying *"Esta en los manos de Dios"* (it's in the hands of God) reflects this assurance. Before something happened, my Tía Anita would proclaim, *"Este va a pasar si Dios quiere"* (this will occur if God wills it). Afterward she would say, *"Este paso, gracias a Dios"* (thank God for making it happen). As a child, I surmised that coming or going, before or after, Tía Anita had it covered.

The final principle—*Gracias: Gratitude, Hope, and Forgiveness*—looks at the enduring faith in the future that ensured the survival of communities of color. The faith traditions in these communities are a foundation for leadership that integrates spirituality with social responsibility.

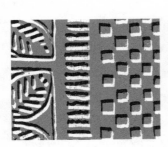

All My Relatives

Universal kinship

Reflect on the meaning and implications of the many sayings that support the belief in human connectedness and the universal human family:

- *Kupia Kumi*—We are one heart
- *Mitakuye oysain*—We are all related
- *Huayucaltia*—We are all brothers and kin
- *Umphakati*—We are all together on the inside
- *Unbuntu*—I am only a person because of other people

In dyads or small groups, stand and repeat these sayings to one another several times (English is fine). The goal is to *experience* human connectedness and to glimpse the ancient belief that human beings are one family.

Explore the emotional or heart aspects of this exercise—how did it make you feel? Discuss the intellectual concepts, such as the scientific basis, particularly quantum physics. Describe the power that comes from understanding that you are part of the *We*—the collective—and are supported by this. Finally, discuss what our society might look like if people upheld this ancient and pervasive belief.

Relationships always carry responsibility

Relating to people as family and kin is not just a feel-good theoretical concept. In fact, the leaders profiled in this book have dedicated their lives to serving people because *relationships always carry responsibility*.

- How have you discerned this sense of responsibility in the lives of the leaders profiled in this book?

- What benefits would our society reap if we followed the path forged by these leaders and rekindled the sense of kinship between people?

The mechanism of exclusion

Blood quantism in the America Indian community and the "one-drop rule" that was imposed on African Americans were mechanisms of exclusion and discrimination.

- Discuss the ramifications of having these types of legal definitions to define people.

- What distinguishes the Latino community and how is their identity different from that of American Indians and African Americans? Why does Yzaguirre believe this could "revolutionize America's race consciousness"?

- There are many stories of people who live in other cultures, adopt the customs, and "become" kin. What experiences have you had in which you felt connected to other cultures? Discuss concrete steps people can take to develop affinities and sensitivities to different cultures.

Living as relatives

The Jemez Pueblo people believe "spiritually we are related."

- How does this define how people should treat one another?

- What are the implications for multicultural leadership?

Recommended readings and resources

- *An Easy Burden: The Civil Rights Movement and the Transformation of America* by Andrew Young (HarperCollins, 1996).

- *Latinos: A Biography of the People* by Earl Shorris (Norton, 1992).

- *Mankiller: A Chief and Her People* by Wilma Mankiller and Michael Wallis (St. Martin's Press, 1993).

PRINCIPLE 8

Gracias—Gratitude, Hope, and Forgiveness

A FEW YEARS AGO, I trudged through the Nicaraguan jungle to the mining town of Bonanza where I was born. The green canopies are lush with banana trees and brazen tropical flowers hanging from vines. Even today, many decades later, there are only three streets. The stark isolation is apparent the moment the cargo plane touches the dirt runway carved in the sea of jungle trees. *How did it happen?* I asked myself. *How did this miracle that is my life ever occur?* My mother and grandmothers would have *no problema* answering—to them it was always *gracias a Dios*—their faith never failed them.

Since serving as a Peace Corps volunteer in Chile over forty years ago, I have listened to thousands of people share their journeys, and I know this reliance on God's providence is not unique. Our collective journeys reflect the unflappable faith and hope that wrap around communities of color like serapes on cold nights. Practicing *Sankofa*—reflecting on our past—reveals the bones of our common journeys and honors the Herculean obstacles our parents and *antepasados* overcame for us to become who we are today.

Migrant workers, sharecroppers, garbage collectors, growing up in shacks with no running water or electricity, immigrants who couldn't speak English—an unlikely pool for the next generation of distinguished American leaders. Yet this was the fertile ground that cultivated the strength of character, hope, and belief in God's grace (or life's goodness) that in turn brought the substance of leadership to communities of color—a past that is reflected in the principle of *Gracias*.

Unos Cuentitos: A Few Little Stories

CROSSING THE RIO GRANDE, Maria Guajardo's parents became migrant workers in the California fields under the searing sun. Her mother only finished the second grade; her father never attended school. Having left their homeland and family, they made all their sacrifices so that their children could go to school.

Guajardo made their dream come true. In fact, she attended Harvard University, obtained a doctorate from the University of Denver, and now serves as Denver's Director of the Mayor's Office for Education and Children. Education, which her parents only dreamed of, has become Maria's passion and life's work.

Ada Deer grew up in a one-room log cabin on the banks of the Wolf River in the Menominee Indian reservation, in the cold windy forests of northern Wisconsin. There was no indoor plumbing, electricity, or running water. She loved to read, and her keen intelligence was noticed by the elders. The Tribal Council awarded her a scholarship to go to the university. Because she was given this opportunity, she saw it as her responsibility to help her brothers and sisters. Four out of five received college degrees. Today, she directs the American Indian Studies program at the University of Wisconsin, assisting many students, Indian and non-Indian alike, in attaining a college degree.

David Wilson remembers his father, who worked as a sharecropper in the Mississippi Delta, learning to read by looking at the newspapers they had tacked to the wall to keep the wind out of their wobbly shack. Sometimes what people do not have becomes the great jewel or prize to be won. Theirs was a deeply spiritual family, and Wilson's father believed God's grace would look after them. Armed with great determination, David became an educator. Today, he is vice president of Auburn University.

Her signature appears on U.S. dollar bills. Anna Escobedo Cabral, the current U.S. treasurer, remembers changing elementary schools over twenty times as her family migrated with the ripening of the crops. Eventually, her father became a laborer because he wanted his children to stay in one school. However, he was injured and suffered spinal disabilities. Not having worker's compensation, he bought an old truck and became a junkman. He would pick up metal trash and creatively fix old appliances and other things he found. Anna was the oldest and helped him sort through the trash. She accepted a scholarship only when her counselor convinced her she could help her family more if she went to college.

 Although there are many spiritual attributes that nourish Black, Latino, and Indian leaders, gracias (gratitude), hope, and forgiveness are three that transformed oppression and need into an enduring faith in life's goodness.

More than four hundred years ago, Ken Salazar's family was among the founders of the city of Santa Fe. Since the 1800s they have lived in the majestic, but economically depressed mountain region of Colorado's San Luis Valley. Salazar grew up in a remote rural area with no electricity or phone lines. His parents were humble and poor farmers, but, as he likes to say, "were rich in values." Stressing hard work, community, and faith, his parents urged their eight children to study hard and pursue their education. They all completed college. Ken is now a U.S. senator, while his brother John serves as congressman from the third district in Colorado.

These childhood stories of leaders from communities of color are not uncommon. They reveal a foundation grounded in faith, sacrifice, service to others, and hope for the future. Without these qualities, our parents would have constantly griped about their unfair situations, become bitter, and simply given up. They might have developed a hateful attitude toward people who did not give them a fair shake or held resentments because the doors of opportunity were tightly guarded.

Although there are many spiritual attributes that nourish Black, Latino, and Indian leaders, *gracias* (gratitude), hope, and forgiveness are three that transformed oppression and need into an enduring faith in life's goodness. The saying "If it doesn't kill you, it will make you stronger" reflects the ability to turn a difficult struggle into an opportunity to develop one's spiritual fortitude. As Jesse Jackson advised, "Suffering breeds character. Character breeds faith. In the end, faith will not disappoint."[1]

Gratitude and Thanksgiving

Gratitude was deeply ingrained in early *We* cultures, in which just surviving was a blessing indeed. Most indigenous cultures had celebrations to give thanks for the cycles of nature, such as the change in seasons, the glorious full moon, and the rain that quenched the earth. One of the most important was the harvest celebration, to give thanks for the first crops that would ensure survival through the cold winter. Gratitude is a transforming force that engenders hope and generosity even when one has little to share or times are difficult. *Gracias*, being grateful, is a key quality that cultivates hope because people concentrate on *what they have*, not *what they lack*.

From before the European conquest of this hemisphere, the seeds of gratitude planted by their indigenous ancestors nourished and sustained Latino people. Because *gracias* means grace as well as thank you, there is an implication that to be happy and to live in what Christians refer to as "a state of grace" or in God's favor, one must be *grateful*. *Gracias a Dios* is a cherished philosophy of life and is almost like a punctuation mark in conversation. When someone acknowledges something good that happened, it is often followed by the refrain "*Gracias a Dios.*" Gratitude embraces an appreciation for parents, family, the community, and the *antepasados*—those who came before. Being thankful is a surefire way Latinos have kept their spirit of optimism and hope alive.

"*Gracias a la Vida*" ("Thanks to Life"), a treasured song by Chilean artist Violeta Parra, is steeped in this pervasive spirit of thankfulness. The song thanks life for giving us our ability to see and to hear, and feet to walk with. Yes, we are grateful for cities, puddles, beaches, deserts, mountains, plains, the stars in the heavens, for the alphabet and words so we can communicate, and for our mothers, friends, brothers, and lovers. We are grateful for both smiles and weeping because they allow us to distinguish happiness from sorrow. Parra ends her song by saying that it is *your song and everyone's song*. "Thanks to life, that has given me so much."

African American spirituality has been fashioned in this tradition. "Praise the Lord," and being thankful for life's blessings, are as central as the hymnal in Black churches.

Historically, this was needed to simply make it through another day and have enough to eat. The poverty and dangers of slavery were everyday threats. Many White people do not have the same awareness of being thankful for *daily survival*. White churches do not emphasize prevailing over pain and hardship in the same way Black churches do. Black people agree that God was a guiding force leading them out of the land of Egypt. This sentiment is reflected in their "national anthem," "Lift Every Voice"—"God of our weary years, God of our silent tears. Thou who has brought us thus far on the way . . ."

Gratitude and thankfulness is an essential reflection of the reverence for life inherent in the American Indian culture. In *Voices of Our Ancestors*, Dhyani Ywahoo of the Eastern Tsalagi (Cherokee) Nation speaks to this connection. "What is praying? To rise in the morning and to thank the sun, and then at midday, when the sun is overhead, thank all of those who have come before. And as the sun descends over the western horizon, say thank you. Oh, a day has passed and another day shall come. I am thankful."[2] In this spirit, American Indian gatherings, community celebrations, and meetings always begin with a prayer of thanksgiving.

Coming from a place of gratefulness and thanksgiving, instead of focusing on lack or needs, replenishes the fountain of generosity that flows from collective cultures. *Gracias* strengthens community. Gratefulness inspires a sense of optimism and hope rather than negativity or despair. This allows people to *keep the faith* during trying times or when faced with limitation. Expressing *gracias* is a great gift that communities of color bring to America; it offers an antidote to the raging materialism that is dividing our nation into a land of haves and have-nots. To be grateful and to give is the opposite of taking more than one's share. Like a spiritual salve, *gracias* can soothe the cultural angst that comes from always wanting more "stuff" than one already has.

Hope and Optimism

In his groundbreaking book *Emotional IQ*, Daniel Goleman defines optimism as the greatest motivator, because it implies a strong expectation that things will turn out all right, despite setbacks and frustrations. He cites research that optimistic people tend to be more successful.[3] Optimism can also be described as hope—an essential trait in communities of color. Hope and optimism was my mother getting on a banana boat with five of her eight children to cross *El Golfo de Mexico*. Optimism is coming to a strange land, struggling to learn English, working two jobs, and seeking education for her children.

A *New York Times/CBS News* poll validated optimism as a Latino cultural trait. The poll noted that 75 percent of Latinos believed their opportunity to succeed was better than that of their parents. Only 56 percent of non-Hispanics thought this was true. Additionally, 64 percent of Latinos thought life would be better for their children. This jumped to 83 percent for Hispanic immigrants who have come here seeking opportunity, but was only 39 percent for non-Hispanics. Hope is what drives Latino immigrants to cross the Rio Grande under perilous and heartbreaking circumstances.[4]

A belief in God's mercy and guidance and an enduring hope that they would overcome is the very substance of African American culture. Dr. Joseph, whose father was a minister, identifies optimism as integral to the Black religious experience: "Every sermon always ended with something about hope. It never stopped with 'things are so bad.' It stopped with 'things may be bad; *however,* there is always the possibility of a better life.'" Without the gift of hope, the Black community couldn't have held on and had the courage to survive slavery and racism. African American leaders have to dispense hope. If people are not hopeful, they won't act to change things. It's not naïve optimism, it is a hopeful realism." A belief in God's mercy and guidance and an enduring faith that they would overcome is the very substance of African American culture, allowing them to thrive under adversity.

Keep hope alive is such a powerful force among African Americans that Jesse Jackson used it as his 1984 presidential campaign slogan. An inspirational refrain in the Black community, hope builds on the perennial belief in the Promised Land—the assurance that one day Black people will be free. Hope was

 Coming from a place of gratefulness and thanksgiving, instead of focusing on lack or needs, replenishes the fountain of generosity that flows from collective cultures. Gracias strengthens community. Gratefulness inspires a sense of optimism and hope rather than negativity or despair. This allows people to keep the faith during trying times or when faced with limitation.

kept alive by hymns such as "Hear That Freedom Train A-Coming, Coming, Coming" and "Woke Up This Morning with My Mind Stayed on Freedom." The hope of justice, noted Martin Luther King Jr., springs from the unrealized promise of America—the promissory note that our country's founders gave to all people that they would enjoy life, liberty, and the pursuit of happiness. This hope has sustained the Black community in their search for equality and freedom.

Just as gravity holds everything to the earth, spirituality is the magnetic force of America Indian culture, binding people together. There is no separation between the spiritual and material world like that which exists in Eurocentric cultures. The Indian worldview is one of wholeness, relatedness, and responsibility. Hope is anchored in dreams, visions, prophecy, and the good counsel of the wise elders and shamans. This hope kept tribes together even when they were removed from their lands and the Bureau of Indian Affairs relocated them to urban areas. Without this hope, tribes would have blown away like tumbleweeds in a prairie sandstorm.

 The Hopi prophesies similarly spoke of a universal tribe that would be a rainbow people because they would represent the iridescent beauty of humankind. They would come to heal the earth, bring peace and understanding, and undo the damage done by the White civilization.

Each tribe has its own prophesies and medicine men, but since colonization the emphasis has been on survival, hope for the future, and the dream of peace. When Black Elk, a medicine man from the Lakota Nation, was only nine, he had a vision about the devastation that was coming, and he was told to urge people to find new strength to survive. Today, Leon Shenandoah is the Tadodaho (Firekeeper, Speaker, or Chief of Chiefs) of the Iroquois Confederacy. In his address to the United Nations in 1985, he spoke of the hope that "the four sacred colors of humans would stand together in the interest of peace." He continued, "We must unite the religions of the world as a spiritual force strong enough to prevail in peace."[5] The Hopi prophesies similarly spoke of a universal tribe that would be a rainbow people because they would represent the iridescent beauty of humankind. They would come to heal the earth, bring peace and understanding, and undo the damage done by the White civilization.

Forgiveness and Reconciliation

Although in this book I have not lingered on the travails endured by communities of color, there are critical leadership lessons we can learn by reflecting on these. As Dr. Joseph so aptly expresses, "African Americans had to come out of desegregation and the pain of racism and work hand in hand with the communities that oppressed them." This could happen only through the practice of forgiveness: "When Martin Luther King Jr. talked about loving the enemy, he was talking about reconciliation. He used the word *love,* not *reconciliation*, but it was the same notion that there had to be forgiveness."

 So one of the key contributions African Americans make to the world is reconciliation. *The challenge of resolving conflict through reconciliation and bringing people together may be as important in the twenty-first century as freedom was at the dawn of the nation states.*

—Dr. Jim Joseph

Dr. Joseph connects this to the African philosophy of *ubuntu*. "*Ubuntu* expresses that one's humanity can only be defined through how one interacts with others. If you damage the humanity of another person, then the whole of humanity is damaged in the process. The African American community has always taught this value. You forgive not only because it is ordained by the creator, but you live in this kind of relationship with other people because it is also in your self-interest."

Reconciliation according to Dr. Joseph is one of the *public values* leaders need to create a diverse society. "African Americans have been schooled on how to tolerate unacceptable behavior and continue working with the people who inflicted these wounds. *So one of the key contributions African Americans make to the world is reconciliation.* The challenge of resolving conflict through reconciliation and bringing people together may be as important in the twenty-first century as freedom was at the dawn of the nation states. In an interdependent world, one of the primary public values must be reconciliation based on tolerance and respect for others."

For Latinos, forgiveness has entailed healing the psychological trauma of the Spanish conquest. Genetically, Latinos are mestizos (of both indigenous and European, but predominately Spanish, parentage). Although that designation is infrequently used in the Northern hemisphere, it is a commonly used in Central and South America. Octavio Paz, the Mexican writer and Nobel Prize winner, described the pain and stigma of being a mixed blood or mestizo as an indelible inferiority complex. He believed that mestizos were made to feel ashamed of their Indian roots. At the same time, they were rejected by their arrogant Spanish fathers, who often did not recognize them as legitimate offspring. This denial negated the very talents and attributes inherited from their European ancestors and denigrated their indigenous roots as well.[6]

Many Latinos credit the marriage of indigenous spirituality and the Catholic faith as the wellspring for the forgiveness and cultural integration that resulted. A symbol of this cultural cohesion is Our Lady of Guadalupe, who appeared as a mestiza with many indigenous symbols surrounding her. At a time when the native people were being extinguished, she spoke in the Nahuatl language, bringing a message of hope that they would survive. She promised to hear their lamentations and to remedy their miseries, pain, and suffering.

As a mestiza she represented the fusion of the two cultures that would become today's Latinos. Guadalupe was the vision and promise of the future. She became a healing force—one that planted seeds of forgiveness and compassion.[7] Today, Latinos recognize that the blood of the Spanish conquistadores runs through our veins and is present in the language we speak, and that many positive aspects of our fusion culture come from Spanish roots. We have forgiven the transgressions of our Spanish ancestors and now consider these forebears as part of our heritage and *familia*.

 Black people faced discrimination and racism by "sticking together." The We *in the song "We Shall Overcome" indicates an understanding that solidarity is their source of strength and salvation.*

Forgiveness also allows people to begin anew. At the start of each year, Cherokee tribal members make a procession to the stream and gather together. People then swirl water above their heads seven times. With each swirl, they wash away any thoughts or actions that are not beneficial for their future well-being. Particularly important is forgiving anyone who had offended or hurt them. Cleansing past grievances allows them to replenish relationships, strengthen the collective, and start with a clean slate each year.[8] This is similar to the Jewish day of atonement—

Yom Kippur—on which people ask forgiveness for transgressions of the previous year. Knowing that intentions are good but that for many reasons a person may falter, forgiveness is requested in advance for any mistakes in the coming year.

Sankofa—looking at history in the bright light of truth—is easier when the process includes forgiveness and reconciliation. Then the truth really can set us free! We can birth new understandings and new pathways. Forgiveness is an ability that was identified by Jesus as the crux of Christian living. It is also a wise and magnanimous leadership trait that allows people to learn from the past, reconcile mistakes, accept imperfections or limitations, and start new beginnings.

 If you look at the world, there are a lot of folks who are searching for who they are, for meaning in life. They have lost that spiritual connection. In my community, I could not even fathom the thought of separating the spirituality of who we are as a people from who I am.

—Benny Shendo Jr.

To achieve our vision of multicultural leadership requires nurturing the qualities of *gratitude, hope, and forgiveness*. These strengthen a leader's ability to validate people for their contributions, as well as to acknowledge their gifts and assets. As reflected in the stories of leaders in communities of color, *gracias* and hope seed a positive and unwavering belief in future possibilities. Spirituality in communities of color is not the "Sunday go to meeting" variety, but a survival and inspirational tactic that protects and nourishes people. Spirituality has served to sustain the collective and unifying force, to integrate social responsibility with spiritual responsibility, and to infuse leadership with spiritual activism.

Spirituality: A Collective and Unifying Force

IN MAINSTREAM LEADERSHIP, spirituality usually has self-development connotations. For instance, Peter Block, in *Stewardship: Choosing Service over Self-Interest*, defines leadership as a commitment to "working on yourself first."[9] Leadership guru Stephen Covey, in his mega-selling book *The Seven Habits of Highly Effective People*, focuses on individual character development and follows in the same vein.[10] When

Andrew Young searched for his own spiritual calling, he looked through a different lens: "Western Christian theology conceives of liberation primarily in personal terms. I needed to see the relationship among ethics, theology, and *socio-economic liberation*."[11]

African Americans, Latinos, and American Indians can testify that their *spiritual roots* are a collective and unifying force that historically sustained them during centuries of toil and discrimination, and today provide the strength and energy for leadership and social action. Indian spirituality reinforces people's collective identity and their relationship as brothers and sisters. Benny Shendo clarifies this: "If you look at the world, there are a lot of folks who are searching for who they are, for meaning in life. They have lost that spiritual connection. In my community, I could not even fathom the thought of separating the *spirituality* of who we are as a people from who I am. It is how we carry ourselves every day." The Jemez songs and ceremonial way of life are as circular and as constant as the seasons, reminding people of their relatedness with each other and with the tribe.

 The Church was the platform from which Black leadership sprang. It was a natural progression from spiritual responsibility *to social and political involvement.*

—Dr. Lea Williams

The waters of Hispanic spirituality run deep. *Fé* (faith) is a deeply seated thread that permeates everyday life and is visible through home altars, the wearing of holy medals, and *estaturas de santos* (statues of saints) and sacred items in visible places—even in cars. Latino leaders tap into this spiritual stream to inspire hope and sustain people's faith that by working together they can uplift the community and improve their lives. César Chávez captured how his faith fueled his activism: "I don't think I could base my will to struggle on cold economics or on some political doctrine. I don't think there would be enough to sustain me. For the basis must be faith."

The term *spiritual responsibility* reflects the integration of leadership, spirituality, and people's welfare in communities of color. Dr. Lea Williams remembers observing this when she was growing up: "The Church was the platform from which Black leadership sprang. It was a natural progression from *spiritual responsibility* to social and political involvement." Walters and Smith note the continuing importance of religion and the church in Black politics and leadership. They state that these are "incubators of political activism, race-group identity and solidarity, as well as a major institution of political leadership and resource mobilization."[12] Perhaps Chavez explained the integration of faith and social action most succinctly. During the *huelga* (farm workers' strike), when asked how they would achieve their goals, he said, "We're going to pray a lot and picket a lot."[13]

Spirituality Is Responsibility Toward Others

THE "BACKSEAT DRIVER" BRAND of religion tells people how to live, what life decisions to make, and what kind of lifestyle they should pursue. Often, however, such religions are not as concerned with providing the economic means, resources, or education that people need to have their basic needs met and to live with dignity. The intrusion of religious and morality platforms into politics has coincided with burgeoning poverty, homelessness, lack of medical insurance, failing education, and a rise in single-parent households. This is meant not to imply a direct cause and effect, only to point out that some religious groups in American have paid more attention to individual morality than to social responsibility.

 When relationships imply responsibility, spirituality is a moral obligation to ensure others' well-being and the collective good. *The leader as community steward and guardian of public values grows out of this conviction.*

When relationships imply responsibility, *spirituality is a moral obligation to ensure others' well-being and the collective good.* The leader as community steward and guardian of public values grows out of this conviction. Seeing people as relatives recognizes a spiritual connection and prescribes that people should treat one another with the respect (and obligation) due a valued family member. In fact, the truest sentiments of the Christian faith follow in this vein. People are described as brothers and sisters and are urged to feed the hungry, give shelter to those in need, and to take care of the sick.

Following this tradition, Andrew Young's family had a biblical creed that guided their lives: "From those to whom much has been given, much will be required." His family had a *living* faith—to serve God and their community, to give back, and to help others who were not as fortunate. Young grew up in a middle-class family in New Orleans. His father attended Howard University and became a dentist. His mother was a teacher. "In my family, faith and a good education were intertwined with the commission to serve others." Hungry strangers who heard of his grandmother's goodness always showed up at her house to get something to eat.[14]

> *I saw my life as one of helping people who were being discriminated against and had no voice.*
>
> —Federico Peña

Federico Peña's family settled in Texas over 250 years ago. His great-great-great-grandfather was a founder of Laredo, and his grandfather had a seat on the City Council. One of his ancestors served in the first territorial legislature, another served as mayor of Laredo, and yet another was president of the school board. In some cultures, this might be the perfect setup to think of oneself as privileged. Yet Peña was taught to never think of himself as better than others. Like his ancestors before him, he chose the path of public service. "I saw my life as one of helping people who were being discriminated against and had no voice."

His life has reflected this commitment. For May 1, 2006—designated as a nationwide "day without immigrants"—he asked the organizers of the Denver March if he could address the group. As a businessperson he certainly would not profit from standing up on such a divisive issue, but he urged people to speak out for what is right: "For those of us who attended religious worship this past weekend, we should conduct a full moral gut check as we watch immigrant workers wither in our deserts, drown in our rivers and die on our highways . . . *I believe that a great people live by their moral and ethical principles every day.* I believe that a nation earns respect when it shows compassion and decency." [15] Peña has also been a leader in Keep Colorado Safe, a campaign to defeat a proposed state constitution that would curtail services for illegal immigrants.

Leadership as Spiritual Activism

LADONNA HARRIS OBSERVES, "In American society, churches are one place, work is somewhere else, education is over there, and none of them relate to each other. For Indian people, *spirituality is the integrating force of their lives and the essence of leadership.*" The separation of spirituality from other aspects of life in the United States contributes to a moral schism whereby leaders can act in unethical and socially irresponsible manners and yet proclaim to be religious and church-going people.

A close look at U.S. history reveals this practice of isolating religion from other areas of one's life. Many European immigrants were fleeing religious persecution and oppressive state religions. The founding fathers purposely protected the nation from this type of government through the first amendment to the Constitution, which states there will not be an official religion and guarantees people freedom of religious expression. President Jefferson further expanded this into the concept of separation of church and state.

Although this concept preoccupies our leaders, the idea of having a discussion about morality, ethics, and spiritual responsibility falls by the wayside. Our congressional leaders are taken away in handcuffs or our president breaks moral codes, all still proclaiming they are churchgoers and good Christians. Perhaps the failing morality in political and in corporate leaders is due not to their lack of church attendance but to the lack of a moral and ethical code that integrates *social responsibility* and *spiritual responsibility*.

Senator Barack Obama believes Americans are looking for a deeper, fuller conversation about religion. In a *USA Today* article entitled "Politicians Need Not Abandon Religion," he

 I believe that a great people live by their moral and ethical principles every day. I believe that a nation earns respect when it shows compassion and decency.

—Federico Peña

stated, "It's wrong to ask believers to leave their religion at the door before entering the public square. Abraham Lincoln, William Jennings Bryan, Martin Luther King Jr.—indeed, the majority of great reformers in American history—were not only motivated by faith, they also used religious language to argue for their cause. To say men and women should not inject their 'personal morality' into policy debates is a practical absurdity; our law is by definition a codification of morality." [16]

Senator Obama is following the tradition of leaders in communities of color, who are expected to have a moral compass that guides their behavior and is reflected in their lives. Historically—as seen in the lives of Andrew Young, César Chávez, and Chief Seattle—leadership, responsibility, and spiritual activism have always been intertwined. Archbishop Romero of El Salvador was part of the liberation theology movement that interlaced social justice and responsibility, particularly for the poor in Latin American countries. During the turbulent 1960s, when California farm workers organized a union to advocate for decent wages and working conditions, they marched in a procession with a statue of Our Lady of Guadalupe leading the way. Chávez uplifted the farm workers' movement with such traditional religious practices as pilgrimages, fasting, retreats, public prayers, and worship services.

The use of fire hoses, billy clubs, and police dogs in Birmingham, Alabama is indelibly etched in America's memory. Andrew Young recounts how the civil rights movement was infused with new spirituality after the use of these intimidation methods and the arrests of their leader. "The marchers were praying and crying to no avail. Then someone shouted, 'God is with this movement.' Over five thousand people marched past the dogs and police singing the old spiritual, 'I want Jesus to walk with me. All along my pilgrim journey, Lord. I want Jesus to walk with me.' Bull Conner, the Birmingham police chief, was shouting, 'Stop them, stop them,' but nobody responded."[17]

According to Young, the paralysis of people who a few days previously had used violent methods to stop the demonstrators was evidence of the spiritual transformation and healing that was taking place. Young embraced the spiritual aspects of the civil rights movement as one that had come to "redeem America's soul." As Martin Luther King Jr. expressed it, "The religious aspect of our quest for justice is a struggle to make our society whole."[18]

Spirituality is integral to every aspect of the American Indians for Opportunity's Ambassadors Program. For example, the identity discussion "Who are you?" and the reflection on personal power "Where do we get our medicine or strength?" has to with a person's spirituality. Spirituality is the personal power or "medicine" a leader carries that allows the leader to contribute to the community and obtain greater consciousness, awareness, and balance. A person's spirit or personal strength will lift that person out of oppression, social inferiority, and self-doubt. Part of a leader's sacred duty is to ensure that the spirit is acknowledged in every aspect of the community's endeavors.

Spirituality in communities of color centers on people. The traditional African philosophy known as *seriti* lends great insight into this connection. *Seriti* is the spirit and power of all life that unites people with each other. It is also the vital life force of an individual and is therefore personal as well. However, *seriti* exists only in the *context of* interaction with others and the community. *Seriti* integrates a person's spiritual integrity with right action toward one's fellow man. One's *seriti* is a reflection of one's moral substance, influence, personal goodness, power, and humanity. The more good deeds one does in life, the more one shares with humanity, the greater one's *seriti* grows. If one does bad deeds, one's *seriti* diminishes.[19]

 Seriti *integrates a person's spiritual integrity with right action toward one's fellow man. One's* seriti *is a reflection of one's moral substance, influence, personal goodness, power, and humanity. The more good deeds one does in life, the more one shares with humanity, the greater one's* seriti *grows.*

Seriti explains why Nelson Mandela, after nearly three decades in jail, did not seek revenge on his persecutors. If he had done that, he would have been taking away from the goodness that comes from forgiveness. By so doing, his *seriti* would have been reduced. Through his forgiving and seeking reconciliation and by doing good, his life force—his *seriti*—and therefore that of his family, clan, and even his nation was enhanced.

Seeing spiritual responsibility as doing good for others has been quintessential in communities of color. This resonates with *seriti* and drives a collective and spiritually responsible form of leadership. Similar to the rising tide that lifts all boats, spirituality is a unifying force that uplifts the whole community. Through practicing gratitude and forgiveness and by being steadfast in their hope for the generations to come, communities of color have emerged as a spiritual force for healing and reconciliation and for creating a world in which people are grateful for what they have been given.

The principle *all my relatives* is based on the expansive view held in communities of color that the well-being of each individual is intricately tied to the well-being of all the people. The leader's role as community steward and advocate for the common good is grounded in the *spiritual responsibility* that comes from seeing people in this light. Communities of color who have weathered the storms of exploitation and kept their values of hope, gratitude, and forgiveness intact can now show the way to a more spiritually oriented form of leadership. The leadership principles from these communities reflect a congruency between the humanistic and democratic values we profess and the action it will take to build a truly authentic, equitable, and multicultural society.

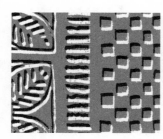

Reflecting on and Applying Principle Eight

Gracias—Gratitude, Hope, and Forgiveness

Practicing *gracias*

Gratitude focuses attention on what one has, not what one wants. It was a spiritual survival tactic for communities of color during centuries of oppression and lack. Practicing gratitude brings a sense of contentment with one's life. It can also be an antidote to the rampant materialism that is dividing our world into the haves and have-nots.

- This week, take five minutes each day and write down ten things for which you are grateful. The song "*Gracias a la Vida*" speaks to being thankful for seeing, hearing, and walking, the beauty of nature, and the relationships in your life. I like to include on my list ordinary things like a good cup of coffee, a warm bath, or a good meal. You will notice as the week goes by that you have a greater appreciation for yourself, the people in your life, and the many things you have.

- I continue this practice by ending each day with a reflection on things that happened that day for which I am grateful. If you try this for at least a week, you will find it makes for a positive ending to the day and may even help ensure a good night's sleep.

- In your organization or group, agree on a regular time for expressing gratefulness and appreciation to others (such as just before the weekly meeting). Start with organizational benefits and then share the talents, support, and efforts each individual brings to the group. If members have difficulty expressing this, use a nice piece of paper with each person's name on which everyone writes positive comments. Develop an *attitude of gratitude* and see people's motivation rise!

 (NEXT STEPS 5 CONTINUED)

- Develop a gratitude habit. Commit to a weekly "gratitude day" on which you make a point of thanking people for their help, ideas, good work, and commitment. An easy way to develop this habit is to name a gratitude day: Marvelous Mondays (to get each week started in a constructive way), or Thankful Thursdays, or Fortunate Fridays (to end the week on a positive note). On this day, send out emails, notes, or make a quick call and thank folks for their contributions during the past week. Mark your gratitude days on your calendar so you develop a habit of thanking folks on a regular basis!

Cherokee cleansing ceremony

Forgiveness is starting over, letting go of old transgressions, and making room for the new. Forgiveness can be an act of community affirmation. "Letting go and cleansing" ceremonies are useful after a contested election or difficult organizational change, to release old baggage, to start on a new track or strategic direction, and with individuals or groups who want to let go of past grievances.

- The group gathers in a circle around a crystal bowl filled with water, symbolizing the Cherokee walk to the river. Usually this happens outside, but this is not necessary. People step up individually, scoop a handful of water and swirl it above, stating what they want to release or whom they would like to forgive. This is not about people who are present, but rather obstacles, situations, or past experiences that stand in the way of growth and power.

- Using a journaling process, people write about grievances or things they would like to "get rid off." They can then reflect individually, share with the group, or both. People stand in a circle and either wad up the paper and throw it into a wastebasket, burn it in an urn, or bury it in the earth. It is important that each person make a statement about what he or she is releasing so that their "community" can support them in this.

Spirituality and social responsibility

- How is spirituality defined in communities of color and what role has it played in their ability to survive and thrive under adverse conditions? How does this spirituality anchor leadership?

- *Seriti,* which integrates one's spiritual integrity with right action toward one's fellow humans, bridges individual spirituality with responsibility to others. Why is this integration a critical need in our world today? Who are some leaders whose *seriti*—energy and power—reflects a strong moral force and goodness toward humanity? Think of people you know and have observed, not necessarily the more prominent leaders.

Recommended readings and resources

- *Long Walk to Freedom: The Autobiography of Nelson Mandela* by Nelson Mandela (Little, Brown, 1995).

- *Our Lady of Guadalupe: Faith and Empowerment Among Mexican-American Women* by Jeannette Rodriguez (University of Texas Press, 1994).

PART FOUR

Leadership for a Multicultural Age—

A Call to Action

HIS FINAL PART IS *a call to action*—an invitation to plant the seeds of multicultural leadership and then nurture their growth and potential. We will take an expansive and organic approach that begins with the individual, extends to the organizational level, considers the need for active participation in our nation, and concludes with the *finale*—the big picture—leadership for our multicultural age!

We begin by looking at a concept known as *destino* in the Latino community, which is similar to an African American's *calling* and the American Indian tradition of the *vision quest*. Becoming a multicultural leader is a *calling* to be part of the global community that is dawning. Once you say *Yes* to the call, you embark on an ambitious journey that starts with a commitment to embodying such qualities as generosity, social responsibility, and service to one's community.

For people to become multicultural leaders, they must understand the difference between *assimilation* and *acculturation*. The American melting pot required immigrants to shed their ethnic and national backgrounds and assimilate. This created cultural uniformity and discounted the contributions that diverse groups made to America. But today, effective leadership requires the ability to acculturate, which allows people to be receptive, skillful, and adaptable to other cultures while staying centered in their own.

By looking more deeply at these two processes, we can discern how acculturation is the portal to our multicultural age.

Next, we will discuss instilling multicultural principles into our organizations that have traditionally operated from a monocultural reference point or in a hierarchical pluralistic fashion. Being able to benefit from cultural integration calls for *egalitarian pluralism,* whereby the unique traditions and contributions of diverse people become part of the organizational framework. The distinctions between *hierarchical* and *egalitarian pluralism* will be considered in depth (a table contrasting their key differences appears in the Next Steps section).

The convergence of the leadership principles of communities of color with American business practices can create a socially responsible environment—one that underscores the role of business in supporting the welfare of our communities and our quality of life. Our exploration of the applicability of multicultural principles to the business arena includes a review of a few corporations that have embraced socially equitable practices. The long-term benefits, effective use, and dissemination of these principles in business, however, warrant additional research and implementation strategies.

We will also acknowledge a number of global pioneers who are following the multicultural principles that stem from communities of color. These leaders are reaching across the world to assist people regardless of national origin, color, class, or race. Four of these enlightened leaders, who embrace the mantle of social responsibility and are breaking the individualistic paradigm, are profiled. They can serve as prototypes of how Anglo leaders can take their place as multicultural leaders of the future.

An authentically multicultural society will fulfill the promise of democracy. To build a more perfect union requires the transformation of our civic culture into one in which *life, liberty, and the pursuit of happiness* are equally accessible and the road to prosperity is open to all people. Multicultural principles provide a blueprint that can invigorate our democracy, enlarge our vision of what it means to be American, and welcome the full inclusion of many cultures and traditions.

The eight principles explored in this book also have a *universality* that cuts across cultures and offer connecting points for building world community. The voices of the leaders contained in this book and the principles that have guided them can position us to be good neighbors in our multicultural age.

The Call to Multicultural Leadership

IN MY LAST YEAR OF COLLEGE, I struggled with an internal tug of war. I was a Latina in a strange intellectual terrain, a culturally alien land. During my four years of college, I never met another Latino student. The University of Florida admitted only two African Americans during my senior year. I finished college before affirmative action, before Latinos became a recognized ethnic group, and before women started filling up the ranks on college campuses. For a Nicaraguan female immigrant from a low-income family to obtain a college education in the early 1960s was as rare as the glorious quetzal bird that floats in the tropical rainforests. Why was I given the prize of a higher education?

Latinos have an intriguing concept known as *destino* or destiny that suggests that outside forces and a greater power guide one's life. *Destino* relates to one's purpose—the content or exact nature of one's life. To understand one's *destino,* one must do some soul searching. Reflecting on family history, significant events, talents and inherent gifts or positive attributes, the circumstances of one's birth, early experiences, and so on, can steer the way to a deeper understanding of one's *destino.* As one embraces one's life journey, *destino* grows, becomes clearer and more encompassing.

Destino is in sharp contrast to the Euro-American belief in individual effort and self-determination. Latinos believe it is impossible to control chance, serendipity, fate, or unplanned events. Life, they feel, is a dance between individual efforts and the lessons, gifts, and experiences life brings. Like an acorn that must be nurtured to grow into the great oak, the seeds of one's *destino* must be nourished and can flourish only with care and effort. *Destino* is the existential core, the "overarching purpose" that Robert Greenleaf believed anchors servant leaders. When Stephen Covey urges leaders to examine their values and principles and develop a personal mission statement to guide their lives, he is asking them to explore their *destino.* This type of reflection provides firm footing when the waters are turbulent and there are tough life decisions to make.

When I was twenty-one and about to graduate from college, I was wading in some very turbulent waters—*what should I do with my life?* I was given many unique opportunities, for which I was deeply grateful. In keeping with *mi cultura y familia* and in the spirit of *We* cultures, I wanted to give back. During my soul searching, President Kennedy was shot. Kennedy was not only an inspiration to my generation, he was revered by

Latinos who saw a charismatic and socially responsible leader who resonated with our cultural values. Inspired by his call to public service, I told my dear parents, "I'm joining the Peace Corps and going to South America."

"*Aye Dios mío!*" If going 120 miles away to college was a cultural taboo, going to the other side of the world was a category five hurricane. What could my *padres* do? I was twenty-one and as stubborn as the mahogany that grows in the Nicaraguan jungle. Telling me over and over that I could always come home, my family watched as their petrified, yet excited, youngest daughter boarded a plane for Santiago, Chile. I was following my *destino*! I was too young to understand it then, but I had answered the call to service, to following the path of leadership, and to becoming a world citizen.

Destino: A Calling and Personal Vision

IN HIS BRILLIANT EXPLORATION of mystical and mythological journeys, the renowned scholar Joseph Campbell identifies answering the call or invitation as the first step in personal transformation. The call beckons a person to a new level of awareness, skill, and increased freedom. The call is a challenge to grow, to engage in an adventure, to delve into the unknown, and to seek greater fulfillment.[1] The leaders whose voices speak to us in this book answered the call to serve their communities, to work for the advancement of humankind, and to don the mantle of leadership.

Traditionally, in many American Indian tribes, answering one's life's calling was done through a solitary vision quest in which one answered the question, "Who am I? What is my vision, and what was I born to do?" A person's vision is power, unique purpose, or medicine. In the American Indian tradition, visions unveil the meaning and purpose of one's life.

A *calling* in the African American community refers to one's life work and connotes a spiritual force that magnetizes a person. When one accepts one's calling, through reflection, prayer, and intuitive insight, the way unfolds. In the Black community, there is a strong connection between one's calling and the uplifting of one's people. Andrew Young recalls the leaders of the civil rights movement: "Everyone had a calling. Most were religious and spiritual leaders who understood that the gospel could be applied to political and economic situations. We were committed to confronting segregation and focused on a specific moral agenda."[2]

At his commencement speech at Connecticut College in 1998, Young counseled students to heed their personal calling. "I want you to look at the world and realize it calls you to leadership. You needn't know where you are going. You only need to take one step at a time. History will lead you down the paths of excellence and creativity."[3]

The time in history in which one lives does indeed influence one's calling. Civil rights, the women's movement, and the emerging of a diverse society are important dynamics that affected my calling and shaped the *shared calling* of Black leaders who confronted segregation as well. There are pervasive movements and social changes that shape and define a whole generation. Leaders must be acutely aware and understand the long-term implications of these movements. To be relevant and effective, leaders must be in sync with the pulse of their times. Therefore, it follows that, given the powerful influence diversity will have in defining the twenty-first century, those who step up to leadership today must also answer the call to multicultural leadership.

Everyone had a calling. Most were religious and spiritual leaders who understood that the gospel could be applied to political and economic situations. We were committed to confronting segregation and focused on a specific moral agenda.

—Andrew Young

Making a Personal Commitment

THE FIRST STEP in making a decision is to establish your intention. Intention is the result you would like to achieve, the ideal you are committed to. Like an arrow headed straight for the bull's-eye, intention is willpower, determination, unerring focus, and an unrelenting belief that you will achieve the desired end. The strongest intentions stir the heart's desire. In reality, the call to becoming a multicultural leader is setting your intentions to serve a purpose greater and nobler than yourself.

The next step is to assess your abilities as a multicultural leader—your background, experiences, exposure to different cultures, and any negative images you may have about certain groups. If you are a person of color, your experience with people outside of your community may be just as limited as that of a White person who lives in the suburbs. A helpful barometer in this process is to understand where you fall on the *assimilation—acculturation continuum* (see Next Steps at the end of this part). This is useful in planning steps to expand your cultural competency. First, let us look at the process of assimilation and its role in forging the U.S. identity. Then we will explore acculturation as a pathway to multicultural leadership.

Assimilation: The Entrada to the American Dream

Assimilation melded one people out of the myriad nationalities that came to our shores, facilitated our national cohesion and character development, and unified our young country. Eager to belong, White immigrants cut ties to their homelands and forgot the customs and language of their grandparents. Assimilation set the tone for a country where conformity, homogeneity, and valuing sameness were the *entrada* to the American dream. *Et pluribus unum*—to make one out of many—was the crucible of the American experiment.

 Assimilation set the tone for a country where conformity, homogeneity, and valuing sameness were the entrada to the American dream. Et pluribus unum—to make one out of many—was the crucible of the American experiment.

Cutting one's roots and losing touch with one's grandparents can be painful and leave a sense of disorientation. People who make such sacrifices often demand that others do likewise. "If I gave up my ancestry and language, why do you insist on holding on to yours? What I am gaining must be worth my sacrifice." The country and way of life people were embracing had to be superior. Assimilation fed ethnocentricity, which in turn bred cultural insensitivity and a predisposition to impose our values on others. The understanding that all cultures are unique expressions of the human experience was as lost as the languages our grandparents spoke.

Today, the English Only movement indicates that some people still see assimilation as necessary to cultural cohesion. (Contrast this with Chile, where a national initiative aims to have all people bilingual in Spanish and English by 2020.) People of color are also pushed to assimilate and fit into the dominant U.S. culture in order to succeed. In communities of color, this has been called *whitewashing*. Raul Yzaguirre passionately reflects on how difficult this is for Latinos: "The road to success that has been offered is to assimilate, change your name, and lose your accent. All those things hold an empty promise that will result in a hollowing out. *'Te quita el corazon'*—it rips out your heart."

His insights reflect the internal and external struggle communities of color have grappled with for generations.

Some of the highly assimilated believe that the United States is the best country in the world—and that people (even in other countries) would be better off if they adopted our values. They rarely venture out of their cultural comfort zone. If they travel, they stay in American enclaves. Assimilated people believe others should "fit in." A person of color who has fully assimilated strives to dress, talk, and act like White people. Although assimilation crafted one nation out of the potpourri that came to America during the formative stages of our nation, as our country evolves into a multicultural nation, assimilation is no longer an adaptive advantage. The path to multicultural competency and understanding today is not assimilation, but acculturation! But wait a minute—can a person shed the skin of assimilation and learn to acculturate?

It Is N-e-v-e-r Too Late to Acculturate

As it was for other students in that era, America's ethnocentric tenor was part of my education. I joined the Peace Corps to help *those countries* south of the border, which I had learned were backward and desperately needed the help of powerful Uncle Sam. Imagine my culture shock to find that Santiago had an old European flavor, with flower-lined *avenidas* that surrounded stately museums and ornate government buildings. Chile was the second oldest democracy in the hemisphere, with educated, informed people. President Frei was Hispanic, as were the senators, the cabinet members, the mayors of all the cities, the presidents of Chilean universities, the directors of television stations, and the heads of its army, navy, and every major business. Growing up in the good old USA, I had no idea that someone of my race could achieve such high-level leadership. Successful people in my childhood were, without exception, White—which is still true for most leaders in top positions.

I realized then that although the land of opportunity had given me many gifts, I had been stripped of my cultural pride and history. The knowledge, contributions, and exquisite histories of the inhabitants before Columbus had been buried like the lost city of the Incas. Thus began the redemption of my Hispanic soul. I embraced my multicultural heritage. *I am Latina and American*. I chose the path of acculturation. Latinos call acculturation *crossing over*—it means a person has learned to go back and forth between cultures and functions successfully in both.

An Invitation to Acculturate

Unlike assimilation, whereby one's culture, language, and background are discarded, acculturation is an *add on*, expanding process. Acculturation requires proactively engaging in cross-cultural experiences, which begins with listening and being open to learning. One must be willing to step out of one's cultural conditioning, gain knowledge of and adapt to diverse perspectives. Acculturation increases one's cultural repertoire, creativity, adaptability, and flexibility, and promotes cross-cultural competency. When people learn to acculturate, they can thrive in different cultural environments.

 Acculturation increases one's cultural repertoire, creativity, adaptability, and flexibility, and promotes cross-cultural competency. When people learn to acculturate, they can thrive in different cultural environments.

One can learn to acculturate by nurturing friendships with people of diverse backgrounds, reading books on other cultures, taking courses that expand one's cultural repertory, joining organizations that serve communities different from one's own, and championing diversity practices at work. Active engagement might also include attending churches of different denominations, learning another language or key words to indicate respect, living in an integrated neighborhood, or traveling to different countries. Many people have hosted foreign exchange students or joined international clubs where they can learn about other countries and cultures. By systematically seeking out these types of experiences, leaders develop a cultural fluidity and adaptability that enables them to tailor their practices and approaches to diverse people, environments, and situations.

On a societal level, to achieve cultural equity and reciprocity, White Americans must acculturate to other cultures' norms and ways of thinking and acting. Reflecting on the principles in this book and integrating these into one's frame of reference can facilitate this process. There are people who have been exposed to many cultures and are successfully acculturated. This includes people of color, Peace Corps volunteers, people who have worked in other countries, our neighbors who are naturalized citizens, recent immigrants, and aficionados of languages and cultures. They can serve as great mentors and guides in the exciting adventure of acculturation.

Yzaguirre explains how acculturation is beneficial for Hispanics and society as a whole: "Hispanic success for both practical and quality of life reasons needs to be,

'I treasure who I am, I treasure my parents, my culture, my language, and I don't have to give any of that up in order to succeed. Indeed, if I keep all those things, it will make me more successful in pragmatic as well as self-fulfilling terms. Latinos have a unique contribution to make to America and we can't do that if we give up our cultural core which makes us who we are." Acculturation allows people to share their cultural gifts and to enjoy the fruits of our multicultural cornucopia.

Remember, assimilation—acculturation is a continuum. Since culture is learned, people can constantly be upgrading their skills and understanding of how to relate to our rich diversity. The important thing is to continue being inquisitive and open-minded and to keep learning about our multicultural age.

Creating Multicultural Organizations

ANSWERING THE CALL TO MULTICULTURAL LEADERSHIP also implies changing organizational structures. Most U.S. organizations today are fashioned around Euro-American culture and hierarchical structures. Although diverse people are included, they must assimilate, adhere to dominant cultural values, and follow prescribed behavior. This is described as *hierarchical pluralism*, and it prevents organizations from genuinely benefiting from cultural diversity.

Dismantling Hierarchical Pluralism

Dr. Joseph explains the limitations of hierarchical pluralism: "Dominant cultural values are at the top and are impermeable. Everyone has to conform to them. People who are different can come in and be included, but they must understand their traditions don't mean anything. Their values are subservient and they must adapt." The underlying message of hierarchical pluralism is *"We who are in control don't have to change because our way is better!"* This translates into people of color having to fit in—read the script, wear the uniform, talk and think like their White counterparts.

To be able to do this, they must identify White cultural norms, which is difficult because the dominant culture is invisible and unacknowledged. Because Whites are often blind to their own existence as a group, as well as their advantages and privileges, they don't understand that *business as usual* is really *doing business our way.* In their creative book on diversity in the workplace, *Leading in Black and White*, Ancella Livers and

Keith Caver coined an interesting term, *miasma*, to emphasize how elusive White culture is to Black managers. *Miasma* is defined as a diaphanous fog—a state of unease, difficult to grasp, but ever-present—a confusing murky environment of misperception and distortion in which Black managers work.

Miasma is based on the assumption that everyone is the same and includes a low tolerance for differences. Livers and Caver further observe, "Blacks often feel that Whites are sizing up their professional potential and suitability by how closely they fit or emulate White middle-class norms." Since miasma is elusive, but real, the actual reason Black managers don't fit in or succeed is never recognized or addressed. Livers and Caver believe this has created a racial divide in corporate America. The result is that Black managers become isolated or estranged and assume a guarded or defensive stance. [4]

People of color who do succeed often shrink their cultural identity. This has led to additional segmentation in communities of color, as their best and brightest become distant from their communities. Many refer to this as window dressing and tokenism, not inclusion. The end result of hierarchical pluralism is that organizations dissipate the vitality and assets of the increasingly multicultural workforce. They do not reap the talents, unique perspectives, knowledge, creativity, innovation, and energy that diversity generates. At the very least, people who are different "check out" and are less participatory and motivated.

 The end result of hierarchical pluralism is that organizations dissipate the vitality and assets of the increasingly multicultural workforce. They do not reap the talents, unique perspectives, knowledge, creativity, innovation, and energy that diversity generates.

Egalitarian Pluralism

The alternative is *egalitarian pluralism*, which opens the door to the values and perspectives of the cultural mosaic that makes up the whole. Egalitarian pluralism is representative of all people in an organization, not just those who have traditionally held power. Organizations must be willing to reinvent themselves by altering their language, structure, and methods of operations. They must change the guard, welcoming diverse leaders to the table to share their perspectives and experiences. This takes deep listening and open dialogue. New forms are created that integrate everyone's experiences, ideas, and unique contributions. *Changing structures, norms, and values is the key to egalitarian pluralism and the foundation for multicultural organizations.*

Operating organizations from an egalitarian framework is new territory to explore and is the challenging work facing multicultural leaders. This exciting venture can begin with discussing and integrating practices such as the leader as equal, collective and shared responsibility, and generosity and reciprocity. Pluralism, which is one of the founding values of our nation, cannot be realized until leadership at all levels, especially the higher echelons, truly reflects our diversity. The values and principles of multicultural leadership enumerated in this book can guide organizations in this transformation. These values and principles also offer people of color, who have *mainstreamed* into dominant-culture organizations, an alternative way of leading that resonates with their communities. By incorporating multicultural principles, they can take the lead in creating work environments that are more accommodating to diversity and do not demand cultural conformity to succeed. These principles validate their abilities as multicultural people and strategically position them for leadership in our global age.

Making Good While Doing Good

The application of multicultural leadership principles in business can create a socially responsible environment—one that upholds the welfare of our communities and benefits people by fairly distributing profits. Federico Peña, who joined the business sector and is currently managing director for Vestar Capital Partners, relates how this benefits business: "What I learned is, you actually develop better business cultures. Just like when I was in politics, people believe in your values, ethics, honesty, and your commitment to support the community and do right by it." There is evidence today that enlightened business leaders are looking to socially sound business practices that are in alignment with multicultural leadership.

John Mackey, corporate chairperson of Whole Foods—a company noted for its equitable business practices—remarks, "There is no inherent reason why business cannot be ethical, socially responsible, and profitable." Whole Foods believes in paying a decent wage (the lowest salary is $13.15 an hour) and provides excellent benefits including health care. They operate through decentralized teamwork that empowers people and encourages autonomy. The company has a "Declaration of Interdependence," which includes an unwavering commitment to diversity, community, and saving the planet.[5]

In 2005, *Fortune* magazine ranked TDIndustries twenty-second out of the hundred best companies to work for. TDI is a specialty construction company that is employee-owned, with annual revenues of $248 million and 1,300 employees. Employees elect the board of directors and refer to each other as *partners.* There are no fancy offices or special perks for executives. The compensation scale designates that no one makes more than ten times the average wage. The CEO of TDIndustries is not robbing his employees of pensions and a decent wage to amass a fortune—unlike the average U.S. corporate CEO, who as of 2005 makes 411 times more than the typical American worker.[6]

This fair wage scale is an example of the cross-pollination of equitable business practices. Retired CEO Jack Lowe remarks, "We got this idea from Whole Foods, where no executive can make more than fourteen times the employee average."[7]

Another example is Southwest Airlines, which marked thirty-five consecutive years of profitability while many airlines struggled against bankruptcy. *Fortune* magazine recognized Southwest as one of the top ten businesses to work for and *Business Ethics* listed them as one of its 100 Best Corporate Citizens.[8] Southwest pays employees more than any other airline, and has a strong profit-sharing plan and stock options. Employees are encouraged to share their cost-cutting ideas, which add to profitability. This employee spirit resulted in the *New York Times* naming Southwest first among airlines for customer service.[9] Providing avenues for people to share ownership and the benefits of their work is a tried-and-true formula for success in communities of color. These companies show that these are sound business practices as well.

Federico Peña believes being socially responsible is good for business. "Big business relies on consumers who need jobs to buy products. If consumers are poor, if purchasing power is declining, companies are not going to be able to sell their products or are going to have to reduce their prices. If you are a smart CEO, you recognize that to have success in the private sector, consumers have to be successful. If we are going to outsource services, we need small businesses that are healthy. This means that everyone has to win. In a way, it is like our relationship to Mexico. When I was with the Clinton administration, we provided loans to Mexico. We knew that as our second largest trading partner, their economy was supporting our economy."

Andrew Young recounts a story illustrating the power that business has in building the diverse and equitable society. People who know their history remember the Birmingham demonstrations where Black people were beaten by police, yet successfully implemented an economic boycott. Many do not know that negotiations with the Committee of One Hundred, the top business leaders in Birmingham, actually ended the de facto segregation practices. By desegregating downtown shops, lunch counters, and public facilities, the business leaders were actually breaking the laws of the state of Alabama. Decades later, when Young went to South Africa, where people were breaking apartheid laws, he surmised, "Anything is legal if one hundred corporate citizens decide to make it legal."[10] Reminiscent of Birmingham, economic sanctions persuaded businesses in South Africa that the price of apartheid was too steep!

If you are a smart CEO, you recognize that to have success in the private sector, consumers have to be successful. If we are going to outsource services, we need small businesses that are healthy. This means that everyone has to win.

—Federico Peña

Since leadership in communities of color has generally arisen from the public and nonprofit sectors, the development of multicultural business models has only recently started emerging. Research on methods for integrating multicultural models and instilling leadership principles from communities of color into the business sector is an inspiring and worthwhile future endeavor. Similar to the challenge of developing multicultural organizations, this is still evolving and there is much more work to be done.

One reason is that companies owned by Blacks, Latinos, and American Indians are small-scale and privately owned. The U.S. Census Bureau reported that in 2002 only 12.7 percent of Hispanic-owned firms had paid employees; about 50 percent of these had only one to four employees, and only 2.2 percent reported fifty employees or more.[11] This would indicate that future efforts to propagate multicultural leadership should include further studies on infusing employee ownership and profit sharing into small businesses. One area where small businesses have made a mark is that of strong community involvement and financial contributions to social issues. Minority Chambers of Commerce are actively involved in providing resources, jobs, and talent to their communities.

In addition to organizations and businesses, our quest to advance multicultural leadership must surely include the public sector, where decisions that affect our quality of life are made and laws that can limit or nourish diversity are crafted. We must remember that pluralism and equality were part of the very bedrock of our nation, and that fulfilling these ideals is the promise of our democracy.

Pluralism and Diversity: The Promise of Democracy

TODAY, LEADERSHIP IN THE PUBLIC AND POLITICAL ARENAS that are responsible for the common good is anemic and needs a civic transfusion. The U.S. democracy was born from the vision of representative government. Yet the exploding cost of campaigns has deformed politics into a money-grabbing pursuit. In 2000, the average cost for a U.S. House of Representatives campaign was $636,000, and for senate races it was a staggering $5.6 million. Even more disconcerting—the biggest spenders won 94 percent of congressional races and 85 percent of senatorial.[12] *These facts have led people to say the United States has the best government that money can buy!*

The disparity between ordinary Americans and elected officials is evident when we note that in 2006, 28 percent of congressional representatives and 33 percent of senators are millionaires. Fewer than 1 percent of Americans overall are in that category. The halls of Congress are also filled with lawyers—42 percent of representatives and 63 percent of senators.[13] This is not to imply that lawyers and millionaires cannot be exemplary public servants and guardians of the public good. However, the rising poverty rates, increasing lack of medical insurance, and low wages are only a few indicators suggesting that today's congressional leaders are not addressing barriers or actively constructing a society that takes care of its people.

Our elected government is further divided from the general population by the inequitable racial and gender representation. Although women make up the majority of our people, they are only 14 percent of senators and a measly 16 percent of Congress. Moreover, in a country whose 2000 census declared that 30 percent of the population was a racial or ethnic minority, *97 percent of senators are White!* But a ray of hope is shining through the congressional window. Perhaps due to the incredible momentum of civil rights, African Americans, who make up 12 percent of the population, hold 10 percent of seats in the U.S. Congress. Hispanics, who make up 13 percent of the population, now fill 6 percent of congressional seats.[14] We cannot, however, solely blame political leaders for being *banditos* of the public funds or lament the fact that diversity and accessibility is not a hallmark of our national government. The concept of "consent to lead" implies that these leaders do what they do because they have tacit consent from the governed; besides, they were elected. There is also the apathy of people who feel they can't make a difference and outright boycotting by voters who refuse to participate and purposefully stay away from the polls. This has resulted in the United States ranking 139th out of 172 democratic nations in voter participation.[15] In the 2004 elections, only 64 percent of eligible citizens casts their votes. Even though this is politically embarrassing, this was the highest participation since 1968. African Americans who struggle for centuries to access the ballot box participated at only 60 percent, while Latinos voting was a discouraging 47 percent.[16] The dismal health of American politics is perhaps the most critical challenge of the new century and is intimately intertwined with the pressing need for multicultural leadership.

The leadership principles in communities of color grew out of historical exclusion; the need for political influence necessitated *community empowerment* and arduous community organizing. Leadership in communities of color rests on a tradition of active citizenship. Voter registration campaigns, mass demonstrations, community education, legal battles, and political activities peppered the social and political movements of the last century. In communities of color, leaders rose up who garnered their authority by working for the public good and addressing barriers that perpetuated inequity and economic disparity. This is the very essence of community stewardship.

Sankofa advises us to remember the lessons of the past. Making good on the promise of justice and equality has required the long-term involvement of a critical mass of people who demanded social responsibility and social reform. Healing American democracy will require a revival of civic leadership—a critical mass of people who are committed to shaping our democracy into a genuinely pluralistic, equitable, and multicultural society. The leadership principles in communities of color offer a blueprint for the regeneration of American democracy, but *there are no shortcuts*. Active citizenship will always be the lifeblood of a healthy democracy.

 The leadership principles in communities of color grew out of historical exclusion; the need for political influence necessitated community empowerment and arduous community organizing. Leadership in communities of color rests on a tradition of active citizenship.

The New Face of Multicultural and Global Leadership

THE LEADERS IN THIS BOOK offer commendable examples of working for the betterment of one's community and country. They are, however, only the tip of the iceberg. Thousands of inspired leaders in communities of color are doing great work. Nonetheless, this is not enough! Multicultural leadership implies being inclusive and welcoming diverse people to the table. Infusing multicultural principles into our organizations and society will require reaching out, building diverse alliances, and starting new partnerships. It is my hope that this book will inspire people from many different backgrounds to embrace the vision of the new world that awaits us and to join with us in creating our multicultural future!

 Multicultural leadership implies being inclusive and welcoming diverse people to the table. Infusing multicultural principles into our organizations and society will require reaching out, building diverse alliances, and starting new partnerships.

For this reason, I have chosen to include four leaders who, unlike the leaders in communities of color we have met, are *White men*. These leaders have broken free of their cultural conditioning and are forgoing individualism and materialism to follow a magnanimous desire to serve humanity. They are taking on the mantle of social and global responsibility, and they offer testimony that the path of multicultural and global leadership is being followed by people of many backgrounds. Although these leaders have all achieved wealth and status, each has looked back, looked forward, and said, "I want a greater purpose in life. I want to do good for humanity." And they have.

We will look at their work in light of the eight multicultural principles. By anchoring their work in these principles, we will unify and integrate a framework that others can emulate.

We should point out that a person need not be rich and famous (like the men we profile here) to have that "Aha!" moment when the search for a meaningful life beckons to a greater purpose. The transformation of our society and world into a benevolent and caring one in which all people are treated as relatives will take the best efforts of all of us. The call to multicultural leadership is an opportunity to grow, to engage in an adventure, and to seek greater personal fulfillment. All are welcomed at the table.

Now let us look briefly at the four men who have answered the call and are stepping over the threshold into our multicultural age.

All My Relatives Live on Planet Earth

If there is any doubt that human beings are connected, think of the first time you saw the photograph taken from space of our exquisite planet, engulfed in waterfall colors of blues and greens, this place we all call home. The sense of interdependence, community stewardship, and civic consciousness that abounds in multicultural leadership also implies a responsibility to protect the natural environment that sustains life. The perils facing our environment threaten the imperative of the seventh-generation rule that we must preserve the world and make life better for our children and for future generations.

Al Gore is now devoting his life to addressing this challenge and is a spokesperson for environmental stewardship and for curtailing global warming. Those who see the film *An Inconvenient Truth* will witness a new Al Gore—one who is on fire with purpose. He is rallying people to change the consumer orientation of their own lives and to exert pressure on the political system through mass citizen education and involvement. By serving a cause greater than he is and motivating people to action, Gore follows in the tradition of leaders in this book. He is preparing one thousand people to present his slide show on global warming and thus is fostering a community of leaders and ensuring continuity.[17] Gore's social stewardship follows the path of a leader as *guardian of the public values.* He is embracing generosity by pledging the profits of his movie and book to furthering the cause of environmental sanity.

All Lives Are Equal

To some people, being the richest man in the world might seem like living on easy street. Bill Gates has chosen a different path. As we have discussed, wealth in communities of color entails *greater social responsibility and generosity.* Following this tradition, Gates has pledged his wealth to the Bill and Melinda Gates Foundation, which rests on two values that reflect multicultural leadership principles—*All lives have equal value* and

From those to whom much has been given, much is expected.[18] The Foundation's values are also in accord with the guiding principles described in this book: being humble and seeking counsel from outside voices; responsible advocacy; treating people with respect and as valued partners; and being a good steward of resources. The foundation's mission is to assist those in greatest need around the globe. Melinda Gates conveys this commitment: "Bill and I are both equally passionate about, how do you lift these people up from poverty? What can be done for the world? What can be done for good?" One shining example is the Global Alliance for Vaccines and Immunizations, which will protect the lives of about ten million of the world's poorest children.[19]

Generosity: Giving Wealth Back to Society

Giving one's wealth back to society certainly reflects the generosity so intrinsic to communities of color. When Warren Buffett pledged his $40 billion fortune to the Gates Foundation, he joined the ranks of leaders who seek to benefit the common good and set the course for the redistribution of wealth. "I don't believe in dynastic wealth," says Buffett. "[That] really strikes me as flying in the face of what this country is really about. We believe in meritocracy and equality of opportunity."[20] This aligns with the principle of the leader as a *guardian of public values* who works for a more equitable society.

To be a *leader among equals*, one must remain an ordinary person, never acting more important than others or parading the trappings of wealth and status. Buffett lives in the same gray stucco house he purchased in Omaha four decades ago for $31,500. He caps his annual salary as Berkshire Hathaway's chairperson at $100,000, which is chump change considering that the CEO of AOL Time Warner raked in $77.3 million in total compensation for 2001, the CEO of Wal-Mart made $17.1 million, and the CEO of Coca-Cola $105 million (in fact, the top-paid CEO in 2005 made a whopping $250 million[21]). Like an ordinary Joe, Buffett prefers burgers or steaks and Coca-Cola to fancy cuisine.[22]

The Rock Star's Crusade for Justice

Bono is an itinerant preacher, troubadour, and world activist for the poorest and most vulnerable people in the world; he has been nominated for the Nobel Prize. The lead singer of the famed Irish Band U2 is challenging the materialistic bent of modern culture. "For a lot of people the world is a desperate place. A third of the people cannot achieve sustenance.

And there is no real reason for that, other than selfishness and greed." He refers to the African principle of *Ubuntu—I am because we are*—as guiding his work.

Bono's campaign integrates spiritual responsibility and activism. "I am wary of faith outside of action. I am wary of religiosity that ignores the wider world." As a *guardian of public values,* he is a lead player in ONE—The Campaign to Make Poverty History, a global partnership between eleven international aid organizations, and the Millennium Campaign, which urges nations to spend an additional 1 percent of their budget to end poverty. "We see that this journey of equity, which came through the civil rights movement in the United States, has now switched to what's going on in Africa. If we really believed that these people were equal to us, we couldn't let this happen. This is about *justice, not poverty.* It is racism disguised by distance."[23]

These four leaders have heard the drumbeat of social responsibility and are following the path of generosity. They are upholding the common good and are uplifting people's lives. As such, they join with multicultural leaders across the planet who are rekindling the flame of our collective humanity and reminding us that there is one human family.

Sankofa—Shaping Our Global Future

$\mathint$ANKOFA, THE MYTHICAL BIRD FROM WEST AFRICA, looks backward and counsels us to retrieve and integrate the past. *Sankofa* also stands with its two feet *facing forward*, reminding us to constantly be creating and nurturing a more inspiring future. We are living in a fluid moment in history. Great cultural shifts are redefining our global landscape. A colorful multicultural bazaar where many cultures intersect and interact is replacing the Euro-American dominance that shaped the past five centuries. The emergence of a global culture that contains within it the jewels of many traditions will be the defining characteristic of the twenty-first century. The principles in this book invite people to incorporate new ways of leading that expand their effectiveness in this increasingly diverse world.

 Sankofa, *the mythical bird from West Africa, looks backward and counsels us to retrieve and integrate the past.* Sankofa *also stands with its two feet* facing forward, *reminding us to constantly be creating and nurturing a more inspiring future.*

These principles—

- Learn from the past

- Have a collective sense of community

- Treat each other as relatives

- Act generously and do not take more than your share

- Practice gratitude, hope, and forgiveness

- Have an indomitable hope for our future

—are all *universally inspiring values* that can uplift humanity and heal our fragile planet. Likewise, defining leaders as *guardians of the public welfare* with a responsibility to tend to the common good is an ancient tradition and one to hold up as the Excalibur of leadership. All cultures benefit from leaders who function as *community stewards*, are honest and respectful of others, have high integrity, and set the standard for others to emulate. As *one among equals*, these leaders share responsibility and develop a community of leaders who can guide the positive evolution of our planet.

Multicultural leadership reflects humanistic values that promote justice and equality and integrate *spiritual responsibility* and *social accountability*. The strife and poverty in our world would not exist if leaders followed these values and became the sculptors of an equitable and caring world. Multicultural leadership also implies global stewardship, which honors the diversity *and* universality of the one human family.

Like the radiant and multicolored flowers in a garden, the multihued birds, or a luminescent rainbow, diversity represents life's vigor, variety, and unending beauty. To craft our global future, this magnificent world must be our vision. Multicultural leaders must anchor our future in our most noble aspirations for the cultural renaissance that awaits us. This shared and inspiring vision will foster a sense of our collective human destiny—one that transcends cultural differences and, like an American Indian prayer arrow, lodges goodwill in people's hearts. Multicultural leaders will be the stewards of this vision, using it as a source of creative power and energy and a fountain of courage and hope. Based on the understanding that *we are all relatives*, this vision of our multicultural future embraces our universal humanity.

Let it be said by the children of the seventh generation that we fulfilled the Hopi prophesies, and we became the universal tribe, the rainbow people who reflected the iridescent beauty of humankind and, just as they prophesied, restored the earth, brought peace and understanding, and healed the damage caused by previous generations.

All that we do now must be done in a sacred manner and in celebration. We are the ones we have been waiting for.

—The Hopi Elders
Oraibi, Arizona[22]

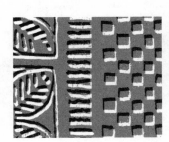

NEXT STEPS

Reflecting On and Applying Part Four

Leadership in a Multicultural age

Assimilation and acculturation

Assimilation has been a historical riptide in America, ushering people into a monocultural way of life. Assimilation is not an adaptive advantage in our multicultural age. Fortunately, people can choose a different pathway and learn to *cross over* or to acculturate. Acculturation is an *add on* process through which people develop cross-cultural competencies

Assimilation and acculturation are a continuum. Where would you rate yourself on this scale?

| Associations center on White culture ◄ ● ►   Many diverse cultural associations |

ASSIMILATION _____ACCULTURATION

−5   −4   −3   −2   −1   0   +1   +2   +3   +4   +5

| Minimal experience with other cultures ◄ ● ►   Seeks out diverse cultural experiences |

ASSIMILATION _____ACCULTURATION

−5   −4   −3   −2   −1   0   +1   +2   +3   +4   +5

| Desire to fit in, conform   ◄ ● ►   Has learned how to "fit in" |

ASSIMILATION _____ACCULTURATION

−5   −4   −3   −2   −1   0   +1   +2   +3   +4   +5

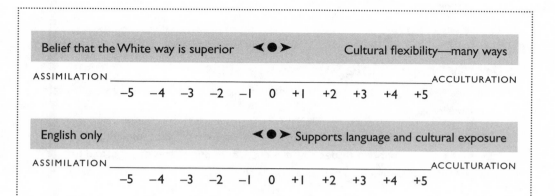

Now that you have considered your own assimilation or acculturation experience, what thoughts come to mind about this? A number of cross-cultural experiences are suggested in this part as ways to increase your ability to acculturate. List a few of these that you feel would enrich your life. Discuss these with others or in a group. Ask for more suggestions. Then make up a Multicultural Menu with delicious diversity-enhancing recipes. When will you do these? How will you keep on track?

In other words, now that you have read this book, how are you going to put more *Salsa, Soul, and Spirit* in your life?

Addressing hierarchical pluralism

Most dominant-culture organizations reflect hierarchical pluralism, whereby people of color need to fit in if they want to succeed. Review and discuss the two organizational paradigms illustrated in the table.

- Have you had experience with organizations that embody hierarchical pluralism? How do these organizations block inclusive leadership and lessen the potential contributions of people of color?

- Select one or two areas from the diagram and analyze them in relationship to an organization you work with or with whom you are familiar. What two or three concrete steps could help this organization align more closely with egalitarian pluralism? What benefits might ensue?

Socially responsible business practices

As noted earlier, being socially responsible and paying employees a fair wage can be very good for business.

- What are some of the ways the businesses profiled here reflect multicultural principles such as generosity, a leader among equals, community stewardship, and being guardians of public values? (Think of an organization as a community of people.)

- What role can (and should) business play in building the equitable society? What are some of the obstacles that stand in the way and what can be done about these?

Revitalizing our democracy

Pluralism holds the promise of authentic democracy, yet today our democracy is faltering. Materialism and love of money have sold our democracy to the highest bidder, and civic engagement has diminished.

- What have you learned about multicultural leadership as reflected in communities of color that can revitalize democracy?

- How can multicultural leadership transform our society so that it reflects the democratic values on which it was founded?

Recommended readings and resources

- *Leadership Is Global: Co-Creating a More Humane and Sustainable World* edited by Walter Link, Thais Corral, and Mark Gerzon (The Shinnyo-en Foundation, 2004).

- *Leading in Black and White: Working Across the Racial Divide in Corporate America* by Ancella B. Livers and Keith A. Caver (Jossey-Bass, 2003).

- *Translation Nation: Defining a New American Identity in the Spanish-Speaking United States* by Hector Tobar (Riverhead Books, 2005).

TWO ORGANIZATIONAL PARADIGMS

Hierarchical Pluralism

- History is seen from the dominant cultural perspective—and believed to be "the truth" or "reality."

- Everyone must conform to dominant cultural values and perspectives. There is only one world view. Ethnocentric.

- Diverse people must *conform* to dominant-culture behavior, dress, norms, thinking, and communication patterns. Homogenous and homogenized.

- Operating rules, structures, and systems are in alignment with dominant-culture values and orientation. Business as usual.

- Intelligence is measured by reading comprehension, critical thinking, and problem-solving—I.Q. standardization. Rational.

- Primary learning is through information, reading and scientific method, use of experts. Analysis.

- Tokenism—one can speak for the many.

- Traditional thinking is sequential and linear. Action- and task-oriented thinking.

- The long-term end is to retain and expand power and to control resources and people.

- Few at the top, generally White males. Privilege, advantage, and entitlement. Inner circle. Clubby.

- Collaboration as a decision-making and team-building tool. Competition-based.

- Scope: pervasive, institutionalized, covert discrimination, normative, dominance unrecognized.

- Cultural patriarchy and dominance.

Egalitarian Pluralism

- History and tradition reflect the experiences and backgrounds of diverse cultures that make up the whole.

- The values, perspectives, and worldviews of all subgroups are respected and integrated. Multicultural.

- Diversity is infused at all levels of the culture, organization, and society—"differences add value." Heterogeneous.

- Operating rules, structures, and systems are dynamic, flexible, responsive to people's needs.

- Intelligence and ability are assessed by a variety of measures (emotional, kinetic, and spiritual.) Emotional, spiritual, and cultural I.Q.

- Different styles of learning and processing information are validated: "we can all learn from one another."

- *Bienvenidos*, inclusiveness is a cherished trait—welcome to the table.

- Multidimensional thinking—there are many paths to the same goal or ends.

- The long-term end is to include equitable representation at all levels of the organization and society. Share resources.

- Many share power and responsibility. Competency, education, hard work are the avenues to success. Empowerment.

- Collaboration as a tool for advancing authentic representation; all voices are heard.

- Scope: interactive, fluid, change-oriented, synergistic, adaptive, encouraging diverse approaches.

- Multicultural: circular, shared leadership.

Notes

Unless otherwise noted, quotations from leaders in communities of color who were contributors for this book come from personal interviews, which were conducted with them, transcribed verbatim, and then coded for common themes and quotes.

Preface

1. From "A Message from the Hopi Elders: The Hopi Nation Elders at Oraibi, Arizona," March 2002, http://www.matrixmasters.com/takecharge/hopi-prophecy.html.

Introduction: Diversity Is Transforming American Leadership

1. U.S. Census Bureau, "U.S. Interim Projections by Age, Sex, Race, and Hispanic Origin," 2004, http://www.census.gov/ipc/www/usinterimproj.

2. Frances Hesselbein, *Leader to Leader*, The Drucker Foundation (San Francisco: Jossey-Bass, 1998).

3. B. Joanne Ciulla, *Cutting Edge Leadership 2000*, Bridge Leaders (College Park, MD: The James MacGregor Burns Academy of Leadership, 2000).

4. Article 1, Section 2, Clause 3 of the U.S. Constitution.

5. The 2000 U.S. Census was the first to allow respondents to select more than one race. Nationwide, 2.4 percent of the population—over 6.8 million—marked two or more races. See http://www.censusscope.org for a more detailed analysis by race (accessed July 1, 2006).

6. For an in-depth understanding of the multicultural history of Spain, see Carlos Fuentes, *The Buried Mirror: Reflections on Spain and the New World* (New York: Houghton Mifflin, 1992), chap. 3.

7. Ronald Segal, *The Black Diaspora* (New York: Farrar, Straus & Giroux, 1995).

8. *Mexico People—2006 CIA World Factbook,* http://www.theodora.comwfbcurrent/mexico/mexico_people.html.

9. See http://en.wikipedia.org/wiki/Latin_America#Demographics (accessed August 1, 2006).

10. Standard and Poor's, *The Hispanic Consumer Market in 1999 and Forecast to 2020* (January 2001).

11. Thomas L. Friedman, *The World is Flat: A Brief History of the Twenty-First Century* (New York: Farrar, Straus and Giroux, 2005), 11.

12. Determining which is the world's second most commonly spoken language is complicated. There is agreement that Mandarin Chinese is first. English, Spanish, and Hindi vie for second place, depending on whether the designation includes only native speakers. The United States, for instance, has the second highest number of Spanish speakers in the world, many of whom are not native speakers. What is certain is that Spanish is the primary language in the greatest number of countries: twenty-three.

For more information, see http://www.cftech.com/BrainBank/COMMUNICATIONS/TopLanguages.html or http://en.wikipedia.org/wiki/Spanish_language (accessed February 14, 2006).

13. For information on Latino subgroups in the U.S. and Puerto Rican population, see www.census.gov/prod/cen2000/doc/sf1.pdf (accessed August 1, 2006).

14. Highlights of Puerto Rican history are available at http://topuertorico.org/history4.shtml (accessed August 28, 2006).

15. W. E. B. Du Bois, *The Souls of Black Folk* (New York: Modern Library Edition, 2003. First published: Chicago: AC McClurg & Co., 1903).

16. Coretta Scott King, *The Words of Martin Luther King, Jr.* (New York: Newmarket Press, 1983), 21.

17. Ywahoo, Dhyani, *Voices of Our Ancestors* (Boston: Shambala, 1987), 111, 225. (Ywahoo is a Cherokee teacher from the Etowah Band of the Eastern Tsalagi.)

18. Paula Gunn Allen, *The Sacred Hoop: Recovering the Feminine in American Indian Traditions* (Boston: Beacon Press, 1986), 60–61.

19. Burt Nanus, "What Is Vision—And Why It Matters," in *Visionary Leadership* (San Francisco: Jossey-Bass, 1992).

Part One: A New Social Covenant

1. Lance Secretan, *One: The Art and Practice of Conscious Leadership* (Caledon, Ontario: The Secretan Center, 2006), 14.

2. King, *The Words of Martin Luther King, Jr.*, 25.

Principle 1: *Sankofa*— Learn from the Past

1. *Sankofa* is an Akan word that means "one must return to the past in order to move forward." A film entitled Sankofa was made by Haile Gerima in 1993 (Mypheduh Films., Inc., P.O. Box 10035, Washington, DC 20018). For additional information, see http://www.duboislc.net/SankofaMeaning.html.

2. Pew Hispanic Center, *Hispanics Gaining Jobs But Suffering Worse Wage Losses in U.S. Labor Force* (Washington, DC, 2006), http://pewhispanic.org/newsroom/releases/release.php?ReleaseID=2 (accessed August 1, 2006).

3. National Center for Educational Statistics, *Drop-out Rates in the United States: 2000* (Washington, DC), http://nces.ed.gov/pubs2002/droppub_2001 (accessed August 26, 2006).

4. A groundbreaking study on the Americas before colonization is Charles C. Mann's *1491: New Revelations of the Americas Before Columbus* (New York: Knopf, 2005). Based on demographic studies, Mann documents that given the death rate of Indians who died from European diseases, the estimates of the pre-Columbian population range from 12.5 to 25 million (see p. 100).

5. Adam Smith, *An Inquiry into the Nature and Causes of the Wealth of Nations*, 5th ed., ed. Edwin Cannon (London: Methuen and Co., 1904).

6. Thomas Hobbes, *Leviathan, or the Matter, Forme, & Power of a Common-Wealth, Ecclesiasticall and Civil*, ed. J. C. A. Gaskin (London: Andrew Crooke, 1651; Oxford, UK: Oxford Press, 1988).

7. Max Weber, *The Protestant Ethic and the Spirit of Capitalism* (New York: Scribner, 1958).

8. Myron P. Gutmann, *Toward the Modern Economy: Early Industry in Europe 1500–1800* (New York: Knopf, 1988).

9. Mann, in *1491: New Revelations of the Americas Before Columbus*, states that "Cortez believed the military conquest of the [Aztec] Alliance had to be accomplished and justified by an equivalent spiritual conquest. The Indians, he said, must be led to salvation" (p. 31).

10. Barry Lopez, *The Rediscovery of North America* (New York: First Vintage Books Edition, 1992).

11. Carlos Fuentes, *The Buried Mirror: Reflections on Spain and the New World* (New York: Houghton Mifflin, 1992), 125.

12. Alexis de Tocqueville, *De la démocratie en Amerique,* published in two volumes, the first in 1835, the second in 1840. English-language versions are *Democracy in America*, trans. and ed. Harvey C. Mansfield and Delba Winthrop (University of Chicago Press, 2000), and *Democracy in America*, trans. Arthur Goldhammer, ed. Olivier Zunz (New York: The Library of America, 2004).

13. Robert Bellah with Richard Madsen, William M. Sullivan, Ann Swidler, and Steven M. Tipton, *Habits of the Heart: Individualism and Commitment in American Life* (1985; updated paperback edition with new introduction, "The House Divided," Berkeley, CA: University of California Press, 1996).

14. Robert Putnam, *Bowling Alone: The Collapse and Revival of American Community* (New York: Simon & Schuster, 2000).

15. Craig Kielburger and Marc Kielburger, *From Me to We: Turning Self-Help on Its Head* (Canada: Wiley, 2004), 34.

16. Scott Allen, "Web of Friendships Unravel, Study Says," *Boston Globe*, June 25, 2006, http://search.boston.com (accessed June 25, 2006).

17. United Nations Development Program, *Income and Poverty: 2005*, Earth Trends Data: Economics, Business and the Environment, GDP Per Capita Income Table 3 (Washington DC: World Bank, 2005).

18. Kim Khan, "How Does Your Debt Compare?" http://moneycentral.msn.com/content/SavingandDebt/P70581.asp (accessed August 28, 2006).

19. Families and Work Institute, *Overwork in America: When the Way We Work Becomes Too Much*, 2005, http://familiesandwork.org/summary/overwork2005.

20. Kielburger and Kielburger, in Roper Organization poll and World Values survey, *From Me to We*, 21–22.

21. Ibid.

22. Ibid.

23. Kielburger and Kielburger, citing "Affluenza," a television program on the epidemic of over-consumption, first broadcast in 1997 by PBS. Produced by John de Graaf.

24. M. Scott Peck, *The Different Drum: Community Making and Peace* (New York: Simon & Schuster, 1988).

25. de Tocqueville, *Democracy in America*.

Principle 2: *I to We*—From Individualism to Collective Identity

1. Norma Carr-Ruffino, *Managing Diversity: People Skills for a Multicultural Workplace* (Andover, UK: International Thomson Publishing, 1996).

2. Michael Boon, *The African Way: The Power of Interactive Leadership* (Cape Town, South Africa: Zebra Press, 1996), 18.

3. Kate Prendergast, "Updating Our Origins; Biology, Genetics and Evolution: An Interview with Steve Jones," *Science and Spirit* 10, no. 5 (2000): 24.

4. Christina Baldwin, *Calling the Circle* (Newberg, OR: Swan Raven, 1994).

5. Riane Eisler, *The Chalice and the Blade* (San Francisco: Harper and Row, 1987).

6. "Modern Forms of *Homo sapiens* First Appear about 195,000 Years Ago," http://www.talkorigins.org/faqs/homs/species.html (accessed December 1, 2006).

7. HRDQ, "Mastering the Change Curve," http://www.hrdq.com/home.htm.

8. For more information on the American Indian Ambassadors program, see Americans for Indian Opportunity, http://www.aio.org/programs.html (accessed August 1, 2006).

9. James A. Joseph, *Remaking America: How the Benevolent Traditions of Many Cultures Are Transforming Our National Life* (San Francisco: Jossey-Bass, 1995), 74.

10. Ibid.

11. Barbara Walters, "The 10 Most Fascinating People of 2005," *ABC News Special*, November 29, 2005.

12. For Albert Einstein quotes, see http://www.heartquotes.net/Einstein.html (accessed August 24, 2006).

Principle 3: *Mi Casa Es Su Casa*— A Spirit of Generosity

1. Boon, *The African Way*, 32–33.

2. Joseph, *Remaking America*, 27.

3. Ibid., 76.

4. Ancella B. Livers and Keith A. Caver, *Leading in Black and White: Working Across the Racial Divide in Corporate America* (San Francisco: Jossey-Bass, 2003).

5. Lauren Gard, "African American Giving Comes of Age," Special Report– Philanthropy 2004, *Business Week*, November 29, 2004, http://www.businessweek.com/magazine/content/04_48/b3910417.htm (accessed August 26, 2006).

6. Joseph, *Remaking America*, 73.

7. Nelson Mandela, *Long Walk to Freedom: The Autobiography of Nelson Mandela* (London: Little, Brown and Company, 1994).

8. *El Mercado Restaurante*, an extensive study commissioned by leading direct-mail media company ADVO, Inc., found that Hispanic consumers spend 20 percent more per week eating out or having food delivered than non-Hispanic consumers. For more information, see www.advo.com/elmerc_restaraunte.html.

9. César Chávez, "Farm Workers Prayer," César Chávez Foundation, www.chavezfoundation.org (accessed December 4, 2006).

10. See Jonathan H. Turner, Leonard Beeghley, and Charles H. Powers, *The Emergence of Sociological Theory*, 5th ed. (Belmont, CA: Wadsworth Thomson Learning, 2002), 43–55. The theory of survival of the fittest, often mistakenly attributed to Darwin, is in fact the work of economist Herbert Spencer. Spencer did base his work, in part, on Darwin's theory of natural selection.

11. David Loye, *Darwin's Lost Theory of Love: A Healthy Vision for the New Century* (San Jose, CA: toExcel/iUniverse, 2000).

12. Marc Ian Barasch, *Field Notes on the Compassionate Life* (New York: Rodale Press, 2005), 12.

13. U.S. Census Bureau, *Income, Poverty and Health Insurance Coverage in the United States: 2003*, Current Populations Reports (August 2003).

14. Holly Sklar, "CEO Pay Still Outrageous," *The Ultimate Field Guide to the U.S. Economy*, May 21, 2003, www.fguide.org/Bulletin/ceopay.htm (accessed June 15, 2006).

15. Stephanie Armour, "What Recovery? Working Poor Struggle to Pay Bills," *USA Today*, www.usatoday.com/money/economy/2004-06-08-low-wage-working-poor (accessed June 1, 2006).

16. U.S. Census Bureau, *Income, Poverty and Health Insurance*, p. 25; correlation of race and poverty for uninsured children.

17. James MacGregor Burns, *Leadership* (New York: Harper Torch Books, 1978).

Part Two: Leadership Styles in Communities of Color

1. Ronald W. Walters and Robert C. Smith, *African American Leadership* (New York: State University of New York Press, 1999), 216.

2. John Naisbitt and Patricia Aburdene, *Megatrends 2000* (New York: Morrow, 1990).

3. Peter Block, *Stewardship: Choosing Service over Self-interest* (San Francisco: Berrett-Koehler, 1993).

4. Walters and Smith, *African American Leadership*, 107.

5. For a more comprehensive description of the collaborative leadership process, see Gill Robinson Hickman, "Leadership and the Social Imperative of Organizations in the 21st Century" in *Leading Organizations: Perspectives for a New Era* (Thousand Oaks, CA: Sage, 1998), 572–580.

6. R. K. Greenleaf, *The Servant as Leader* (Newton Center, MA: The Robert Greenleaf Center, 1970).

Principle 4: A Leader Among Equals— Community Conferred Leadership

1. Norma Carr-Ruffino, *Managing Diversity*, 232.

2. See *Océano Dicconario Inglés: Español* (Barcelona: Oceano Grupo Editorial, S.A., 2002). The Jemez Pueblo use the term *cacique* for their traditional governing body, a group that represents the various clans and religious leaders. This usage is an artifact of the Spanish conquest dating back to 1540 and is indicative of the amalgamation of indigenous and Spanish languages and cultures. In Spanish *cacique* means chief or can also connote a political boss.

3. National Community for Latino Leadership, Inc. (NCLL), *Reflecting an American Vista: The Character and Impact of Latino Leadership* 1, no. 1, January 2001. NCLL is a national organization founded in 1989 whose mission is to develop ethical, responsible, and accountable leaders on behalf of the U.S. Latino population and the broader community. See http://www.latinoleadership.org/.

4. As cited in Joseph, *Remaking America*, 209.

5. Lea Williams, *Servants of the People: The 1960s Legacy of African American Leadership* (New York: St. Martin's Press, 1998), 28.

6. Antonia Pantoja, *Memoir of a Visionary* (Houston, TX: Arte Público Press, 2002), 61.

7. Antonia Pantoja, presentation to the National Hispana Leadership Institute, Washington, DC, September 1989.

8. Walters and Smith, *African American Leadership*, 117.

9. Pantoja, *Memoir of a Visionary*, 84.

Principle 5: Leaders as Guardians of Public Values—A Tradition of Activism

1. Pantoja, *Memoir of a Visionary*, 98.

2. Pantoja, presentation to the National Hispana Leadership Institute, September 1989.

3. Williams, *Servants of the People*, 46.

4. Pablo Freire, *The Pedagogy of the Oppressed*, trans. Myra Bergman Ramos, special anniversary edition (New York: Continuum, 2000).

5. Peggy McIntosh, *White Privilege and Male Privilege: A Personal Account of Coming to See Correspondences Through Work in Women's Studies* (Wellesley, MA: Wellesley College, 1988).

6. Ibid.

7. Andrew Young, *An Easy Burden: The Civil Rights Movement and the Transformation of America* (New York: HarperCollins, 1996), 252.

8. Andrew Young, interviewed on *Frontline*, July 21, 1995. http://www.pbs.org/wgbh/pages/frontline/jesse/interviews/young.html (accessed May 10, 2006).

9. Federico Peña, speech at "We Are America" march, Denver, CO, May 1, 2006, insidedenver.com/drmn/other_business/article/0,2777,DRMN_23916_4668821,00.html.

10. Martin Luther King Jr., letter from Birmingham Jail, April 16, 1963, http://www.africa.upenn.edu/Articles_Gen/Letter_Birmingham.html.

11. Martin Luther King Jr., http://www.brainyquote.com/quotes/authors/m/martin_luther_king_jr.html (accessed December 7, 2006).

Principle 6: Leaders as Community Stewards—Working for the Common Good

1. Greenleaf, *The Servant as Leader*, 7–8.

2. Antonia Pantoja, interviewed by Lillian Jimenez, executive director of the Latino Educational Media Center, New York, January 18, 2002. This interview will be included in a documentary film entitled *Abriendo Caminos* about Pantoja's life and contributions.

3. National Community for Latino Leadership, *Reflecting an American Vista: The Character and Impact of Leadership.* Andy Hernandez and Alfred Ramirez, 2001.

4. Pantoja, *Memoir of a Visionary*, 84.

5. John White, *Black Leadership in America* (New York: Longman, 1994), 191.

6. Williams, *Servants of the People*, 17.

7. Walters and Smith, *African American Leadership*, 46, 122.

8. Andrew Young, *Frontline* interview.

9. Nancy Gibbs, "The 5 Best Big-City Mayors," *Time*, April 25, 2005, http://www.time.com/time/magazine/article/0,9171,1050214,00.html (accessed December 7, 2006).

10. John Gardner, as listed in *Direct Quotes: Contemporary Consultants* (1996; a printed workbook available from Mary Jo Clark and Pat Heiny, P.O. Box 52, Richmond, VA 47375). From speech delivered by John Gardner to Leadership USA, November 18, 1995, Pomona, CA.

11. Williams, "Dynamic Times Call for Dynamic Leaders," in *Servants of the People.*

12. Mandela, *Long Walk to Freedom*, 24–25.

13. National Community for Latino Leadership, *Reflecting an American Vista.*

14. James M. Kouzes and Barry Z. Posner, *The Leadership Challenge*, rev. ed. (San Francisco: Jossey-Bass, 2003).

15. Carr-Ruffino, *Managing Diversity*, 332.

16. Pantoja, quoted in "Puerto Rico Profile: Dr. Antonia Pantoja," *Puerto Rico Herald*, November 17, 2000.

17. Walters and Smith, *African American Leadership*, 123.

18. Ibid., 211.

Principle 7: All My Relatives—*La Familia,* the Village, the Tribe

1. Young, *An Easy Burden*, 14.

2. Boon, *The African Way*, 74.

3. Natalie Angier, "DNA Shows Humans Are All One Race," *New York Times*, August 22, 2000.

4. M. J. Wheatley, *Leadership and the New Science* (San Francisco: Berrett-Koehler, 1993).

5. Williams, *Servants of the People*, 185–186.

6. Pantoja interview, January 2002.

7. Joseph, *Remaking of America*, 73.

8. Boon, *The African Way*, 31–32.

9. Joseph, *Remaking of America*, 79.

10. Dr. F. James Davis, *Who Is Black? One Nation's Definition* (University Park, PA: Penn State Press, 2001).

11. Andrew Young, *A Way Out of No Way* (Nashville, TN: Nelson, 1994), 131.

12. Ibid.

13. http://chavez.cde.ca.gov/ModelCurriculum/ Teachers/Lessons/Resources/Biographies/Middle_ Level_Biography.aspx (accessed December 4, 2006).

14. "Current Population Survey 2004," Bureau of Labor Statistics and U.S. Census Bureau, http:// money.cnn.com/2004/08/26/news/economy/ poverty_survey (accessed December 4, 2006).

15. "Hunger in USA Rises by 43 Percent over Last Five Years," based on analysis of a 2004 USDA report, "Household Food Security in the United States," Center on Poverty and Hunger, http://www .centeronhunger.org.

16. http://en.wikipedia.org/wiki/Homelessness_ in_the_United_States#Statistics_and_demographics (accessed December 4, 2006).

17. John F. Kennedy, http://www.brainyquote. com/quotes/authors/j/john_f_kennedy.html (accessed October 17, 2006).

18. Young, *An Easy Burden*, 163.

19. Williams, *Servants of the People*, 144.

Principle 8: Gracias—Gratitude, Hope, and Forgiveness

1. Jesse Jackson, speech to the Democratic Party National Convention, 1984.

2. Dhyani Ywahoo, *Voices of Our Ancestors*, 133.

3. Daniel Goleman, *Emotional Intelligence* (New York: Bantam Books, 1995).

4. *New York Times/CBS News* poll based on telephone interviews conducted July 13 to 27, 2003, with 3,092 adults throughout the United States, www.nytimes.com/packages/html/ politics/20030806_poll/20030806poll-results.html (accessed January 10, 2006).

5. Leon Shenandoah, chief of Onondaga Nation and Tadodaho ("Firekeeper") of the Haudenosaunee, address to the General Assembly of the United Nations, October 25, 1985, http://nativenewsonline. org/history/hist0722.html (accessed September 12, 2005). The Tadodaho can be described as president, spiritual elder, and principal chief of the Grand Council, the eldest democracy in North America. This Confederacy originally included the Mohawks, Oneidas, Onondagas, Cayugas, and Senecas. The sixth nation, the Tuscaroras, migrated into Iroquois country in the early eighteenth century. See http:// www.onondagalakepeacefestival.org/2004/Leon.htm or, for a historical perspective, http://www.ratical. org/many_worlds/6Nations/EoL/chp2.html (accessed December 6, 2006).

6. Octavio Paz, *The Labyrinth of Solitude*, 2d ed. (New York: Penguin USA, 1977). First published in Spanish in 1950, *The Labyrinth of Solitude* is considered one of the most enduring and powerful works ever created on Mexico and its people, character, and culture. Paz won the Nobel Prize for literature in 1990.

7. To understand the importance of Our Lady of Guadalupe at the time of the conquest, read Jeannette Rodriguez, *Our Lady of Guadalupe: Faith and Empowerment Among Mexican-American Women* (Austin, TX: University of Texas Press, 1994). According to the Catholic Church, her apparition is the Patroness of the Western Hemisphere. Her influence as a cultural icon, if not as a religious figure, is evident in the myriad images and writing about her in the United States and many other countries.

8. Ywahoo, *Voices of our Ancestors*, 41.

9. Block, *Stewardship: Choosing Service over Self-interest.*

10. Stephen Covey, *The Seven Habits of Highly Effective People* (New York: Simon & Schuster, 1989).

11. Young, *A Way Out of No Way*, 31.

12. Walters and Smith, *African American Leadership*, 77.

13. César Chávez, National Farm Worker Ministry, http://www.nfwm.org/worshipresources/ cesarquotes.shtml (accessed December 7, 2006).

14. Young, *An Easy Burden*, 15, 23.

15. Peña, speech at "We Are America" march.

16. Barack Obama, "On Religion: Politicians Need Not Abandon Religion," *USA Today*, July 10, 2006.

17. Young, *A Way Out of No Way*, 83.

18. Young, *An Easy Burden*, 299.

19. Boon, *The African Way*, 35–38.

Part Four: Leadership for a Multicultural Age

1. Joseph Campbell, *The Hero's Journey: Joseph Campbell on His Life and Work*, 3rd (centennial) ed., ed. and introduction Phil Cousineau, producer/foreword author Stuart Brown (Novato, CA: New World Library, 2003).

2. Young, *Frontline* interview.

3. Andrew Young, commencement speech at Connecticut College, 1998, http://www.conncoll.edu/events/speeches/young.html (accessed December 5, 2006).

4. Livers and Caver, *Leading in Black and White*, 18–24.

5. Charles Fishman, "Whole Foods Is All Teams," *Fast Company*, April 1996, http://www.fastcompany.com/magazine/02/team1.html (accessed July 27, 2006).

6. Sarah Anderson and John Cavanagh, Chuck Collins and Eric Benjamin, *Executive Excess 2006*, ed. Sam Pizzigati, Institute for Policy Studies and United for a Fair Economy, 2006, http://www.faireconomy.org/reports/2006/ExecutiveExcess2006.pdf (accessed December 5, 2006). The authors note: "Since we first started tracking the CEO-worker pay gap in 1990, it has grown from 107-to-1 to 411-to-1 in 2005. Today's gap is nearly 10 times as large as the 1980 ratio of 42-to-1, calculated by *Business Week*. If the minimum wage had risen at the same pace as CEO pay since 1990, it would be worth $22.61 today, rather than the actual $5.15."

7. Phone conversation with TDIndustries' retired CEO Jack Lowe, May 1, 2006, http://money.cnn.com/magazines/fortune/bestcompanies/snapshots/1311.html (accessed March 15, 2006).

8. William F. Achtmeyer, *Southwest Airlines Corporation,* No. 2-0012 (Hanover, NH: The Center for Global Leadership at Tuck School of Business at Dartmouth University, 2002).

9. Mitchell Schmurman, "Southwest's Magic Formula: Low Costs, Low Fares, High Pay," *Dallas-Houston Star-Telegram*, May 24, 2006.

10. Young, *An Easy Burden*, 248–249.

11. U.S. Census Bureau, "Survey of Business Owners" 2002 data: Hispanic-Owned Firms Employment Data.

12. The Center for Responsive Politics, "Money Wins Big in 2000 Elections," http://www.opensecrets.org/pressreleases/Post-Election2000.htm (accessed January 5, 2006).

13. *American Government Online, The United States Congress Quick Facts: The 109th Congress,* http://www.thisnation.com (accessed July 10, 2006).

14. Ibid.

15. *U.S. Voter Turnout Up in 2004, Census Bureau Reports. May 2005.* http://www.census.gov/Press-Release/www/releases/archives/voting/004986.html accessed December 5, 2006.

16. Politics and the Economy: Election 2004, http://www.pbs.org/now/politics/votestats.html (accessed December 5, 2006).

17. Albert Gore, *An Inconvenient Truth* (New York: Rodale Press, 2006).

18. "From those to whom much has been given, much will be required" (Luke 12:48). One of two values of the Gates Foundation, this was also the family creed for Andrew Young and is a guidepost for leaders in communities of color who have succeeded despite overwhelming obstacles.

19. Bill and Melinda Gates Foundation, http://www.gatesfoundation.org/AboutUs (accessed July 15, 2006).

20. Charlie Rose, "Warren Buffett Makes Historic Gift to the Bill and Melinda Gates Foundation," *The Charlie Rose Show*, June 26, 2006.

21. Larry Kantor, "Brilliant Careers: Warren Buffett," *Salon*, August 13, 1999, http://www.salon.com/people/bc/1999/08/31/buffett/index1.html (accessed July 15, 2006).

22. Jann S. Wenner, "Bono: The Rolling Stone Interview," *Rolling Stone*, November 3, 2005, 56–58.

23. "A Message from the Hopi Elders: The Hopi Nation Elders at Oraibi, Arizona," March 2002, http://www.matrixmasters.com/takecharge/hopi-prophecy.html.

Subject Index

A

Abernathy, Ralph, 122
Aburdene, Patricia, 79
accountability. *See* social
    accountability
acculturation, 20, 181–82,
    185–89, 202–3
acquisitive cultures, 35, 36, 54
activism
    active citizenship, 100–103,
        105–6, 153
    barriers of exclusion, 70,
        106–12
    exercises and resources,
        114–15
    public values, 19, 73, 80, 93,
        98–100
    rekindling American, 112–
        13, 195
    role of leader in, 96–98, 100–
        101, 133, 173–76
African American leadership
    activism and, 79–80, 98–101,
        124–25
    community servanthood,
        88–90, 120, 122–23
    culturally effective
        communication, 126–
        27, 139–40
    profiles of, xiv–xv
    psychology of oppression
        and, 108–9, 190
    spirituality as springboard
        for, 170–71, 174
    See also civil rights
        movement

African American Leadership
    (Walters, Smith), 77–80
African Americans
    calling, 181, 184
    collective culture of, 12–14,
        51, 53–54, 146
    cosmology of connectedness,
        148–49, 152, 158, 167,
        175, 179, 199
    distinguishing race and, 104,
        150, 151
    generosity of, 59–60, 63–65,
        68
    gratitude/hope/forgiveness
        in, 29, 163–67
    slaves/slavery, 12–14, 53, 127,
        149, 164
    song and soul, 12–14, 53, 64,
        65, 165–66
All my relatives. *See*
    global family; social
    accountability
ambassadors, 130–31
American Indian leadership
    activism and, 101–3
    as community-conferred,
        85–86, 141
    community servanthood
        and, 121
    culturally effective
        communication, 127–
        28, 130–31, 139, 140
    profiles of, xv–xvi
    psychology of oppression
        and, 107–8, 110

American Indians
    blood line and tribe, 149–51
    circular view of, 15–17, 77,
        139, 166
    civil rights movement, 101–2
    collective culture of, 51–52,
        84–85, 147–48
    hope/generosity/forgiveness
        in, 29–30, 61–63, 65, 68,
        164, 168
    tribal governance/
        sovereignty, 102–3, 141
    vision quest, 181, 184
American Indians for
    Opportunity Ambassadors'
    Program, 52, 107, 108, 123,
    174–75
ancestors, veneration of, 28–
    29, 42–43
Anglos
    communication processes of,
        127, 128
    as dominant culture, 106–7,
        186–87
    ethnocentricity of, 8, 30, 102,
        186–87, 205
    global pioneers, 196–99
    psychology of oppression
        and, 107–10
    white privilege, 80–81, 107,
        110–12, 114, 205
Anthony, Susan B., 117
apathy, 108–9
Asian Americans, xi
ASPIRA (to aspire), 97–98,
    124

213

Names Index

About the Author

Juana Bordas is president of Mestiza Leadership International, a company that focuses on leadership, diversity, and organizational change. A former faculty member at the Center for Creative Leadership (CCL), she taught in the Leadership Development Program—the most highly utilized executive program in the world. As founding president and CEO of the National Hispana Leadership Institute—the only program in America that prepares Latinas for national leadership—she forged partnerships with Harvard's John F. Kennedy School of Government and CCL to provide training for Hispanic women. Juana is a founder and was executive director of Denver's Mi Casa Women's Center, recognized today as a national model for women's empowerment.

Juana's previous publications include the essay "Passion and Power: Finding Personal Purpose," in *Reflections on Leadership* (John Wiley & Sons); "Latino Leadership: Building a Diverse and Humane Society," which appeared in the *Journal for Leadership Studies*, and "African American Leaders: Guardians of Public Values," which appeared in the inaugural issue of the *International Journal on Servant Leadership*. She is a contributing author of "Leadership in the 21st Century" in *Rethinking Leadership* (Sage).

Juana served as advisor to Harvard's Hispanic Journal on Public Policy and the Kellogg National Fellows Program. She received the Wise Woman Award from the National Center for Women's Policy Studies and was inducted into the Colorado Women's Hall of Fame. Currently, she is vice president of the board of the Greenleaf Center for Servant Leadership and a trustee of the International Leadership Association.

A former U.S. Peace Corps volunteer, Juana received the Franklin Miller Award from the Peace Corps for her lifelong commitment to advancing communities of color. The *Denver Business Journal* selected her for their 2003 Outstanding Women in Business Award for her efforts in promotion of public partnerships and nonprofit involvement in the business arena. She was recognized by the National Organization of Black Elected Legislative Women as a Colorado Pioneer for her "Legacy of Outstanding Leadership." In 2006, Juana received the Leadership Legacy award from Spellman College's Center for Leadership and Civic Engagement.

About Berrett-Koehler Publishers

BERRETT-KOEHLER IS AN INDEPENDENT PUBLISHER dedicated to an ambitious mission: Creating a World that Works for All.

We believe that to truly create a better world, action is needed at all levels—individual, organizational, and societal. At the individual level, our publications help people align their lives with their values and with their aspirations for a better world. At the organizational level, our publications promote progressive leadership and management practices, socially responsible approaches to business, and humane and effective organizations. At the societal level, our publications advance social and economic justice, shared prosperity, sustainability, and new solutions to national and global issues.

A major theme of our publications is "Opening Up New Space." They challenge conventional thinking, introduce new ideas, and foster positive change. Their common quest is changing the underlying beliefs, mindsets, institutions, and structures that keep generating the same cycles of problems, no matter who our leaders are or what improvement programs we adopt.

We strive to practice what we preach—to operate our publishing company in line with the ideas in our books. At the core of our approach is *stewardship*, which we define as a deep sense of responsibility to administer the company for the benefit of all of our "stakeholder" groups: authors, customers, employees, investors, service providers, and the communities and environment around us.

We are grateful to the thousands of readers, authors, and other friends of the company who consider themselves to be part of the "BK Community." We hope that you, too, will join us in our mission.

Be Connected

Visit Our Website

GO TO WWW.BKCONNECTION.COM to read exclusive previews and excerpts of new books, find detailed information on all Berrett-Koehler titles and authors, browse subject-area libraries of books, and get special discounts.

Subscribe to Our Free E-Newsletter

BE THE FIRST TO HEAR about new publications, special discount offers, exclusive articles, news about bestsellers, and more! Get on the list for our free e-newsletter by going to www.bkconnection.com.

Participate in the Discussion

TO SEE WHAT OTHERS ARE SAYING about our books and post your own thoughts, check out our blogs at www.bkblogs.com.

Get Quantity Discounts

BERRETT-KOEHLER BOOKS ARE AVAILABLE at quantity discounts for orders of ten or more copies. Please call us toll-free at (800) 929-2929 or email us at bkp.orders@aidcvt.com.

Host a Reading Group

OR TIPS ON HOW TO FORM and carry on a book reading group in your workplace or community, see our website at www.bkconnection.com.

Join the BK Community

Thousands of readers of our books have become part of the "BK Community" by participating in events featuring our authors, reviewing draft manuscripts of forthcoming books, spreading the word about their favorite books, and supporting our publishing program in other ways. If you would like to join the BK Community, please contact us at bkcommunity@bkpub.com.